Women and
Culture Series

The Women and Culture Series is dedicated to books that illuminate the lives, roles, achievements, and status of women, past or present.

Fran Leeper Buss
Dignity: Lower Income Women Tell of Their Lives and Struggles
La Partera: Story of a Midwife

Valerie Kossew Pichanick
Harriet Martineau: The Woman and Her Work, 1802–76

Sandra Baxter and Marjorie Lansing
Women and Politics: The Visible Majority

Estelle B. Freedman
Their Sister's Keepers: Women's Prison Reform in America, 1830–1930

Susan C. Bourque and Kay Barbara Warren
*Women of the Andes: Patriarchy and Social Change in
Two Peruvian Towns*

Marion S. Goldman
*Gold Diggers and Silver Miners: Prostitution and Social Life on the
Comstock Lode*

Page duBois
*Centaurs and Amazons: Women and the Pre-History of the Great Chain
of Being*

Mary Kinnear
Daughters of Time: Women in the Western Tradition

Lynda K. Bundtzen
Plath's Incarnations: Woman and the Creative Process

Violet B. Haas and Carolyn C. Perrucci, editors
Women in Scientific and Engineering Professions

Sally Price
Co-wives and Calabashes

Patricia R. Hill
*The World Their Household: The American Woman's Foreign Mission
Movement and Cultural Transformation, 1870–1920*

Diane Wood Middlebrook and Marilyn Yalom, editors
Coming to Light: American Women Poets in the Twentieth Century

Leslie W. Rabine
Reading the Romantic Heroine: Text, History, Ideology

Joanne S. Frye
*Living Stories, Telling Lives: Women and the Novel
in Contemporary Experience*

E. Francis White
*Sierra Leone's Settler Women Traders: Women on the
Afro-European Frontier*

Catherine Parsons Smith and Cynthia S. Richardson
Mary Carr Moore, American Composer

Barbara Drygulski Wright, editor
Women, Work, and Technology: Transformations

Lynda Hart, editor
*Making a Spectacle: Feminist Essays on
Contemporary Women's Theatre*

Dignity

Dignity

Lower Income Women Tell of Their Lives and Struggles

Oral Histories
Compiled by Fran Leeper Buss

Introduction by Susan Contratto

The University of Michigan Press
Ann Arbor

LIBRARY OF CONGRESS CATALOGING IN PUBLICATION DATA
Main entry under title:

Dignity : lower income women tell of their lives
   and struggles.

   (Women and culture series)
   Bibliography: p.
   1. Working class women—United States—Case
studies.   2. Urban women—United States—Case
studies.   3. Women, Poor—United States—Case
studies.   4. Women—Employment—United States—
Case studies.   I. Buss, Fran Leeper, 1942–
II. Series.
HQ1426.D54   1985   305.4'3   85-990
ISBN 0-472-10061-0
ISBN 0-472-06357-X (pbk.)

NANCY ROSENBERGER

To Agate, Leda, Ruth, and Wilma

Acknowledgments

Initial funding for this work came from a United Church of Christ Leadership Development for Women grant. I have also received assistance from the University of Wisconsin at Whitewater, where I have held the position of Honorary Women's Studies Scholar.

Over a hundred women have helped me in the writing of this book, and it would be impossible to thank each of them personally. Many women provided contacts for me and informed me of groups and organizations where I might find people to interview. They made telephone calls, wrote letters, drove me to meetings, and opened their homes to me while I was in their area. Others helped me transcribe tapes and type copies of the stories. I especially appreciate the efforts of Olgha Sierra Sandman, Mary Nack, Ellyn O'Grady, and my primary typist, Lou Zahn.

I also want to thank my friends Agate Nesaule, Ruth Schauer, and Pat Shibles, who read manuscripts and gave me personal and technical aid; my mother-in-law, Leda Buss; and Marilyn Hutchinson, Debra Hoffman, and Anne Griffiths. I do not believe this book would have been written in this way without the deep support, assistance, and love of my husband, David, and our three nearly adult children, Kimberly, Lisa, and Jim.

The people who were essential, of course, were those women who opened their lives to me, told me their stories, and took me into their homes and families. To them I will always be grateful. Because of my promise to them of confidentiality, I cannot list their names, but I will always remember them and the gifts they gave me. Finally, special friendships developed during the writing of this book, and those women friends I especially love.

Contents

Photographs

All photos are by the author, unless otherwise indicated.

Introduction
Susan Contratto

In this book we hear eleven women's voices: that of Fran Leeper Buss and those belonging to the ten women whose individual stories she has uncovered. Buss originally envisioned a project similar to the book *Working*, in which Studs Terkel interviewed people representing a wide variety of occupations; Buss's focus, however, would be the work lives of lower-income women. Soon, she has said, her conception of the project changed.

> I couldn't just limit the scope of the interviews to the women's work lives, or for example, the economic issues faced by displaced homemakers. The totality of the lives kept coming out, with work and economics only an important segment. I became deeply moved by each woman, especially by the ways she tried to find meaning in her life and how she tried, almost desperately at times, to explain that meaning to me so others would see it. They all wished that their thoughts and experiences would be recognized as worthwhile by the outside world, and my listening to their stories was one way of achieving that.

Locating her subjects through political and friendship networks, Buss conducted and recorded these interviews in homes, cars, neighborhoods, and workplaces. While she did not have a fixed agenda, she did have a list of topics that she hoped to cover in each interview.

> Each woman's family, cultural, and economic background and
> its effect on her

The circumstances of her birth and childhood, as well as the
history of her mother, father, and grandmother

Childhood goals, friends, mentors, and perception of life; and
understanding of life

Menarche and adolescence as they related to her personally,
with friends, and in terms of cultural expectations

Her marriage (or lack of marriage, in a few cases): its problems,
strengths, and differences from what she had expected

Her experiences as a mother, if she was one

Any experiences of incest, rape, battering, sexual harassment,
etc.

Her work and economic life

Issues dealing with old age

Buss felt a reciprocal involvement with these women. Because of her
firsthand knowledge of poverty, single parenting, sexual exploitation,
and illness, she felt an empathy that led her to reject the dominant
research paradigm of researcher/subject polarization where the re-
searcher benefits while the subject is left unchanged at best and exploited at worst. Buss has said, "I . . . believe that it would not have
been ethical for me to enter these women's lives, write down a lot of
their conditions, and then just walk out." Her method, including
continuing involvement with her "subjects," is one of qualitative feminist research.

The ten women whose stories are recounted here comprise a varied group. Four are white, three are black, one is a Native American,
and one is of Japanese ancestry. They range in age from thirty-three to
seventy-two, though more than half of them are over sixty-five.

In some ways, the characteristics of the women chosen for this
volume reflect the demography of poor women in America: blacks
made up about one-third of those receiving public assistance at the
time of the 1980 census, although only 11.7 percent of the population.
The elderly, though not comprising half of all lower-income citizens,
are certainly statistically overrepresented among America's poor.

In other ways, Buss's sample is skewed: of the total United States
population in 1980, Native Americans represented only 0.601 percent, Japanese Americans only 0.309 percent. Nor do the geographical
regions represented here illustrate the range of poverty in the United
States: of the states having the lowest per capita income, New
Hampshire, Maine, and Vermont ranked 27, 38, and 40 respectively
in the 1980 census, with 50 being the lowest.

But each of these women is more than a number, more than a
member of an aggregate. By listening closely to these stories, we can

hear how lives are shaped by being poor, being female, and being a member of a minority group. We can also learn how these women struggle and survive; how they fight, often effectively, sometimes dramatically, to be powerful within and in spite of the structural constraints imposed on their lives.

Being born female is usually an unambiguous biological event, and much of a woman's developmental experience revolves around bodily growth and change. But experiencing childhood as a little girl and then becoming a woman is a social experience, as well. From the moment of a female's birth, others respond to her with specific assumptions and behaviors based solely on her gender. The growing girl eventually becomes self-conscious about her femaleness in situations where being a boy or a girl makes a difference. Besides her conscious sense of what it means to be a girl, she often develops certain "typical" female personality characteristics. Empathy, caring, nurturing behavior, and other relational skills are not consciously chosen, but can often feel like the core of a woman's being. (See Miller 1976; Chodorow 1978; Gilligan 1982; and Ruddick 1982 for a discussion of the development of these personality traits.) We see in this book that being a woman not only involves these three elements: biology, society or culture, and personality, but is strongly affected by poverty and ethnicity as well.

As you read each interview, you will feel that you have met a whole, complex person whose story stands on its own. Yet you may also share my experience: hearing in one story, and then in another, familiar echoes of women's experience. As a psychologist interested in women's development, I hear these echoes in the context of our deepening understanding of women's experiences. If I were an economist, a sociologist, or a child development specialist, I would introduce this volume quite differently. The stories of these individual lives offer rich possibilities.

Biological Determinants

For the women you will meet here, the biological events of menarche, childbirth, and menopause not only mark the passage of time but also take on social and economic meaning.

Nearly all of them found menarche fear-inspiring: the ill-prepared, sometimes completely naive pubescent girl is dismayed and ashamed at what is happening to her body. Josephine says,

> I needed a mother to talk to me as I was growing. My aunt and my grandfather had always told me that if a boy just rubbed his

hand on your arm you was going to have a baby. And I was taught to have a baby was something awful, but they didn't tell anything else. So when my first period came I was very frightened. I knew that I had no kind of contact with a boy, but I was afraid they'd think I was playing around. My period had started overnight and my bedsheet was all bloody, and I was bloody. I got up and got those things off when the family had gone to work. I made up the bed and everything, but I kept bleeding and I didn't know what was wrong. We had an artesian well that we drank the water from back farther in the yard. It was a small spring where the cow and the horse got their water. I went down to this spring and got in that spring and washed and washed. But every time that I'd step out I'd take a leaf and wipe myself, and I would see more blood on it; so I got back into the water. I stayed in that spring until that water chilled my blood and I passed out.

Had she had a mother, Josephine suggests, she might have received information that could have forestalled her panic.

Irene, in contrast, was taught about menstruation by her grandmother. The complex nature of and associations surrounding this biological fact are apparent in her account of an incident that occurred when she was a student at a Bureau of Indian Affairs school and worked in the home of one of the staff members:

Of course, by then they had washing machines, but she didn't like washing machines. She claimed they ruined her clothes, so she enjoyed watching me over a scrub board. And she didn't always soak the baby's diapers when the baby soiled them. So I'd have to scrub those darn things till they were white. But there was a turning point. One day I got there and she said, "There are some things in the bathroom in a bucket to be washed, and I want you to get at them right away. Clean them good."

Irene would wash feces from the baby's diaper, but even in the face of sure punishment, she refused to wash another woman's menstrual blood. She believed that menstruation was dirty and dangerous, that frightening diseases exuded from a woman's body. Part of the power of this incident is that the woman for whom Irene worked knew precisely that Irene would be broken and humiliated by violating such powerful, unarticulated but shared taboos.

Menstrual information concerns the facts of what is happening or will happen to a young girl's body, but it also carries the shadowy and often frightening cultural meanings of female monthly bleeding. Beliefs about menstrual pollution are common to every class and ethnic group, though the particular form they take may vary. What does it feel like to know that regularly, because of your femaleness, you spread dangerous dirt and disease? That you should not have intercourse? That you are not allowed to participate in religious rituals? That you are unclean? These ideas become an indelible part of the female sense of self.

These women often became pregnant early in their lives. Maria Elena had her first baby at fifteen; Darlene, Helen, Josephine, and Mary were all pregnant at sixteen. Again, social experience and economic circumstances affect this biological event. A surprising number of these first pregnancies resulted not from ignorance about contraception, but from a more basic lack of information about human reproduction. The notion that children learn about sexuality from each other, from watching farm animals, or from sex education classes is simply not borne out in the stories of these women's lives. Darlene, for example, married Virgil when she was fifteen and became pregnant within a few months. She says: "I also didn't know the facts of life. I thought I did, but I didn't. I thought it was just people being together; I didn't know there was the sexual part of it. Mom never had talked to me about it." As with menstruation, their lack of accurate, basic information about sexuality left these women vulnerable and frightened. In some cases it also made them responsible for caring for young children when, as mothers, they were hardly more than children themselves.

Because they were poor, many gave birth at home. In this country, midwife-assisted home birth was common well into the twentieth century, particularly in rural and lower-class areas. Darlene, now aged thirty-three, was delivered at home by her great-grandmother. Though Darlene's own six children were apparently delivered by a physician, her pregnant aunt relied on her own grandmother. From a middle-class perspective, it is easy to idealize midwife-assisted deliveries; for these poor women, home birth was scary and potentially life threatening.

When medical professionals do manage childbirth, a woman's poverty often adversely affects the way she is treated by them. Lee, unmarried and pregnant with her first baby at age twenty, went on welfare. Afraid that she would have to put the baby up for adoption if she got medical attention, she did nothing until her seventh month, when, overwhelmed with panic, she went to a local hospital. To her dismay, she found she had not lived in the town long enough to be eligible for free services: "Then I just got desperate and started crying and the doctor decided to waive the rules." Lee's story provides numerous examples of a woman trying to gain control over her reproductive capacity, appealing for assistance appropriately, and when it is refused, resorting to dangerous alternatives. Already the mother of four young children, and strained nearly beyond her ability to care for them, Lee asked a woman physician for a tubal ligation, since other means of contraception had not worked; the physician refused. Lee had four more pregnancies, two of which were terminated with self-induced abortions.

None of these women talk about menopause. The physiological symptoms that many women experience in conjunction with menopause are relatively unobtrusive. Debilitating menopausal depression tends to occur in those women whose sense of themselves is tied up in motherhood; they grieve the loss of a capacity, that of bearing and nurturing children, and the grief is profound because a major part of their identity is lost. The women you will meet in these stories do not fit the psychological criteria of candidates for serious menopausal depression, since most of them are involved in critically important work in addition to their mothering. As will become clear later, their sense of themselves as mothers carries few illusions of unrealistic power and responsibility.

More likely, for some of these women the loss of reproductive potential was somewhat of a relief, since each child born is an additional economic responsibility. For women already living at a subsistence level, the fear of unwanted pregnancy is enormous. Furthermore, even when contraceptive methods are available, religiously sanctioned, and safe, they are still expensive. Middle-class women under thirty-five can hardly imagine what life was like before the advent of the pill and of birth control clinics where the consent of a woman's parents or husband was not required. Many of the women did not make a choice between motherhood or work; they were among the relatively stable numbers of women who, though the mothers of small children, had to work in the paid labor force if their families were to survive. For a woman to arrange child care when she has little to spend and an inflexible work schedule is very difficult. Sometimes the children suffer from makeshift arrangements; inevitably the mother suffers.

Social/Cultural Determinants

Throughout these women's stories we hear them describe the social experience of being female. For the most part, this experience is not positive or even neutral. Most often, when talking of themselves as social beings for whom femaleness is of central concern, the preoccupation is with a sense of limitation, inequity, and exploitation. Lee, self-reflective and analytic, tells how her father wanted a boy. As a child, she often played with boys and relished their same freedom, exploration, and excitement, but when she became a teenager, she realized that she had to give up such freedom and instead become a girl, whatever that meant. Her emotional confusion over maleness and femaleness is clear in an adolescent memory: a soldier walks her home from her job as a cashier at the local movie theater, and tries to rape her; she bites him in self-protection. We applaud her spirit, then read that a few days later, the soldier and the medic who treated him confronted Lee with the evidence of her attack on the soldier. She says, "I really felt sick, pale and weak because it was hideous. But it was just done in panic because I had never been helpless before and that was the only way out." Behind this statement lie layers of paradoxical guilt and shame: a nice girl would not have "invited" the attack, a nice girl would not have retaliated, a nice girl would not have acted that way at all.

Other females in childhood and adolescence are less verbal about the limiting quality of being female. It is simply a reality that prevents them from running away, and makes them vulnerable to sexual exploitation and to segregation by sex. It also propels them into early marriages. Helen, at sixteen, married a man of fifty-one who promised to bring her younger brothers and sisters out of an orphanage. Mildred married when she was seventeen. She describes dating:

> One night when I was sixteen we were sitting in the drive-in, and a guy parked next to us and slammed his car door into ours. He came over and said, "Hi, my name's Harold. I'm sorry I bumped you."
> And I said, "Oh, well, I'm Mildred," and that's how we met. We dated for about five or six months and then decided to get married, which was ridiculous. I think a lot of the reason I decided to get married was just because I was so unhappy. . . . It seemed thrilling, but it wasn't. It was stupid, very stupid, but I thought it was all going to be so great.

While little girls cannot run away, older girls can do so by getting married. When seven of these women were teenagers, they married men they barely knew to escape childhood living arrangements. The reasons are many. Poverty, of course, is a major factor: jobs are hard to find or nonexistent; their own family's subsistence is marginal, and there are younger, more dependent mouths to feed. Mildred suggests another factor: "I thought it was all going to be so great." The fantasy of linking marriage and romantic love finds particularly devoted adherents among those young women whose daily lives and future prospects are relatively bleak.

The exceptions are interesting. Mary T., the daughter of Japanese immigrants, married a man she had known since elementary school. Although the marriage was not formally arranged, it was an appropriate one, meeting the needs of both families and of the community. For Mary, continuity and community seem to have replaced escape and romantic love as motivating factors for marriage. Though poverty was a presence in the lives of Mary T. and her family, perhaps the American Dream still held promise for them as relatively recent immigrants to America.

And Lee, already the mother of one child and expecting another, married Ed in her early twenties because, in her words, "So out of sheer being worn down, I went ahead and got married to be polite, to keep from hurting his feelings."

Women's physical weakness, as defined by muscle-to-fat ratio, is one of the reliable cross-cultural differences between men and women. While clearly biological, this difference also affects women socially; being weaker also means being less powerful in social relationships. While not inevitable, the social aspect of physical strength is historically true, even though modern technology has rendered such physical differences relatively unimportant. What has become clear is that men's abuse of their power over women is all too frequent in families, in the community, and at work. These women's worst experiences remind us of what it means to be a member of the weaker sex. (In thinking about the abuse of women as victims of incest, rape, battering by husbands, and sexual harassment and exploitation on the job, it is hard to imagine an analogous experience for men, one where the potential of sexual and aggressive exploitation is always present. Possibly it is what men imagine prison to be like.)

While the abuse of power toward women happens regardless of socioeconomic class, poverty certainly limits these women's options. Darlene, horribly beaten by her husband, knew she could not return home because she would impose too great a financial burden on her parents. Mildred describes the trap of sexual harassment in a work situation that she simply cannot afford to leave.

Recent scholarship on abuse of power shows that such abuse is structurally defined as permissible. Rape, for example, has been viewed historically as an accepted act of male conquest. In peaceful communities, female sexuality is often held up as the problem (she was seductive, she "wanted" it, she "was asking for it")—only recently has marital rape become legally actionable.

These lives reveal the psychological scars of years and years of hardship: depression, at times severe; substance abuse; resignation; and frustrated rage. More interestingly, however, they also show strength, drive, and determination. These women push on. While they are sometimes victimized by their sex, their poverty, and their minority status, they are not passive victims. They take care, they take responsibility, and they work for change. Sometimes their arena is family, but it often extends beyond. Many of these women are individually successful because they feel a sense of purpose in their lives; if asked, they would tell you that their lives had made a difference to family, friends, or an even wider circle. But to label these "success stories" is naive, since the structures of oppression severely limit these women's chances for success. Horatio Alger stories are about white males, and for poor people they can appear only as fantasies about other people living in quite another world.

Men move in and out of these women's lives. Of the ten, only Mary T. has a long-standing traditional relationship with a man. Fathers disappear; marriages don't last; protectors end up being abusers; husbands or lovers or fathers die. The women have no illusions about institutional support either: bosses, the government, and the welfare system are not caretaking but adversarial. Land ownership does not equal security; again and again the company, large landholders, city, state, and even the federal government strip ownership from the poor and the powerless. These women know just where they stand. They have no fantasies of being rescued and they understand the structural constraints on their effectiveness against these oppressors.

Perhaps it is this awareness that makes these women so free of mother blaming. In spite of what mainstream psychology would describe as debilitating deficiencies in nurturance, these women are neither paralyzed nor bitter. One could argue that due to their need to devote so much energy to practical, "worldly" struggles, the poor lack the psychological luxury of self-reflection and don't, therefore, recognize the "poor mothering" they received. Others might contend that poor people who have not been well educated are not familiar with the intricacies of self-reflection that might lead to such a recognition. In contrast, these women recognize the clear limits of mothering both as their mothers practiced it and as they themselves practice it. They do not share the middle-class myth of maternal power. (For further explication of this myth as it affects both women and psychology, see Chodorow and Contratto 1982; and Contratto 1984.)

Over and over again, these women say of their mothers, "She did the best she could."

And they themselves do the best they can. They are each engrossed at some point in their lives in taking care of children, and with preserving and encouraging growth and change. The ten women here have a total of thirty-nine children of their own. Sarah raised her dead brother's children; Helen took care of her younger brothers and sisters, retrieving them from an orphanage after her marriage; and Josephine went from Chicago to Memphis to fetch her daughter's children, who were in physical danger from her daughter's husband. Several worked taking care of other people's children, often a very important experience for them. Crusty, irascible Sarah softens noticeably when describing the children for whom she cared. Josephine took in foster children and Helen took care of several retarded adults when her own four sons were grown and had families of their own.

For these women, caregiving is often extremely difficult. Irene, as a single mother with four small children, joined the circus to feed and clothe her family. Josephine, already a widow with a one-year-old child at eighteen, describes her daily, chronic uncertainty over having food for her baby. Darlene describes the backbreaking physical labor, like hauling coal, performed well into each pregnancy to earn enough to feed her children. And Lee speaks of the unremitting guilt that has been a part of her psychological life since discovering that her husband was sexually abusing their daughters.

Partly as a result of real hardship, partly out of an implicit recognition of the limits of maternal power, these women, without feeling a mother's harsh self-recrimination, seem to let their children live independent lives. Their children are often not successful. Hattie, for all of Josephine's struggle in rearing her, becomes an alcoholic with uncontrolled rages toward her mother. Josephine is afraid of her daughter; Hattie's behavior is painful for her to acknowledge, but she does not hold herself responsible for the person that Hattie has become. Absent from her story are maternal "shoulds" and "oughts." Sarah matter-of-factly describes her childrearing and its outcome:

> Stayed home with them. And my auntie too and my mother too. We do fine when we were there [in the South]. Then I brought them up here [to the North] and they start getting in trouble. I don't know why they get in trouble. I guess 'cause of their dad.

Sarah offers two explanations for her children's difficulties. Implicitly, she suggests that the South is a better place to raise children and the family's move was not good for them. Explicitly, she speculates that her children might have inherited their father's personality. Both explanations are possible, given what little we know about why children get into trouble in later life, but they are explanations rarely heard from middle-class women, who seem quick to take responsibility for their children's problems. At the very least, a guilty mother is one who has not acknowledged the constraints on her own maternal power.

All of these women extend caretaking beyond the family. Sarah and Josephine have both taken care of other people's houses and children. Josephine was a cook in a house of prostitution, and Helen not only cooked extravagantly for her family, but became the proprietor of a restaurant where she could feed all sorts of people. Helen's love of food and of feeding others make parts of her story mouthwatering.

Two of the women, Irene and Mary T., have extended their lifelong struggles with racism to include teaching children about their cultural heritage. At the time of the interview, Mary T. had been active for many years in a Japanese cultural school, and Irene had been involved in preserving the oral history of her tribal people.

Darlene, badly abused by her husband, talks about spouse abuse with other women in an Appalachian community center and helps them find the resources to care for themselves. Lee, herself the mother of six children, works with parents in self-help support groups.

The work of these women is extremely important to them—they are consciously and voluntarily involved in improving the living and working conditions of their friends, neighbors, coworkers, and children. Three of the women are labor union organizers: Maria Elena, the daughter of a migrant worker and a migrant worker herself, is an activist in the United Farm Workers union; Mildred and Mary, garment factory workers, participate in the fight to unionize textile workers. They have had some measure of concrete success, too. Maria Elena celebrates the opening of the community center she has dreamed of, and Mildred and Mary see J. P. Stevens forced to live with the union.

But even their successes, impressive as they are, illustrate the magnitude of the problems they face and their own relative powerlessness. None of them hold positions of power and authority within their unions, since typically these visible positions go to men while women, with their better "people skills" do the daily grassroots work. (See Wertheimer and Nelson 1975; Lawson and Barton 1980.) Further, the larger structural system circumscribes their successes. Shortly after the victory over J. P. Stevens, for example, the company began closing plants and laying off workers in the South. Though the bad economic situation may have been beyond the control of the company, a company executive deferring his salary increase for a year suffers little in comparison with a laid-off worker facing hunger and cold.

Hunger and cold: these words provide a fitting conclusion. With this book Fran Leeper Buss has given us a stirring picture of how poor women struggle and survive. To survive with dignity in the face of hunger and cold is what these stories are all about.

A bibliography containing suggestions for further reading appears at the end of this volume. This list of selected books and articles was compiled with the assistance of Cynthia Palmer, and represents only a sampling of the rich and exciting scholarship on women now becoming available.

Susan Contratto, former director of the Women's Studies Program at the University of Michigan, is a psychologist with a private practice in Ann Arbor. She received her doctorate from the Harvard University Graduate School of Education and has taught courses in psychology and women's studies for over ten years. The author of numerous publications examining women's roles and psychological development, she also serves as vice-president of the board of the local Domestic Violence Project.

Lives of Dignity and Purpose

Fran Leeper Buss

The old white woman I was staying with in the mountains of Kentucky considered it her God-given duty throughout life to visit "the sick and the afflicted." She had given birth three times, raised her two surviving children, and cared for her miner husband throughout his work life, his long illness with black lung disease, his death and burial. She had served as a midwife when the need was great and there was no one else to do it. She had cradled her own young baby in her arms as the infant slowly lost ground in her fight for life, singing and talking to the child as she faded. But the old woman's overall conviction and purpose in life was that she was to bring whatever solace and care she could to those in desperate need.

Despite increasing senility, she remained physically strong. She led me up a green hollow to the dilapidated cabin of an even more elderly and emaciated woman, a woman crippled and starving, living in an eight-by-eight-foot cabin without toilet facilities who was cared for only by a retarded boy. Only old Rosie seemed aware of the sick woman's circumstances, and it was Rosie's belief in her mission, despite her increasing inability to remember details of the present, that eventually brought some aid to the crippled woman.

At other times I met with a young black woman in the beastly hot and noisy apartment that she shared with her two young daughters and her mother in a crowded public housing project in Montgomery, Alabama. Life churned around us during those visits as people attempted to escape from the overwhelming heat into the treeless shadows of the projects. The young woman had given birth to her first child at sixteen and after her divorce tried to provide for them on her own. She had found work in the notorious J. P. Stevens textile mills in Montgomery and became active in the union drive that was intended to alleviate some of the poor working conditions in the mills. One night she was fired because of her organizing efforts and barred from the other factories in the area. When no work was available, she and her daughters went on welfare, trying to exist on a total income of $180 a month.

While her children climbed on and off her lap, she spoke of the time when her pregnancy forced her to quit high school, her attempts to provide for her babies, her close relationship with her mother, the self-respect she acquired as she worked for the union, her moment-by-moment financial struggles, and her hopes and fears for the futures of her daughters and herself.

During the four years of research for this book, I met, worked with, and stayed with many women. I listened intently as they told me of the struggles and triumphs in their lives. I heard them speak of the universal experiences of women made especially sharp and piercing by their poverty. Through laughter and tears they told me of their experiences with menstruation, pregnancy, motherhood, contraception, and abortion; of their struggles with rape, sexual harassment, battering, abandonment, death, and poverty; of marriage, divorce, and widowhood; of friendship and love; and of racial, sexual, and economic discrimination. They also spoke of their belief systems and how they came to find dignity and meaning in their lives. During these times I became overwhelmingly aware of the vulnerability of women created by the cultural role women have been assigned and their biological ability to give birth to children in an often nonsupportive and cruel social system.

On the whole, the women whose stories appear in this book are survivors, and they are often not the desperately poor. For each of these women who have somehow made it through all the barriers of class, racial, and sexual discrimination, there are those who did not survive. Those women's stories tend not to be told, because they are not very visible, because they are so vulnerable that publicity would be dangerous, or because they have died or have been too "beaten down" to discuss their lives.

The fragility of the survivor status these women have attained under dismal circumstances seemed especially clear to me one hot summer afternoon in rural Georgia. I was visiting with a small, dark, thirty-four-year-old black woman whose voice was low and quiet and who appeared as if she tried to take up little space in life. Her trailer was in relatively good condition, but its furnishings indicated her poverty. A window overlooked a wheat field, a breeze blew through her curtains, and we could hear birds singing outside. In almost a whisper, the woman described the poverty of her childhood, her family's lack of food, and her mother's life, including twenty pregnancies that resulted in nine children who lived past young childhood. Of these nine, one girl died of unknown causes, one boy died of leukemia, one boy was shot, and two boys died in a car accident. Then, of the four remaining children, one boy was totally disabled so that he could not walk or speak, and his aging mother still takes care of him. The elderly and fragile mother, therefore, had three functioning children out of the twenty to whom she had given birth.

I interviewed seventy-two women but only ten stories are told here, and it was very difficult to choose whose stories should be included. However, I have tried to present somewhat of a balanced picture in terms of rural and urban backgrounds, age, race, and life situations. I certainly did not choose these specific women because one's story was more important than another's; such a judgment would be impossible to make. Some of the women whose stories I heard eventually received higher education, through great effort. Their education helped them attain leadership roles in social action groups, which made it easier for me to locate them in the first place. Also, several women in the book are in middle-income brackets at the present time, but because of financial struggles throughout childhood and young adulthood, and the insights that these women have shared with me, I have decided to include their stories. I want to emphasize that these stories are not statistically representative of a cross section of women from lower-income or marginal-income situations.

The stories told by the women in this book did not occur as monologues, but were the product of a developing relationship between each woman and myself. As much as I tried to be objective and encourage each woman to take the lead in what we discussed, by asking certain questions, responding in specific ways, and choosing which material to include in the final editing, I have certainly influenced the final telling of each story. Because of the influence I had, it is important that readers have some knowledge of my background, beliefs, and interests.

I did not enter these women's lives as a total stranger to the life experiences they describe. I am a white woman who grew up in a primarily working-class neighborhood in a small city in the Midwest. Our neighborhood bordered on some of the most impoverished areas in our community, and when I was young, my mother pointed out to me the disturbing inequities between the neighborhoods.

I was married relatively young and divorced when my three children were preschoolers and we were living in the West. Following my

divorce, my struggle to support the children became especially difficult. At one point, I worked four part-time jobs and spent more than
50 percent of my income on child care. Food stamps were crucial to
our physical and emotional survival, and we went on welfare for a
period of time. It was during this time that I came to understand the
importance of the strength women can give each other. Despite this
valuable resource, I became ill and received several years of extremely
poor, indigent medical care. I also personally experienced sexual violence and institutional violence against women and the poor.

Then I married again, and with the assistance of my present husband and those close to us, I became healthier and finished my education. During those years I did community organizing with other low-
income women, founding a women's crisis and information center,
and thus came in contact with many other women experiencing some
of the basic struggles of life. I have continued community organizing
throughout the years and am presently on leave of absence from the
ministry of the United Church of Christ and am teaching women's
studies part time at the University of Wisconsin at Whitewater.

The political visions that have shaped my writing were formed by
my personal experiences, work in community organizing, a long-term
involvement in groups working with justice issues, a training in liberal
and radical Christian ethics, and a fourteen-year commitment to feminism. I am deeply interested in the means by which people find
meaning in life and what religious, philosophical, or ethical under-
standings underscore their courage, commitments, methods of con-
fronting suffering, ideas of justice, and efforts to change themselves
and the world. I try to understand how individual women from different backgrounds experience the events common to most women, and I
care a great deal about the support groups that develop among women
to help them through the tremendous struggles associated with poverty
and discrimination. I have been strongly aware of my limits as a white
woman speaking to women of color and from cultures other than
mine, and I appreciate the depth with which those women have shared
and tried to tell me of their experiences.

I traced the women to interview through various means, beginning
with suggestions made by friends from across the country, then working through newspapers, political action groups, and religious action
groups. Frequently, the women I interviewed referred me to their
family and friends. While doing the research, I stayed with or near the
woman being interviewed, and her comments were tape-recorded in-
formally in a number of sessions. In transcribing the tapes, I have
edited the comments for clarity and cohesiveness. Despite these altera-
tions, I believe I have maintained the integrity and individuality of

their statements. Approximately half of the women also read their own story after I had written it. Some wished to have their name and other identifying information changed to protect their privacy. These changes are noted in the individual story introductions.

It would have been impossible for me to experience all that went into this book without it affecting my life profoundly. I have become personally involved with most of the women, maintaining friendships through letters, the telephone, and visits. I have also tried to help them locate resources when specific needs have arisen, but primarily the total experience has deepened my political conviction that we must all struggle to make our society more just.

Statistics are important. According to the 1980 census, taken close to the time when the interviews were done, 75 percent of poor people in the United States are women. Female-headed households represent 15 percent of all families, but they are over half of all poor families. Seventy percent of female-headed households live in poverty. Minority women especially suffer. Two-thirds of all poor black families are headed by women. Almost half of all families headed by black and Hispanic women live in poverty. The unemployment rate for black women is over 18 percent and over 15 percent for Hispanic women, compared to 9 percent for white women. Being employed does not necessarily lift women out of poverty as it usually does for men. Three out of four full-time working women earn less than $10,000 a year, one of three earns under $7,000. (These statistics are taken from a handout published by the Women's International League for Peace and Freedom 1983.)

Most of these interviews were done in the months before the beginning of the Reagan administration and its consequent cutbacks in social services and similar programs for the poor, who are primarily women and children. Many of the women in these pages and the people they love have been directly affected by such cutbacks, through the loss of employment, unemployment or training aid, welfare, food stamps, utility assistance, medical programs, industrial safety measures, old-age programs for the poor, rehabilitation programs, child care help, and federal prenatal and postnatal nutrition programs. If the interviews were being done at this moment, much more immediate desperation would be described. It is the lives of people like the women in this book and their loved ones that are being sacrificed in the name of various economic theories.

In addition, these cutbacks are occurring when the Equal Rights Amendment has been defeated and at a time when some of the major programs designed to combat racial and sexual discrimination, such as voting rights legislation, affirmative action, and busing to achieve school integration, appear to be in jeopardy. The struggle against injustice seems to be losing ground.

Yet, despite all the hurdles these women faced, many of their stories have a heroic quality. Each person dealt with the universals of being a woman in her own way, struggling with each event and passage in her life according to her own ethnic background and personal manner. While fighting against the forces of discrimination, violence, and economic hardships, she also searched for meaning in her circumstances and consequently created a unique life of dignity and purpose. Stories of such struggles follow.

*I'm not afraid; I'm not afraid. . . . I
raised my daughter the best that I could.
I've never sold my body to nobody. I've
never stole anything. I've never been
arrested. And you can go places and find
that I have a record of working. It's just
that I grew tired of domestic work, and I
wanted a home of my own. That's the
way it was, so I can face my God.*

—Josephine Hunter

When a Milwaukee urban renewal project forced Josephine Hunter to sell the home she and her husband had lovingly cared for, the home in which they had raised four grandchildren and thirty-five foster children, Josephine ended up with almost no profit to represent a lifetime of unending work. She cried and pleaded and went to a lawyer, hoping to stay in her home or at least receive what she felt would be a reasonable profit from its sale, but nothing worked; she was forced to sell a fourteen-room duplex for $10,000.

The small amount of cash that remained after the house closing was rapidly eaten up by the costs of her husband's final illness, his funeral, and some medical bills of her own. Finally, aware of the vulnerability of a lone, crippled old woman, she spent her final $1,000 on an alarm system that promised her some personal safety. The benefits of sixty years of hard work were now gone.

Josephine lives today in the rented main floor of an old duplex right outside the area razed by the urban renewal project. Josephine is black and her home is in a largely black neighborhood dotted by recently built projects and subsidized single-family homes; Josephine is largely cut off from the outside world and spends her days isolated and watching TV. Nevertheless, she does attempt to maintain a home for her retarded thirty-seven-year-old grandson Robert. He works days and is gone most evenings, but his company is immensely important to Josephine.

The house she keeps is cheerful and clean. There are numerous knickknacks set carefully around with a number of artificial plants and flowers. Her front bay window contains six large pots of African violets, and in the mornings, rich, deep colors shine through a high stained-glass window. Throughout the house she has carefully arranged hand-made lace, embroidered, and crocheted goods, and she displays stuffed animals won by Robert at carnivals.

In warm weather Josephine often sits out on her porch watching the events of her neighborhood, but once inside, she keeps her doors locked and bolted against danger year round. She was mugged not too many years ago, and that fear is always with her. It is a sad commentary that, at the end of her life, so much energy and money must go into ensuring her personal safety.

Josephine herself is a short, wide woman of seventy-two who moves about slowly and stiffly with the help of a cane. Her skin is light brown and freckled, her white and gray hair pulled back into a bun. Josephine's face is marked by the creases and lines of age, but it has also retained a rather youthful, narrow shape. We sat at her dining room table as we talked, and she shared her story with fullness, detail, and vigor, revealing herself and her keen observations of her world. Josephine chose to use her real name.

Josephine I was born in Memphis, Tennessee, in 1907, so I am seventy-two years old. My mother had three children and I was the middle child. She died when she was twenty-five, following childbirth. She had childbirth fever and there was nothing that they knew for it. My mother's people were part Negro and part Oklahoma Indian, and my father was part white and part Negro. His father was an Englishman. My mother's people did not like my father because of his mixture of birth and because he was Catholic. Since they were dark they didn't think of the mixture of birth on their side. When my mother died my father was not allowed around us. There was a neighbor who knew him, though, and once in awhile I got to see my father through her. But he died when I was fifteen or so. To this day I can't really see why my mother's people hated him.

My mother's people were not as poor as some. My grandfather had bought his own property which was on the outskirts of the city. It was a simple house with four rooms. My mother and her two brothers and one sister were born there, and then I was born there too. In the summer my grandfather had his garden where he raised vegetables. He also had a cow and some chickens, so we had eggs and milk.

The only memories I have of my mother was when she was in bed and I was seven. Do you know what turnip greens are? She would have me go to the market or a peddler would come by and I would buy them. Then she would have me bring into her room the greens and two pans and a trash piece of paper. She would put it on the floor, and I would sit beside the bed, and she would show me which to put in the pan and which to throw away in the trash. After I had finished picking the greens she would show me by measuring with her fingers and hands about how much salt pork I should put in the pot. Then it would cook. I also had been taught to wash the greens, and if the water was real dirty, she would hold up five fingers meaning I should wash them that many times to know that they were clean. That's the way she taught me, and that's what I can remember of her.

For two weeks that's the way things were with us. She was in bed and the baby was near her. Then the baby died one morning and she died in the afternoon. Who knows what the baby died of? They didn't have a doctor, just a midwife who was very old. We called the midwife Grandma Bates. All Grandma Bates knew was that my mother had a fever. They put jimsonweed on her. It was a weed that grew out in a field and had a white bloom on it like a morning glory, only the bloom was much larger. The weed had an awful odor, something similar to horse manure. They would gather these weeds, bruise them, and put them in a towel or a rag and tie them round your head, and it would draw the fever out. So they put them around my mother's head, and they put them across her belly.

The next thing I knew the undertakers came and took my mother away. She was dead, but nobody told me. I guess she died on a Monday, and they brought the body back on Wednesday evening. At that time her people had what they call a wake. It was at the home and on the door there was a long piece of white ribbon tied up in a bow. They called it a crepe. If a person was young, like my mother, it was white, middle-aged it was gray, and old like I am now, it was black.

They put my mother in a white coffin across the bay window in the front room. The house was full of people, going in and out, in the backyard as well as the front yard. It was September and very, very warm. They sang, they prayed, and they told jokes and drank coffee all night. When I got sleepy one of the neighbors told me to go lay down on the daybed in the same room as my mother's coffin. Well, I laid on the daybed, and my mother was laying over there in this box, as I called it. I didn't know what it was.

One of the neighbors came to me when I woke up the next morning, and she said to me, "Now you better get a good look at your mother. You'd better look until the time for us to take her body to the church because you won't see her anymore."

And I said, "Why? And why is she in that box and don't talk?"

Well, the neighbor just patted me on the shoulders and said, "Just look," and she went away from me.

I do remember they put a white dress on me and they combed my hair. It was real thick at that time, and they put it in three braids and put a white ribbon on each of my braids. Then we rode out to the cemetery in what was called a hack pulled by two horses.

I remember being squished between my uncles and aunt. It was a few years before I really understood what happened.

Nobody really took care of us after that, my older brother and myself. We stayed with my mother's people, but my aunt was a single woman and was too busy trying to find a husband to be with us. The men were busy going out, like men do, and my grandfather was too busy chasing young women.

In the summertime before and after my mother died, my grandfather's brother would take my older brother and myself to the country to live on a farm. In the country they ate in a different way than we did in town. They would go out in the field, and they would gather what they were gonna have for supper and then cook it. Well, I would go with them and gather what we call butter beans there and lima beans here. They also grew watermelons, and, oh, they were so sweet.

I remember that I didn't have the proper clothes to wear. It would get to be about 102 or 104 or 105 degrees in the summer, and I can remember in July one year when I was little that I had a red plaid wool dress. That's all I had to put on. All my life I had wanted to be clean and cool. In the summer I'd play all day with the other kids with the red wool dress on, and then the other kids would take a bath. Of course, they lived with their parents and had more. When we took a bath we used to sit a tub of water out in the sun and the water would heat up. I'd take a bath too like the other kids, but I'd have to put the same dirty clothes back on.

One of our neighbors seen me, and she knew what I was trying to do, so she called me over. She gave me a complete outfit, a draws, a drawsbody, which are underclothes, and a dress of her daughter's. And, of course, she rolled up my dirty clothes and said, "You can take them home." Oh boy, that was the happiest day of my life. I could take a bath and put on clean clothes.

It was hard to feel my family loved me when I was little. I didn't know, when I'd wake up in the house one morning, if I was going to sleep in the house with them that night. They'd all be going out. I do have to give them credit, though. They never believed in leaving me in the house alone. I had to go to the neighbor woman's.

And she was glad to see me. In fact, she was so good to me I started to call her my godmother. She always would put some milk in a saucer for me, and she made hot corncake bread and would give me a whole cake of this cornbread, very hot off the griddle. That was a treat. And every day, when I came home from school, she had something hot to give me to eat. She taught me how to cook and everything, and when she died I really lost a friend.

Her son was good to me too. I called him my cousin. They gave me the first real nice pair of shoes that I ever had. They were black patent leather, bought for Easter. They called them "Mary Janes," and they had a strap across the front of them. The son bought me those and his mother bought me a white eyelet dress, with a big, white satin sash. I had a new dress, new slip, new pants, and new socks and shoes. That particular Easter you couldn't ask me anything, nor could you tell me anything, I was so proud.

My family never gave me anything. I never knew what it was to have a nickel in my hand to go to the store or to buy an ice cream cone or a piece of candy. But the kids in the neighborhood knew that I wasn't getting anything, so if they got any they gave me a piece. The only money I got this godmother and her son gave me.

We had a movie on the corner there, a little theater, and they ran movies for kids on Saturday afternoons. It took a nickel and a card to get in. See, you'd go to the store and you'd buy something and they would punch the card. Then it'd take one of those cards filled out and a nickel to get into the movie. My godmother started trading at that store so she could have the card. Then, when she filled it out, she would give me a nickel, and I could go to the show. Sometimes she gave me a dime, and I could get a bag of popcorn, too.

She and her son meant so much to me. After I got older and understood I said that God just gave her the feeling to feel for me, because I was no relation to her. She didn't have to do that. And her son didn't have to give me anything. I was not her responsibility. When they died it was like I had lost my best friends. But I kind of got used to death, just looked like everybody was dying around me.

I went to school when I was a child, a segregated school. It wasn't too far away. I could run to it and I ran practically all the time because I'd be late. As soon as I got a little older they had me working all the time. I'd work before school in the morning, and when I got out of school I had to run to make dinner. I couldn't play along with the other kids.

My teachers were all Negro and they were strict. We had to know our ABCs when we started there and even some of the multiplication tables, from the ones to the threes. There was no kindergarten. The teacher had a long chart on what was like wrapping paper, yellow and green. It was about as long as both arms stretched out. It had words on it like "cat," "dog," or "mouse," and sentences like "See Johnny run. Johnny can run. Johnny has a ball." Instead of books, that's how we learned. And we learned to write large. If you tried to print she'd hit you on the knuckles and tell you, "You write." So even today I write large and clear.

We had two teachers that told everyone in the class, "You've got to learn to read, you've got to learn to write, and you've got to learn to understand what you read and write." And even today I'm darn glad I went to that school.

The times with my family were hard for me when I was little. My granddaddy's people did give me food. I can't say they didn't give me something to eat, and I had a bed to sleep in. Sometimes it was clean; sometimes it wasn't. But I didn't have proper clothes to wear. And when I was little, before my godmother started helping me, I went for days and days without my hair being combed. It was thick so that when they finally combed it I would cry because it hurt so much.

When I got large enough I had to get up at four o'clock and five o'clock in the morning and make breakfast for all of them. I had to make biscuits from scratch and have them all ready, a really big pan, and I fried meat. I had to have it all on the table when they got up. My aunt would wake me up and say, "Time to get up and make breakfast." Then I would wrap their lunch for them to take to work.

After they went to work I had to clean the table, wash the dishes, make up the beds, and go to school. Then, when school was out I had to come home and finish what I hadn't been able to do before I went to school and make the supper and have it done before five-thirty. In between that, the kids would be out in the street playing ball, and I would run out and try to play with them and at the same time watch my supper. If it burned I got a lickin'. But I'd still take a chance and go out there in the traffic and play a little ball. I got a lickin' more than once because it burned. It didn't burn real bad, but you could taste it. I was smart enough to take it from one pot and put it in another to try and keep them from knowing, but they could taste it. Of course, I was cooking all the time on a coal and wood stove.

I needed a mother to talk to me as I was growing. My aunt and my grandfather had always told me that if a boy just rubbed his hand on your arm you was going to have a baby. And I was taught to have a baby was something awful, but they didn't tell me anything else. So when my first period came I was very frightened. I knew that I had no kind of contact with a boy, but I was afraid they'd think I was playing around. My period had started overnight and my bedsheet was all bloody, and I was bloody. I got up and got those things off when the family had gone to work. I made up the bed and everything, but I kept bleeding and didn't know what was wrong. We had an artesian well that we drank the water from back farther in the yard. It was a small spring where the cow and the horse got their water. I went down to this spring and got in that spring and washed and washed. But every time that I'd step out I'd take a leaf and wipe myself, and I would see more blood on it; so I got back into the water. I stayed in that spring until that water chilled my blood and I passed out.

A girl from next door come down to bring their horse and there I was. It was just the way my arms fell that kept me from drowning. She ran and got her mother, and they found the sheet where I was trying to wash it. They took me home and I got OK, but it was a year and a half before my period came back.

My brother was two and a half years older than me, and he tried to help me with the family, to stand up for me, but they were hard on him too and his standing up didn't work. So, when I was twelve, he got tired of it and ran off. He didn't tell me before he left, probably because I would have cried, and he didn't want to see me cry. He felt that it was just better that he get up and go.

My mother's people were really angry. My granddaddy said, "If he comes back, I'll beat him to the inch of his life." But he never came back. We never heard from him. I don't know if he went up to the railroad and caught a freight train or what. I cried and I cried, day after day, until finally the old lady, my godmother, told me, "Well, there's no need of crying. He's gone and you just have to make the best of it."

But after he left I had to do his work and mine too at home. He had brought in the coal and wood, so then I had to bring that in nights, and on Saturdays I had to bring in double amounts because it was a sin to cut wood on a Sunday. So I had to cut double wood on Saturday and lug in double amounts of coal.

Things stayed hard and as I grew older I seen the other children having more. If I'd been a boy I could have run away but I couldn't. I got to the tenth grade in school, but I didn't have the proper clothes to wear, and my godmother was dead and her son was gone, so I didn't have anybody to depend upon.

There was a boy named Ernest that came around who had been a friend of my brother, and when I was sixteen he asked me to marry him. Well, to me I'd seen a way of having a better home; so at sixteen I married him, and we lived pretty good and happy. I got pregnant real soon but when I was six months I was going up some open steps carrying two lard buckets full of water, and my foot went through the hole in the back of the steps and I fell backwards. I lost the baby and had a hard time. Then later I got pregnant with the one living child I have. Giving birth at seventeen was bad because I knew nothing, and every time she tried to come out, I'd draw up. So she had to tear her way into the world.

Then, when I was eighteen and my baby was six months, my husband took sick. He came home from work one night, and the dinner was all prepared except for making cornbread. So I made the cornbread and when it was ready I called him, but he didn't answer. I went into the other room where he was and he was just laying there. I ran my hand across his face and he had a fever. I shook him and I couldn't wake him up.

His mother lived four doors down the street, and I ran down there to get her to come up. She did and said, "Ernest isn't dead, but he's unconscious." So we called an ambulance and rushed him to the hospital.

When we got to the hospital they said it was meningitis. There was an epidemic then and people were dying with it like sheep with the rots. They strapped him in bed, face down, with a strap as wide as my hand against the back of his head, but even with the strap, his neck pulled back and was broke and he died.

I had no money but his mother had a little insurance that she used to bury him. That's something I never did understand. At the funeral she had this Baptist preacher, and that man stood in the pulpit every bit of a hour and a half, hoopin' and hollerin'. He'd shout, "Well, Brother Fields is gone to God, and I can see him flying around in heaven."

And I said to myself, "How in the devil can he see him flying around in heaven?"

"Yes, I seen Brother Ernest. I know the angels came down and took him away, and I can just see them going off together."

And they'll sing the saddest songs there ever was and people were crying and fainting. You are worn out. You are frazzled. Just wilted down. And, then, when you are sitting there, they have the coffin open the whole while. There it is before you, almost like a table to sit at. It's open and I'm sitting there, right there on the front seat, and I got to look at it, or I got to look up at the preacher. Afterwards, for a long, long time at night, when I would go to sleep, I could hear the screaming and those people.

I cried at Ernest's funeral. I realized that I was left all alone, and nobody really cared, even Ernest's mother. So I cried and I cried for months afterward. I'd just sit and for no reason at all the tears would just start rollin'. And I couldn't stop them. By the time I was twenty, I'd lost my mother, my father, my youngest brother, my older one, my first baby, my husband, and my godmother was gone. I was all alone with Hattie Mae, my baby, and we had nothing.

I stayed where we were living; there was no place to go and we were bad off. Then a friend that knew my father came over, and he said, "How're ya living?"

"I'm not living. I'm just here. If I don't have the money to pay the rent next month I don't know what's gonna happen."

He said, "How much is the rent?"

"It's a dollar and a half a week." We had two rooms, a front room and a combination bedroom and kitchen.

Then my father's friend paid my rent for five weeks. So I knew I had a place to stay. And he went to the grocery, and he bought some beans, white beans and rice and neckbones and some pig tails. It was just common food, but it was better than what I had. And he also gave me a dollar and seventy-five cents in cash money because turnip greens and spinach was a penny a pound. And I bought spinach and I bought what we called side meat in the South; you call it salt pork up North. I would cook the greens with it. So we survived.

I had to find something to do and some way to take care of my child. There was an old lady that lived next door to me. She was in the condition then that I'm in now. She had no one to help her, and I asked her if she would keep my child while I went out to find work.

I said, "Now, you know I have no money to give you."

"Well, I will do that for you if you will do one thing for me. The rent man is gonna put me out, and I have no place to go."

So I says, "Sure, I will take you in. I'll just turn my front room into a bedroom." So she kept the child for her room and board, and I got a job child nursing. I walked to work two and a half miles and back every day to make five dollars a week. At first I only worked a half day on Saturdays and not on Sundays. The work enabled me to pay my rent and to buy a little food for this old lady and my child.

I had to learn to make do those years. I walked around with newspaper and pasteboard in my shoes. The shoe tops would be looking good, and I would polish them to keep you from thinking I didn't have any shoes on. I earned only five dollars and I had to pay my rent of a dollar and a quarter, and I had to clothe my daughter and myself and buy food with what was left. The old lady liked graham crackers, and you could get a good-sized bag if you went to the National Biscuit Company and got the broken ones. So I would walk a mile twice a week to get the broken graham crackers for her. Then, when I came home, I would warm up spinach and neckbones and we would eat. Sometimes we ran out and, in order for my daughter to have food, I wouldn't eat. There was no welfare then in Memphis, and if somebody didn't give you something, you just didn't get it.

There were a lot of things to take care of in the house. I had to buy fifty pounds of ice for our icebox. The box was wood, with a tin lining, and you put the ice in on the top and the coldness come down. It had a spout where the ice melted and run down and threw it into the backyard. Of course, there was no toilets in the house then. You either went outdoors to an out-of-doors privy, or, if you were lucky, you had a toilet on the back porch. We had a washstand by the door, and it had a round hole cut in it where the bowl sit. When you were through with the water you pitched the water out the door. We had a coal and wood stove, and on the back of the stove was a reservoir for water. You would fill up the reservoir with cold water, and as long as there was fire in the stove, you had hot water.

When we did laundry in the summertime, we had a big iron pot that would sit out in the yard, and you made a fire under this pot. If your white clothes didn't suit you, you put lye in the water before it got hot and would let it boil. Then you'd drop your white clothes into this pot of boiling water, and you'd take a paddle and churn them up and down. After you cooked them so long a time, you took this paddle and would bring them out and put them in a bucket of hot water. Then you'd take them over to your tub and rinse them out. When you were through washing your clothes, you'd hang the tub up on the nail on the side of the house.

Of course, we didn't have very many clothes, so I'd wash our clothes out overnight when I got home from work. I'd hang them in the kitchen and let them dry and get up early the next morning and press them. I wanted my daughter to be clean when she went to school, and I wanted her to have a better education than I had.

I didn't have to chop the wood I needed. I was able to buy it cut. I never could buy a ton of coal. But when the coal trains were coming into Memphis, pieces of coal would fall off on the side of the track, and they'd pick up the coal. Then they would bring it around to various houses to sell, and you could get a cropper-sack of coal for fifty cents.

One time my child-nursing job ended, and I became a cook for a house of prostitution. A friend of mine, who worked there, had an operation, and I worked for her until she was well. I had needed a job real bad. This was a house with eight girls. They were all white but there were Negro houses too. There were five houses like that on the street, altogether. That way the men knew where they wanted to go and what they wanted to do there, and no one went down to that place looking for them. When you walked into the front door of the house, it was just like any other living room. The bedrooms were all upstairs and that's where the carryings on was did.

They all worked nightly but they also had customers that would come and sometimes stay seven days or eight days. Then, if a particular girl was with a particular man, she did not see anyone else during that time. She was not, as they called it, on call. But if a particular person wasn't around, they was on call for anybody that came in.

There was a girl, Rosie, who was with a man from Texas. He owned cattle and oil and they called him Big Tex. If he came there for seven days, he brought seven steaks for himself and seven for the house woman, or mother, as they called her. And that was the first time I'd ever seen a steak three and a half to four inches thick. When he was there I had to prepare this steak for him, and he would eat it for breakfast.

This particular fellow, Tex, said that I cooked the meals for him as well as the colored woman that he had in Texas that he called "Mammy." She was getting too old to cook, so he offered me her job to go to Texas to cook for him.

I told him, "No, I don't want to go that far." But he found out that I had a child, and he took Rosie downtown and bought my little girl five dresses, six pair of socks, and two pair of shoes. He said that was his way of showing appreciation for me. Then he gave me $150 cash money. But I still said no, I just didn't want to go. But with that way of spending, the women there had to take good care of him.

The women there educated me. They told me what life was and the things that you went up against. One of those girls told me that had she known when she went into that business the things that she had to go through, she would never have gone in it. Everything in those houses aren't done natural. When one of the men comes in and pays the woman to get you, you've got to do whatever he wants did. And any way that he wants it did.

She said, "You are making an honest living. Continue to work that way because I can't get out of it now. There isn't anything in this life, any way that they want sex did, that I haven't had to do. It's all right to cook for us and go home before the action comes, but don't ever sell your body. Don't sell your body."

Yes, they talked to me. They told me that they went in that business when they were young and had nothing else to do. The ones who talked to me were in their thirties, and you never got over forty in that business because the men didn't want them that old. So they always had 'to bring in young ones. Sometimes they had a rough night, as they called it, and on those mornings two or three of them would ask me to bring their breakfast up to them in bed.

Out of the money that they made, over half of it had to go to the woman in charge. They sell their body and that woman got over half of it. But with Tex it was different. When Tex walked in to be with Rosie, he would give the housemother $300, and he told her, "Whatever I give to Rosie is Rosie's damn business, and you are not to bother her about it." Of course, the mother may have said something to Rosie about it after Tex left. We'd never know.

I remembered their advice and I didn't fall for anything even though I had a child to take care of. I had boyfriends and, yes, I went to bed with them, but I never sold my body.

I had a boyfriend, Stokly, that really was nice to me. He ran on the railroad as a Pullman porter, and during the time we were together he was hauling soldiers. Once he sent me a wire from Bowling Green, Kentucky, that said I should meet him in the station. When I went there he had a large split basket with two handles on it. In it he had a whole slab of bacon. And that was the first time I knew that canned peaches come in two-gallon cans, because he gave some to me. Peaches, pears, apricots, whatever they were serving the soldiers, he'd have some of it in his basket when he'd come. He and the cook were good friends, and he had told the cook about me being his girlfriend.

And all the tips Stokly got, he would give them to me. He'd say, "Your rent is due. I'm giving you this. It'll keep you and the child going. You need fresh meat, you need fresh vegetables." And he's given me as much as twenty-five dollars just on tips he got. That plus the food.

But when he wasn't on the road, I didn't go to bed with him in my house. I had a child and I respected her. When he asked me to go to bed with him, he took me to where he roomed, and I would spend an hour with him. And he would come over to my house and sit around, laugh, and talk and play with my child.

The one thing I didn't like about him, though, was that he

liked to gamble. I didn't like that and I felt that, yes, he would be ever so nice, but then I says to myself, "Who knows? He's a single man and if he throws away all his money gambling now, it's no responsibility but himself. But if I marry him and then he threw it all away, I would suffer and my child would suffer."

So I told him, "I won't marry you 'cause of the gambling. Not unless you give it up."

He answered, "Well, I've been gambling all my life, ever since I was fourteen years old. I'm not going to give it up just for you."

"Then if you don't want to stop we just can't be friends." And that's the way we broke up.

I felt I had gone through enough with my childhood and bringing up my daughter until I got on my feet, so now why marry someone just to say I had a husband. And sex has never been a great big thing for me. I always felt that if I got in a panic, I had a syringe with a long water hose that I could use and relieve myself.

Of course, at that time no one took any pills to prevent babies. But you could take a jar of Vaseline or any other grease that you had and grease yourself real good before and it wouldn't stick. Then afterwards we would get up and go to the bathroom and strain ourself to pass water. And if you didn't use grease you could use a syringe and flush yourself out afterwards. Also, you didn't lie down with a man at a certain time after your period. That's how we did it.

Most of the time when I was in the South I worked as a domestic, doing child nursing or cooking. Down there I don't care how poor white people were or how rich they were, they always tried to have somebody come to work for them, unless they were extremely poor, and I never worked for an extreme poor person. I always looked to try to work for somebody that could help me. Didn't need to go and work for somebody as poor as I am 'cause they couldn't help me.

When you worked for a family of people like the Goldsmiths and the Leakers and the Wolfs, where my name was Josephine Fields, in the neighborhood I was known as Josephine Goldsmith. When you worked for those people you were known by their surname. Other times they said, "the nigger Goldsmith." But the people I worked for never called me nigger, at least not to my face. The other word they used to put us down was to call Negro kids "pickaninnies," like they aren't even people. I could never accept that word.

I was mixed-up about all the names when I was little, but when I'd gotten large enough to understand, I took the dictionary and looked up the word *nigger*. It said a nigger is a person of a low standard. That means, according to the dictionary, he can be white, he can be green, he can be yellow. He doesn't have to be black. So it doesn't belong to me. I'm not a nigger.

We usually had to work long hours, like with some jobs I had Thursdays and Sundays off and with some jobs I had Thursdays and every other Sunday off. When I was working as a cook I would have every other Sunday off because the child had a nurse and the nurse would get off Wednesdays. So on Wednesdays I didn't have to cook because it fell to my duty to look after the child. But that meant that I had to stay there until nine that night because the mother and father would go out to dinner, and they needed me to take care of their child. And every other Sunday the nurse was off, so that meant every other Sunday I had to babysit.

The average white woman in the South is lazy. They figure that the black people, as they call us, is glad to take care of their kids and work, but they don't think about our kids. I had to be there at eight every morning to make breakfast before the man went to work. The only lunch I made would be for the nurse, the child, and myself, because the woman was out somewhere playing bridge. Then they'd come home about five-thirty, but it'd be six-thirty when I put the dinner on the table 'cause they'd be getting ready to go out. Then I'd serve the dinner, wash the dishes, and go home to my child around eighty-thirty. It was nine o'clock before I got home to see my child. But it wasn't just me, it was everybody. That's the way it was and it isn't much better than that today. They get a little more money, but the same thing is going on.

We didn't have holidays like Christmas and Thanksgiving off either. You had to cook the Christmas dinner and serve it. The later they ate, the later you were getting off. Sometimes it was around six-thirty or seven before they started to eat. Even here, in the North, I had to cook the holidays. Their holidays, too, if they were Jewish.

I only had one job that I was ever fired off of. It's 'cause of the way white men deal with Negro women in the South. If a white man takes a liking to a Negro woman, she is got to leave town or something. Because if she doesn't leave, she will never get along there.

I went to work for a family where the man was a doctor. He had two children, a girl and a boy. His wife was ill and I was hired as a cook. Out of the two months I worked there they gave two parties. I had to cook and do the dishes for the parties. They had a butler who served the meals. After the first party the doctor said he would take me home. Well, I thought that was nice because my home was a long ways away, and the buses there were running only once an hour. It was eleven o'clock at night, so I told him I would appreciate him taking me home.

When it was time I went out and got in his car. He went about six blocks away from his house and then pulled over and started to make advances. I said, "I'm not that type of person. I was hired to cook for you, and that's all I expect to do."

So he said, "All right, I'll take you home."

Well, I thought it was all over. Two weeks went by and they had another party. This time I had spoke to the butler; he was a colored person, too. I says, "Will you help me to get my dishes up, and will you take me into the city so I can take a bus from there? I've got to get home early tonight."

He said, "All right." So the butler and I stayed and we washed the dishes.

Then the doctor come back to say, "I'll take you home."

"No, you won't take me home. I have another way of getting home."

I didn't tell him that this other fella said he would take me home, but the doctor guessed that, and he said, "Well, you'd better stay and make some coffee because we need another pot."

The butler had a wife and a sick child, so he couldn't wait for me and he left. When I got the coffee made I decided to walk home even though it was six or seven miles. I was sneaking out the door when the man seen me running and went after me. He caught me and told me that he liked me, and I was going to be his woman. He said, "You don't have to work here; you can stay home. I'll support you. I know you have a child."

"I don't want you under no circumstances."

Then he put me in the car and started to drive me into town. I waited until I got good into town, and then I opened the car door fast. He grabbed for me. At that time I had long fingernails, and I scratched his face, and, right away, I jumped out of the car. I was in the city so he couldn't run after me.

The next day I didn't go to work. I called his house and told his wife that I had quit and I told her what happened. She said, "Well, you were the first one that ever fought back. The others just give in."

I said, "I don't want him and I don't want him running after me. Will you please put my money in the mail?"

She said she would, but I waited three days and it didn't come. On the fourth day he came. He stood outside my house and called me and said he was gonna pay me, but he wanted to get in the house. I had the screen door locked between us but he jerked the door loose.

He came in and I fought him. Then I grabbed my rolling pin and hit him over the head with it and broke the rolling pin. He threw the money down and yelled that I would never put my foot in his house again.

I says, "I'm never coming to your house, and you better not ever come to mine!"

He shouted, "You damn nigger! You think you're so much better than anybody else."

"Yes, I'm far better than you," and he left.

Things like that go on down there. Once a colored woman is hooked up with a white man she can't see her own friends, and no Negro man can ever speak to her. Yes, the white man may buy you a home, and he may furnish it up swell for you, but once he comes there and does what he wants with you he goes out with his friends and there you sit. I knew that went on because there were several women in the neighborhood that it had happened to, and I just wasn't going to be in it.

I was lucky to live in Tennessee; right across the river is Arkansas, and once you got in Arkansas, anything could happen to you. That's where the Ku Klux Klan were. There were not too many in Tennessee unless they left Arkansas and came over to Memphis. Then they usually ran after the sharecroppers and colored women. If any of them take a liking to you, you'd better get out of there and get away or you gonna go with them.

Life was hard for colored people when I lived there. Still is. I knew of farmers, sharecroppers, who especially had hard times, so hard that the man would have to slip away in the dark. I knew of one man and woman who worked a farm and had three children. Every season they planted the crop; every season they picked it. They lived in shacks, just a room and a kitchen. There was what they called a store, but it's really a commissary where they went to get food. When they were planting the cotton they got plenty of food from the store. Then during the growing time it was cut off, but during the picking they got plenty of food again. Every year the boss told them they were gonna get out of debt, but every year when the season was over they owed him more than they did before. Because he said that they had eaten up their profit at the store.

Well, the man and woman grew tired of that, and one night they sat down and talked and decided that he would leave. So, on a dark night when the moon wasn't shining, he put on dark clothes and put red pepper in his shoes and slipped away. The red pepper was in case the boss missed him and sent bloodhounds after him. Then with the red pepper in his shoes, the bloodhounds couldn't smell him. He also took a couple of boxes with red pepper in them, so he could throw some behind him when he went. If the boss had caught him, the boss and his friends would have probably beat the man to death.

Once the man got away he had to trust somebody to speak to his wife and tell her that he made it safe. Then he got a job and sneaked money back to his wife. In the meantime she kept working, and when she got enough money she told the boss she was going to the next town to visit some of her people. The person that she visited had already bought the railroad tickets for her and her children. They took her to a town further away, and they caught the train and got away. Yes, life was hard for them.

There were lots of ways of controlling people there. For instance, my people didn't have any trouble voting in Tennessee. Of course, women didn't vote but men did. They always registered and voted and paid the poll tax, my two uncles and my grandfather. But then you had to vote whatever way they decided that you should vote. You couldn't be independent and go in and vote for whoever you wanted to. If they decided you had to vote Democrat, that's the way you had to do it. They didn't have secret voting booths.

And there were the people who ran the wards and the precincts, and whatever they said, you did. A white man, Jim Mulcair, ran a saloon in my area and was one of the biggest people there is in that business. We lived in the Eleventh Ward, in the Fifth Precinct, and Jim Mulcair was the boss. If a colored person got in trouble there and he'd been patronizing Jim Mulcair's saloon, regardless what he did, he got out. Because Jim Mulcair said so. And if you weren't patronizing his saloon, you didn't get out.

Mulcair had a colored woman, Estelle, and she had two kids by him. He supported them and everybody around there knew it was his kids and he didn't deny it. Whenever he wanted to he'd go down to Estelle's house and stay there. Her mother and father was there, but there was nothing they could do about it. If he didn't want to go to her house but still wanted her, he'd call her up on the phone and she went to him. Other than him, she couldn't go anywhere or have any friends.

Women were treated according to how light or dark their skin was. Estelle was fairly light, so her two daughters were very, very light and it was easier for them. A woman of my complexion or about a half a shade or a shade lighter got by, but if she was real black, she just had it hard. If a dark woman got a job, it was cleaning a house or doing laundry. You never even got a job child nursing. It was the roughest of work that a dark woman got.

Yes, it was hard for Negroes in the South, but not just Negroes but for poor whites, too. Out from the cities in the country, white and colored kids, if they were poor, only go to school June, July, and August. You see, the cotton crops and the corn crops or whatever they're growing is growing at that time. So they can go to school for those months. Then in the fall, when the corn is ripe, they have to go to the fields and pick the cotton, the corn, soybeans, or whatever. Then, when all of that is picked and laid aside, that's when they go back to school.

In January is the beginning of the term. Then in the spring it's time to till the soil, and the further south you go, the earlier it is. So they till the soil and the kids on the farms have to go and plant the seed. So they're out of school again in April, May, and June. It's probably going on today; it was when my grandchildren were little. That way, the poor kids get very little school.

I made sure my daughter went through high school and even two years of college, but when she was nineteen years old she told me she was determined to get married.

She said, "If you don't consent, we'll run off."

"Well, you don't have to run off. Wait until Thursday when I'm off. Do you want a big wedding?"

"No, I just want to get married."

"All right."

I bought a cake and new clothes and they got married. He was an entertainer and a heavy drinker, though, and before long she was drinking and smoking hard too. She got pregnant but lost the baby at six months and then had another baby, Robert. Then came a little girl, Joanne, and another baby who only lived two hours because he was blue from all her drinking and smoking.

Finally, I decided I wasn't getting anyplace. I was only making twelve dollars a week and my child was grown and the old lady was dead. A young woman I knew in Tennessee, a Mrs. Feinstein, had moved to a suburb near Milwaukee, Wisconsin, and she offered me twenty-five dollars a week plus room and board to work as her housekeeper and cook. Even with the twenty-five dollars, it wasn't any pay for all the hours I'd work. And I never received social security, not till I quit doing domestic work altogether. For all those years I'd worked, I didn't have anything for my future.

I did the cooking and just had to keep the dining room, the breakfast room, and the kitchen clean. She had a cleaning woman to do the rest of the house and a laundress to do the wash. So I moved North and stayed working for her for seven and a half years.

One day I was out in the afternoon, and I saw fire trucks and a crowd standing around, but I couldn't see the fire. An older man was standing there, and I asked him, "Where is the fire?"

He said, "In some of those old houses over there."

"Oh, someone might get hurt."

He answered, "Yes, they might." He looked at me and said, "You don't sound like you're from around here. Are you from Virginia?"

"No, from Memphis, Tennessee," and we got talking. His name was Fred and he was a big, kind, white-haired Negro man who was twenty-one years older than me. We got on real swell and when I was gone he wrote me letters and in one he proposed. I was thirty-five years old when we were married. He stayed in the house where I worked, and Fred worked in a factory for International Harvester.

Fred was born in Louisiana, right on the state line of Arkansas. His family would cross from Louisiana into Arkansas to pick cotton and other crops. They owned a horse, wagon, and a couple of mules, what you call rolling stock, so that anytime they needed to they got ready to up and go.

With all their working it was hard for the kids to get an education, and Fred only went to second grade in school. He was large and the kids teased him, so he just never went back. He was a smart man, though, and was an inventor, too, designing machines where he worked at International Harvester. He was a real intelligent man, and a good one, too.

Earlier, when Fred and I had been married for about a year, I became ill, and Miz Feinstein said, "Oh, oh, we're gonna have a little pickaninny running around here."

I turned to her and looked at her very, very funny and hard and said, "Whatcha mean?"

"You're pregnant."

"Yes, I'm sick, but I know I'm not pregnant."

"How do you know you're not?"

"I'm still coming around; I have the curse. Whenever I'm pregnant it quits."

"Oh, well, this is another time, and it doesn't have to happen that way."

I didn't say anything about her saying "pickaninny" at that time. I was very sick; I knew I had to go to the doctor and I didn't have one. Also, I knew my only way of getting back at her was to leave her home, and at that time Fred and I were living there 'cause you couldn't find a place to rent or to buy or nothing. So, the word just stayed there inside of me.

I did talk to Fred about it. Well, Fred had lived still further south than I did, in New Orleans, and he had heard, "You damn black nigger" all the time. Also, he knew how people were burned at the stake and all, so he wasn't as upset as me.

He said to me, "Well, what are you gonna do about it?"

"It's nothing I can do about it right now. You know I'm sick and I can't get out to look for a place to live and I know you can't either, but that word will be there, and when I bring it to the surface, you can bet your bottom dollar I'll have a place to live. That's when I'm gonna tell her about it."

So I kept working and got sicker and sicker, and finally Miz Feinstein said, "I'm gonna take you to the doctor."

"That's good; I want to go to the doctor. I'm not afraid of going to a doctor."

So we went and he examined me. He was a friend of Miz Feinstein and he called me Josie. He said, "Josie, you're not pregnant."

"I know I'm not pregnant."

"Well, I'm going out to tell Miz Feinstein." So he went out and she finally believed what I was saying.

Then he came back in and finished the exam and said to me, "Josie, you have a tumor. It's ripe. That's why you've been so sick. We'll have to operate."

So I had my operation and recovered, but the word she'd used stayed with me. I worked two years longer for her after she said that. During those two years I never mistreated her children, her mother, or her father, or anybody that come up. I just went on as if nothing had happened, but during that time Fred and I bought a house together. Fred bought a dining room set, we bought a bedroom set, and we bought a used kitchen stove and a used coolerator. I had a living room set, nothing fancy, but it was ours. And with the extra bedrooms we closed the doors. It was two weeks to Christmas when we got it together.

I worked on Miz Feinstein's Christmas dinner and she gave me a blanket. She thought I would be using it upstairs. I thanked her and she said, "You don't have to come so early tomorrow. You cooked Christmas dinner and everything, so why not come around eleven or twelve o'clock?"

I said, "Miz Feinstein, I will not be here tomorrow at eleven o'clock or any other day."

"Oh, you're starting some more of your foolishness!"

"No, I'm not. I have my own place now. I'm gonna stay in my own home."

"Well, what you doing that for? You're always doing something silly. You got a home here."

"Miz Feinstein, I got a husband. My husband works out to International Harvester, which you know. And he don't get off until twelve o'clock at night. He has to take a shower to come home, and it's one-thirty and two o'clock when he gets out here. That's one of the reasons."

"What's the second reason?"

"Do you remember when I was so sick, and you carried me to the doctor, and before you carried me, you said that I was going to have a little pickaninny?"

"Well, I didn't mean anything by it."

"You said it. You know that's what's said in the South about a Negro child. He is called a pickaninny. You know I come from there and you know it's resented."

"Well, why didn't you say something about it before?"

"I had to wait until the opportunity presented itself. And today, it has presented itself."

"What am I going to do? I don't have any help!"

I said, "That's not my problem," and walked out. I walked out.

Three weeks later she came over to my house. "Oh, I know you're living in a dump."

"No, I'm not living in a dump. You are welcome to come in and see it."

So she came in and she seen it and she was surprised. Then she said, "Haven't you got over your madness? Don't you want to come back to work?"

"No. I will never work for you again." And I never went back to work for her again. You see, I have a terrible temper.

The house we bought and moved into was a duplex, and we rented the other half, but the renters didn't take care of it. I had heard about taking foster kids, and, being Catholic, I talked with the priest, and my application to do foster care was accepted. I said, "They need a home and I'll be helping somebody, so why try to rent the extra room when it is being destroyed." Fred was happy too, so we took them in.

I think I could count about thirty-five foster kids that I had. Out of the thirty-five, there was four that we called our own children because those four were the first children that we took in and they were young. There were three boys and a girl.

Things had got bad with my daughter, though. When we got married Fred hadn't met my daughter, and so we decided to go visit her after the wedding. I went down there a week ahead of Fred for one purpose. I knew she didn't clean house well, and I wanted to get there and clean the house up before he came. When Fred came down I met him at the station and the house was all clean.

She had two children, Robert and Joanne, but she and this boy she married weren't getting along. The two weeks we stayed at her house, he was staying out all night with other women and the other women would call Hattie Mae. He didn't buy not one nickel's work of food the whole time we were there, and yet he come home every evening to eat.

So, after we left, she wrote and said she wanted a divorce. Fred said, "Get her a lawyer down there," and we bought the divorce. After she could leave we brought her up and put her in a house. But when she got up here in the city she began to run to taverns, and she wouldn't cook or take care of her kids.

After a while she took the kids and went back down to Tennessee, and she married again and had two more children. They went out to live in the country, and her husband treated them real, real bad. For one thing, Robert and Joanne didn't go to school enough to say they was in school. School wasn't going most of the time because of the kids needing to work the crops. But more important, Hattie Mae's husband wouldn't give Hattie Mae any food for herself and the two more kids she had with him. Joanne was five, though, and he said he would give Joanne anything 'cause he was gonna grow her up to be his woman. Sometimes when Joanne asked for some milk he'd walk to the grocery store and get some. He made a mistake, however. He made the statement about growing Joanne up to be his woman at a little country grocery store on the corner, and a lady who worked there heard it.

She inquired around and knew that I lived up North somewhere. She had never met me but she got my name and address somehow and sent me a special delivery letter, telling me that I should come down and get Robert and Joanne.

She said, "When you come to Memphis don't go around there before you stop here."

I read the letter and handed it over to Fred, so Fred said to me, "How soon can you get away?"

Well, I had a houseful of foster kids at that time too, so I said, "Today is Friday; I'll leave Tuesday morning." So I got food together for the foster kids and then I left by Greyhound bus.

I rode all night out of Chicago and got into Memphis at eight-thirty the next morning. I then went to the house where my two uncles lived. They were surprised and I told them what I was doing there.

Well, the older and the younger one both said, "We'll go in with you," and they put a gun in their pocket.

But God so had it that when we got there Hattie Mae's husband wasn't there. Somebody told him that I was there and that my two uncles were coming. Hattie Mae knew why I was there when we walked in, but she didn't know how I found out and I never told her. She was glad for me to come and take them. We stayed there waiting until ten that night. Wilma was a baby and Hattie Mae hadn't had any milk to feed her, and there was no food in the house to feed Robert nor Joanne nor herself. So my Uncle Henry carried me back up to the store.

When I walked in the store the lady looked up and said, "I wrote you, didn't I?"

"Yes."

There were two or three people in the store. She said, "Well, come in over here and sit down. Let me finish these customers and we'll talk."

When she got all the customers out she locked the door so no one else could come in. Then she said, "I was hoping you'd come, but you didn't answer so I didn't know."

"I didn't have time to answer. I'm running a foster home and I had to get together food for the children that's there at the house so I could come."

"All right." Then she was the one that told me about Robert, who was seven at the time. She said, "Hattie Mae's husband has hit that little boy Robert over the head with an iron pipe and Robert's been in the hospital. He's very mean to Robert but he sometimes gives things to Joanne 'cause he's going to grow Joanne up to be his woman. He brags about that. But the only time they eat is when little Robert goes out in anybody's garden and steals whatever's edible. He don't steal enough to sell, but he steals enough for all of them to eat.

"Half of the time when he steals a cabbage, there's not even a little meat in the house, so he'll come up to me and tell me he needs a piece of meat to cook the cabbage with. And then I give it to him. And the neighbors now have learned that he won't steal no more than for him and the family to eat during the day. He also will go to three different neighbors and will milk their cow, so that the baby and all the rest of 'em can have milk."

Hattie Mae's husband was saying he was gonna grow Joanne up to be his woman and yet he would kill Robert! So, I went back to get the kids, Joanne, Robert, Robert's younger half-brother, and the baby. But when the half-brother heard I was going to take them, he unlocked the door, ran out, and went to his father. So the man took the boy and left, and I've only seen the child twice in my life. But I took the other three back up North with me.

At that time, when we first had little Robert, he was just as crazy as a bat because of his head being hurt and what happened. He'd sit down at the table where he'd see food, and he would eat and eat and eat and then have to run downstairs to the bathroom to vomit. He'd eat like that 'cause he seen the food, and he was afraid it wouldn't be any more. He thought if he could fill his stomach, he wouldn't be hungry.

When it was time to put him in school he just couldn't learn. They sent us down to city hall and from city hall to the Mayo Clinic to see about his head. The doctors at the clinic said, no, they wouldn't operate on him, to leave him 'cause he was young and his skull might lift. They gave us letters, Fred had one and I had one, saying he couldn't be in school. They told Fred to take him fishing and anyplace else to entertain him, and told me to take him downtown shopping with me, and if anybody stops us, to show them the letter. Well, we did as they said, but Robert was retarded. Nothing could change that. He finally went to a special school and then to vocational school.

Later, Hattie Mae had another son who I raised from six years old. He always was in trouble and nothing we did seemed to work. The police were at the house so much because of him, that every time I got back to the house I'd look up to see the squad car. I thought they were coming there even if they weren't coming, but nine times out of ten they were.

The doctor said that was one of the causes for my ulcer, and that was one of the beginnings of me getting these nervous shakes. I can remember before I first got those shakes; I was sitting out on the porch and I saw squad cars coming both ways. Fred was living and I said, "Oh, my God. Here comes two cars. They did something terrible," thinking of my grandson. God knows, if I knew I had to go to the bathroom I'd a went before, but just sitting there, before I could get up, I passed water up there on the porch. And that's when the shakes began.

The littlest girl, Wilma, was cross-eyed, and when she was with my husband and me, we paid for an operation for her eyes. She was two when she had the operation, and it cost $2,500 to bring a specialist from New York to do it. The hospital didn't charge anything. And when the specialist came out of the surgery, the doctor at the county hospital said, "Miz Hunter. This is the doctor that did the work for you."

I put my hand out to say thank you, and he walked by me as if I didn't live. That hurt me so bad.

The other doctor said, "Just don't worry about it. Your child's eyes is gonna be fine."

I told him, "Thank you," but I went home and told Fred and I cried. Fred said, "Don't worry about it. If she sees, that's all right."

During those years we had all those kids, the first four, the grandkids, and others we'd take. And Fred loved those kids. He really loved 'em. Once, I never will forget, all the boys had did something, and I said I was gonna give 'em a lickin'. Fred took those kids in the house and told them, "Put a pie pan in the back of your pants. When your Ma hits you, she won't hit you, she'll hit the pan." And those crazy kids put that in there, and when I hit them, the pan made a noise. I became so tickled I sit down and starts laughing, and we all laughed and that was the end of the whipping. He would do things like that.

Now if they did something real bad and he got angry with them, he'd make them hold their hand out, and he'd give them three to four licks in the hand, but they would be licks. When they were all grown, they told me, "He hurt! But your whipping, you could of hit us all day and you didn't hurt us."

I didn't have any trouble with the kids from the Catholic Society, John, Dennis, and Stephen, and the little girl, Linda. Of course, I hear from Linda quite often. She lives in New York. It was the kids from the county that gave me trouble, and my youngest grandson, and my granddaughter, Joanne.

When Joanne got to be fourteen or fifteen she started running around and playing hooky from school. She got tangled up with a boy that I had in the foster home, and she come up with a baby when she was sixteen. I forgave her for that and tried to get her to go back to school, but then she started hanging out with her mother who had come back up here, and she started drinking and things just went from bad to worse.

The baby's father's people took it. I just refused to do it. I said I had did my part. And I tell them today, "If anything goes wrong, don't come to me." I said, "There is no law in the United States to make a grandmother and a great-grandmother and a great, great-grandmother take care of anybody." Besides, what do I have to take care of them with? I'm just living off my husband's social security.

During a lot of the time when I had the foster kids I also worked full time as a nurse's aid. After Fred retired I took the nighttime eleven to seven shift in nursing homes because it was the easy shift. I tried to plan things together. For example, if strawberries were in season and if I had an easy night, I'd buy a case of strawberries on the way home, and when I got home I'd pick them, sugar them down, and let them sit two or three hours. Then I'd say to Fred, "Maybe I'll lay down. Wake me up at three. Peel the potatoes for supper and before you wake me up, put them on to cook with a little salt in them." We'd have a half a bushel of potatoes for a meal.

Then at three the kids would be coming in, so I'd get up, we'd eat, and then after the dishes would be all washed up, I'd put the strawberries on for preserves and let them cook. Then, maybe at seven, I'd lay down again or maybe I didn't. It just depended on the way I felt. Finally, I'd finish cooking the preserves off because I would leave my house at ten-thirty going to work at eleven.

Today I pray God for one thing only. I don't want to get physically any worse off than I am now. If I get to the place where I can't look after myself and help myself, then I don't want to live. It's bad enough now. I don't want to ever go in any convalescent home. I know what goes on in them from all my years of work. I don't care how nice your family is to the nurses, they grow tired of you when you get to be old and cranky.

And sometimes you're in a nursing home, and your family don't come to see you, and you are laying there seeing everybody else have company. That's bad too. I've seen them lay there and face the wall and cry because nobody comes to see them. If that happens you are there with nobody to come and ask you how you feel. The nurses are going to come in and do what they have to do for you and get going. They haven't got time to give you a lot of pampering and attention.

Also, the nurses work too hard. They get more money now than when I worked, but it still isn't much. It's mostly women making little money and doing hard, hard work. When I worked at one sanitarium fifteen years ago, I got $175 every two weeks, and that was top wages. Also, that's where I got beat up.

I was working the seven in the morning till three shift, and I had to go out on the bus line at four-thirty in the morning in order to catch the first bus and then transfer to get to the sanitarium. It was winter and dark and as I was crossing the alley to get to the bus stop, two young men sneaked up out of the dark and surprised me and said, "We know you have money in your pocketbook. Give it to us!"

"I don't have but a dollar." I didn't; I just had my meal ticket, one dollar, and a pass.

They said, "We know better. You just got paid by the city. Give it to us."

"I haven't got paid." And then they started to beat me, and I began to scream.

A man who lived across the alley heard my screams and came running outside with his gun and fired it into the air two times. By then the teenagers were running down the alley where they dropped my pocketbook and got away. The police came and took me home.

You see people with one black eye? I had both of mine black at the same time. In order to see, I had to hold my head way back and look up and try to tilt it enough to see sideways. And for a long time I could hardly see a thing. Fred didn't want me to go back there, and I got another nursing aid's job, but for a long time I was very scared.

I worked there until Fred got sick. He had leukemia and just got worse and worse until his blood looked like water and even his eyes changed color. So finally I couldn't take care of him at home, and he went into the hospital for the last time. Fred had been very nice to me. He had been very nice to my daughter. He had been very nice to my grandchildren and the children we cared for, and to just die that way with so much sickness.

He died conscious because at five-thirty that morning the priest had gone in to give him his communion. Then the nurse went in to give him his medication. Even when he was so sick he always had some kind of something to say. He said, "Well now, the priest has been here giving good, and now here you come with the devil's work." He meant that medicine. She gave him his medicine and went out, and when they went back in to put him up in bed for his morning breakfast, he was dead.

When he died I was at home. I had a premonition, but I didn't know what it was. It was during the riots here, and they were going around burning houses, and the house next door to me had been burnt, but it didn't burn down. I was sleeping at night and I woke up suddenly around two o'clock in the morning. I went to the front door and looked out in the street to see if something was happening, but I seen nothing. So I laid back down but I couldn't go to sleep. I was just turning, just turning.

So I said, "Well, there's something wrong, but I don't know what it is so I might as well get up."

I had taken my curtains down and washed them, but I hadn't got them up. I was going to put them up the next day. Since I couldn't sleep I got up and put those curtains up all over the house. And I had my four grandchildren and these four children that I said I loved so much and two other foster kids in the house, so I made breakfast. Then I took the dinner bell that I had, which was the way we called the kids sleeping upstairs, and I rang the bell.

All the kids came down and they ate and the dishes was washed. Then John, the boy that lives in Chicago, says to me, "Mama, what in the world is wrong with you? Do you know it's six o'clock, and you have put all the curtains up over the house? You have made the breakfast. We have washed up the dishes, and you're telling us to go to school. And we don't go to school till a lot later than this."

The telephone rang. John was closer to the telephone, so he picked it up and said, "Hello." Of course, it was the doctor asking for me.

Then John said to me, "Mama, it's a man on the telephone. What would he be calling you for?"

"I don't know," and I went over to the telephone.

The man said, "Miz Hunter, County General Hospital calling."

I hung the telephone right up.

Johnny said, "Mama, you didn't say nothing but hello. What's wrong?"

"Nothing. Just let me sit here. He'll ring back and when he rings back, if it's what I think he's going to say, I don't want to hear it."

So he rang right back and he told me, "Don't hang up," and he told me what was wrong.

So I told the kids, "Fred is dead."

"Daddy can't be dead."

"Yes, he is, that's what it's all about."

The doctor realized when I hung up the first time that I was real upset, so he told me, "When you do come to the hospital, come to the desk and ask for me."

So when I got there, the nurse went and found him, and he came with a needle and gave me a shot right away. Well, just right then and there I became like steel. I identified Fred; I rubbed his face and all and just stood with my hands clasped and looked at him. No tears. The priest came and he talked with me. He said,

"Take it easy," and still no tears came, and the whole while that anyone was there or even through the funeral no tears came.

Then, at last, one night when the house was quiet and the kids had gone to bed, I was just sitting up. I looked over to where Fred had a chair that he would sleep in, and to me it seemed I just seen him there. I looked away from him and when I looked back again I seen nothing. Then the tears just started rolling. They just rolled.

I sat and I cried all night and all the next day. I would stop but I would fill up, and the tears would spill again. I did that for about a month and then there were no more tears. They had just vanished.

And what's the need? The Bible tells us that we should weep when a child is born. The Catholic priests'll tell you that. We should weep when a child is born 'cause it's coming into the world of sin, and who knows what that child will face in life? The Bible also tells us when a person dies we should rejoice. They're leaving a hard, hard world. But we do it backward. When a baby comes in we grab it and hug it; we kiss it and we say, "Isn't it sweet? It's a lovely child," but we shouldn't think that way. As I've gotten older and have lived through so much I've kind of understood a little bit, so I just don't see it that way.

Not only did I lose Fred, but before too long I lost our house, too. The city decided to buy all the houses around where we lived to tear down for urban renewal. I loved my house; it was the house where Fred and I lived and raised all those kids.

We had paid $9,250 for the house, and when we got it, it was in a very poor condition. We put a cornerstone siding all over it that was guaranteed not to burn in fire. We put inlaid linoleum in both kitchens, up and down. We tore out the sink because the house was full of cockroaches before we came, and we put formica top over the sink and the back of the walls. We painted and papered the rooms and added a bathroom and so much more. We filled in our backyard and built a fence and planted rosebushes and various flowers so that from the time of the spring until it got cold, there were flowers.

I fought the city, but lost, and after I knew for sure they were coming to take it, I started packing. When the time did come that I had to get out, I called the movers. I cried all the night before and all that day, and the day that I walked out of the house and closed the doors, the tears were just rolling. I just couldn't help it. I moved over to a small rented duplex where I live now.

After I left people broke the back door down and broke in to steal what was takeable. They stole the bathroom fixtures, the light fixtures, and everything else. Then, when I had been gone two weeks and before the city could tear it down, it was set afire. Somebody went on the inside into the attic and started it. The firemen said that somebody had poured gasoline from the attic all the way down to the basement, and it was burning a long time on the inside before it was discovered. You see, when we were remodeling it and putting on the siding, they'd told us the siding would not burn.

After the fire I went around the remains just to see if the siding had burned, but it didn't. The siding had melted and run together like tar. I walked all the way around the house, but I didn't try to go in. I didn't know if something would fall on me if I did, and I didn't have no business in there anyhow. But the tears came down.

Well, after my kids grew up, the four foster kids that I really loved along with my grandchildren, I decided I didn't want to take care of any more foster kids, but I also didn't want to go back in nursing. So I went to work for the welfare up here. I had to wait to get in at welfare, and, meantime, I worked in the laundry. I didn't like it because it was so hot, and I was usually soaking wet from my head to my feet. Then I took a cold, but finally I got in at welfare and worked for seven years giving emergency food allotments to people who needed them.

Through all that time, and even today, things are so bad with my daughter. She's just a habitual drunkard and there's nothing that I could do about it. She refuses to go to the lockup or the treatment center. So to me she's dead and she's not dead. I don't go out to look for her or to bother about her, one way or the other, and I do say that if she would die somebody will go to the store where Robert works and tell him.

Dennis knows where she lives and not long ago I said to him, "Won't you tell me so I can go get her?"

He said, "No, Mama. I don't want you going to that hellhole. Because that's all it is."

So I lay down at night wondering, and the very first time that I hear somebody was mugged and killed on the street, I sit by the TV, and the minute the paper comes I look to see if it's her.

Hattie Mae and Joanne were not my only disappointments, because one of the foster boys that I raised, he is in the business of being a pimp. Now, he don't bring them around me, and I don't go where he lives because he lives in Chicago. He knows that I don't approve of it, but, he says to me, "They want to sell their body for me; let them do it!"

I said, "But you wasn't raised that way. Why are you doing this?"

"Oh, if I don't do it, somebody else'll do it."

My grandson Robert, who lives here with me, knows he does that, and Robert don't like it either. And the boy that I raised that became a lawyer, he didn't approve of it. Really, the family, as we call it, don't care for it.

I try to talk to him. I say, "Now, you are twenty-seven years old, almost turning thirty. When are you gonna quit this? Look, each day you are getting older. Now, you've only had one job in your life and that's not much. You went to welding school and you could make good money.

"Suppose you live to be as old as I am? Those women will not be able to keep you up because after so long a time their bodies are gonna wear out. Then they won't have any social security and you won't either. And I'm not gonna take care of you, so don't get that in your head. I'm not gonna take of you. So what're you going to do?"

He says, "Well, I don't know."

"That's something to think about. Now look at Robert, who was the only child that I didn't think would amount to anything because he was hit over the head with this lead pipe by his stepfather, but Robert is doing so good." But he doesn't listen and I can't think of anything else to say.

Some of the kids turned out real good, though. And Robert has always worked and his bosses feel so good about him that he's only had two jobs. He was working as a boy and he works as a man. He's never married and he lives at home with me. He was hurt so bad and he turned out so good.

One night when I was working for welfare I came home from work, my grandson and I ate dinner, and I went to bed and went to sleep. I woke up the next morning and couldn't move my legs. Just overnight! I was in the hospital for eight weeks, and to this day they don't know what happened. I still cannot walk very easy and have to move with a cane. So I'm not able to work.

I'd like to be working, but there is nothing I can do. I don't like the idea of just sitting, holding my hands. I get so bored, doing nothing much but watching TV. I've done so many things. I was a Red Cross worker and a civil defense worker, and now I sit at home. I don't see my friends very much anymore; they can't get out to see me any more than I can get to see them.

There isn't but one thing that I worry about, and I don't worry about that too much. Robert is young and he has to go out and enjoy himself, and when he goes out sometimes he'll stay all night. Then I don't like to be left here by myself. I have a pistol that I keep, and I know how to use it. And I have a little alarm box that I keep with me at all times. If I hear a noise all I have to do is press a button and the alarm will go off. The alarm will sound downtown, and they'll know it's me. I had to put $200 down to pay for the alarm and have been paying the rest for a long time. It will come to about $1,000 when I'm done paying for it, and it was about the last money I really had.

I only had $450 left from all my years of work. With me being sick and everything, it's gone. When Fred was sick he went to a private hospital, and they kept him up there until they had drained out all his insurance, and then they told him he'd better go to the County. So there was that bill. When he died at County, I owed them over $3,000. Then Fred didn't have any burial insurance, and I had to pay for the funeral with the money from the city taking our house. Then there were other things that came along. I had been sick, I owed a doctor bill, and then the money was gone.

I live off Fred's social security of $230 a month; mine wasn't worth as much as his. If Robert wasn't living with me, I don't know what I'd do. Of course, I get the supplemental and it helps to pay my doctor bills. But it's a very tight way to live after so many years of working.

The only other worry I have is Robert. I worry that he's so free-hearted; he'll give anything to anybody that anybody needs and that concerns me for him. Other than that I don't worry about him. He's got a job and knows how to live.

I've pretty much finished with my worries and plans. And as for dying, that don't worry me. My legs are too stiff to get down on my knees to pray, and so every night I say my prayers in bed, flat on my back, but God hears them anyway. I says to God, "I thank you for letting me see the day. I thank you for the night that I have seen. And if it's your will that I go to sleep and don't wake up, it is you that I'm asking to take my soul."

I'm not afraid; I'm not afraid. I feel that upon this earth I've taken in the foster kids, and I raised them to the best of my knowledge. I knew what it was to come up hard, and I raised my daughter the best that I could. I've never sold my body to nobody. I've never stole anything. I've never been arrested. And you can go places and find that I have a record of working. It's just that I grew tired of domestic work, and I wanted a home of my own. That's the way it was, so I can face my God.

*But I can say, I've been with the best and
the worst in my life, and the secret is,
they're all people.*

—Helen Drazenovich Berklich

The people in the sepia-colored photographs stared out across time. In the first photograph, taken in 1915, an immense young woman of about seventeen sat stolidly with a plump baby propped on her lap. Her dark hair was parted down the middle and pulled back behind her ears, and she gazed forward intently and soberly. A little boy about one and a half years old stood next to her, and a young man with a full mustache stood behind. I studied the young woman's face, trying to see if it held any clues of the immense amount of labor and struggle she would experience before she died at twenty-nine. I picked up no such hint, just a look of resignation and endurance. The baby was Helen, the woman I had traveled to northern Minnesota to interview, and the young woman in the photo was Helen's mother—Big Mary, as she was called.

The other photograph, taken fifteen years later, was of Helen's wedding party, made up largely of Yugoslavian immigrants like Helen's mother, father, and new husband. The same intense stares were captured in this photo; sixteen-year-old Helen, dressed in white, was sitting front and center next to her new, fifty-one-year-old husband. Again, I searched the photograph of Helen's face for clues of the fear and shame she described experiencing during her wedding, but found none. Instead, her full face and serious expression stared unrevealingly into the camera.

When I first met sixty-five-year-old Helen Drazenovich Berklich, I was quite stunned by the force of her personality. She swept me into her house and welcomed me with a big, booming voice which still carried the eastern European accent of her parents. She was a large, white-haired woman who swayed when she moved, and wore flowing clothing of deep purple and violet; her low-cut blouses provided easy access to the handkerchief she kept tucked inside her bra in case she cried. She grasped me on both arms, looked intently into my eyes, and said "Frances, I'm going to tell you just how it was, just how it is, Frances."

Helen immediately sat me down at her dining room table and began to feed me and to talk. She offered me food constantly, and her moods quickly jumped from outbursts of laughter to sharp anger, tears, and laughter again. Her whole body shook when she laughed, and she used dramatic gestures, frequently touching me to accent her words. During our five days together, we talked of many deaths; when speaking of the dead, she would hastily cross herself and say, "May God rest her soul." She was a generous and hardy woman who swore constantly but almost as frequently referred to her religion.

Helen cared for four retarded adults in her home and maintained a continual interchange with the three who were present when we talked. She called her boarders "the kids" and watched them with steady devotion. They came to her for advice on many details of their lives, such as the clothes they were to wear for Easter, letters and bills they had received, and the complications of their pets. Helen frequently asked them for their opinions of the subjects we discussed, laughed and joked with them, and was physically affectionate with them.

Helen lived in a small city on the Mesabi Iron Range. The range stretches across northeastern Minnesota in an area about 100 miles long and 2 to 10 miles wide. The iron ore in this area provided jobs for Helen's family and the other families in the area who had emigrated from various European countries. The immigrant men worked in the mines; the women grew gardens, kept animals, maintained homes, and ran boardinghouses for unmarried miners.

From the 1890s through the early part of this century, the immigrants left their respective countries to escape poverty and war. But life was also hard here for these newcomers, who often arrived as adolescents without family. Groups such as the Finns, Italians, Yugoslavians, Serbians, and others lived together in little neighborhood enclaves of a block or two as they worked long hours, learned a new language, and adapted to the new land. For many of these women and men, life was short and filled with endless labor. During this time the face of the range changed irrevocably as great, gaping canyons and pits were carved out of what had been pine-covered ground. It is from these beginnings that Helen's story is told. She chose to use her real name and told her story as she lived it, with passion and exuberance.

Helen   The village in Yugoslavia that my mother and father came from is very poor. My father only got to third grade; that was the last time he remembered going to school. He had basic intelligence but he couldn't read. His parents would say, "You got to go in the hills and take care of the sheep." He would sit up in the hills, and at night he'd hear those wolves and he was scared.

Also, there were wars fought over there. Those countries seem far away from each other, but they're practically right across the road. Their boys would have to go to war, and I think my father and my husband ran away from the old country partly because they were gonna be next to go to wars. They were thirteen, just young kids. My father didn't have a passport, but this other kid had one and he changed his mind, so he gave my father his passport, and my father came on that kid's passport. Later, he tried to get his citizenship papers, but he couldn't get them because there was no John Shebly that came over here. So my father never got to be a citizen.

They had agents over there recruiting people to come to this country to work. My God, the kids thought they were coming to the land of cream 'n honey. I've heard people talk about when they came. They were in third class on the boat, in the hold. It sounded like it was just horrible. There were a whole bunch of people just pushed in together. But, then, when they arrived, they looked up and saw the Statue of Liberty, and it was just like God in front of them. It's true, all they had ever known was poverty and wars.

Two of those young boys he came with were my mother's brothers. They were all about thirteen and they went to a lumber camp in the woods, north of Duluth in Minnesota. Of course, they didn't speak English when they came. They all worked together cutting trees. Then the two brothers asked my father why don't he send for my mother, who was their young sister, to bring her to this country and get married. So my father saved the dough for her.

My mother's family was very poor when they raised her, and they were strict, strict, strict. There was none of the premarital stuff with those old honkies. If you came home with a baby, you were dead. She was fifteen when she came to marry my father, and, of course, she'd never seen him.

They were married in 1914 and my father worked on the ore docks and my mother took in boarders. And she had babies every year, nine by the time she was twenty-nine. The first died and then I was the oldest. She also had a store and bootlegged. And she ate. I think eating was her outlet for her unhappiness because when she was married, she was a beautiful, tall, thin lady, and then she got to over 400 pounds. She weighed all that and was six feet tall, so people called her Big Mary.

Her boarders were lumberjacks who would come out of the woods. They came like every three months for a vacation of two or three days. They'd come to the boardinghouses, and then they'd get moonshine and they'd get drunk and eat well and just lay around, and then they'd go back to the woods. I can remember it so well. She also had to take care of the store, so she had to learn to read and write English.

In Yugoslavia they have this idea about prestige for men. To this day, those women over there carry bundles on their head, and they're carrying the pails of water or whatever, and they're way out here pregnant, and the men are walking behind them carrying nothing. When I visited Yugoslavia I said to the man I was with, "Why isn't that guy helping his wife carry all that?"

And he said, "Ohhh, that's a shame. A woman has to be worthy of her man, so she has to do all that kind of work." And sure enough, this is true. And let me tell you, my father was kingpin. God, he had prestige like you wouldn't believe. Because his wife was real worthy. [Laughs hard.]

I don't remember too much of when I was real little, but I do remember finding some great big matches. There were two men sleeping on a bed, and I started a fire under their mattress. I don't know if I owned up to it or not. I was just a real angelic type. [Laughs again.] Also, our mother was working all the time, and we played in the old train depot for fun.

People loved my mother. There was a Bethel home by our store, and she fed more poor guys out of that home. She was a person with compassion, too, but I got it all. The first kid gets the whole load. I had to do lots of work. I didn't mind the work, but she'd whip me. Let me tell you, with the old school, the sun rises and sets on the first son. I don't know why. I was the first born that lived, but then when Emil came along, my mother adored him. Steven, who was the second brother, used to get lickings too, but Emil could get by with everything. It wasn't Emil's fault; my mother and father just put all their worship on him. Then it got so that wherever I went, Emil went with me. And I never, till the last day, got away from Emil.

I took care of all the little kids while my mother ran the store. And I'd take lickings for them. The kids would lie like hell and say I'd done things, but I'd rather take the lickings than let them get them.

I did have a special friend, Mary. We used to play house and then we'd pretend we were actresses. We'd put on pointed shoes, the ones you use the buttonhook with, and we'd get beautiful flowerettes from Goodwill for a penny. And then we'd perform. We'd act out movies like *Tin Can Alley* and *Run Sheep Run*. We played the silent movies with our long dresses and those button shoes. She had a younger brother who was with us too. Her mother was so good to us kids, really so good. Now, see, her mother was home and could cook and care for us. My mother was in business so she couldn't be the kind of sweet mother that they had. But we never realized that. I didn't understand my mother like that till now the last ten or twenty years. We felt real bad that our mother couldn't be at home with us like other mothers could be. Mary and her family moved back to Yugoslavia.

My mother had all of us children at home except for the last baby. She was very sick by then, and she had her in the hospital. Afterwards, the baby, Katherine, was taken to a children's home in Duluth, and the rest of us were sent to the St. James Orphanage. My mother died when she was twenty-nine years old. [Begins to cry.] She had nine children, a store, and twenty boarders. My father was up here working on the iron range at the time. He used to work on the iron-ore docks in Duluth, but then those folded up or laid off, so he came up here and worked the mines.

The day before my mother died, Emil and I went to see her at St. Luke's Hospital. I was twelve and Emil was ten. We took the streetcar and when we got there she was dying. We didn't know it, though. She said, "You kids go on back. I don't want to see you; it hurts me." Then, the last words she ever said to me were, "Helen, take care of your brothers and sisters." She was so sick. I can still see her. Then she died that night.

The next day the sister let me call the hospital, and I asked, "How is Mrs. Shebly?"

They had no idea I was the daughter, and they said, "She died."

I went down to the playroom of the orphanage and just hollered and screamed. [Cries hard.] So I took my brother Emil, and we went by streetcar to Crawford's Mortuary. That's where she was. They had her laid out on the couch; they hadn't put her in the coffin yet. We stood and looked at her.

Poor thing. She didn't have nobody with her. A baby every year and all that hard work. Her kidneys failed from all that bull work. My father was working at the ore docks and mine, and she always had everything ready for him. That was the prestige thing again. When I think of it, there couldn't have been love and helping each other with them.

They couldn't bury her then because it was such a horrible day. She died on the twelfth of December, and they put her in a vault and postponed the funeral till in the summer. So when it came time for her burial the next summer, my sister Ann and I walked out from the St. James Orphanage to the cemetery. Emil and Steve, my brothers, were waiting for my dad to come. They didn't show up and Ann and I were the only ones there when they put my mother in the ground. Then, afterwards, my father came with three carloads of friends, all ploughed and drinking. My mother and father had earned a lot of money, and my father drank all that up.

Those were bad depression days, the days when we went to the orphanage. Honest to God, they couldn't afford nothing, really. There were not many funds for the orphanage and my father couldn't pay. For breakfast, the thing we had most was skimmed milk oatmeal with Karo Syrup on it, and on some mornings, we had peanut butter sandwiches and cocoa. And on Sunday two girls would go up to the kitchen and get a pan that had our meal in it. And those pans were full of day-old rolls that the bakery would send out. That was our dinner.

We had our chores. We ironed and did lots of work. I varnished the whole rectory; the rectory held 300 kids. I scraped and varnished the hallways. I also worked in the baby department. Enjoyed it, I'm not complaining, enjoyed it, and worked in the kitchen with Sister Louise.

Christmas was a good time, though. On Christmas we'd really have a big meal. God, we'd look forward to Christmas. All the people in the different companies would send great big presents and food galore. And then, one Christmas, I got the most beautiful doll I ever got in my life. I saw it, I opened it, I held it, and I gave it to Sister and I never saw it again. They put it away because we had no time to play.

And I want you to know, I felt the fires of hell burning many a time. We were taught not to do things, not to lie. Don't tell stories, don't steal, don't do this or that. We were taught that hell was the punishment for sins.

We never got the same food as the nuns and the priests got. Once I was working in the kitchen and was in the walk-in cooler, and there was the most beautiful slice of beef, a whole platter of beef sitting there. And I ate a great big piece. I don't think I even chewed it. I just swallowed it down. You know what day that was? Friday. And that night we had holy hour. Now don't say that you can't culture people and train them. I could feel that fire of hell. I cried. I was upset. Sister Julianna got me when we got outside, and she said, "Helen, what is your problem?"

I said, "Sister, I ate meat today and I'm gonna go to hell!"

And she said, "Oh, don't worry about that. God'll forgive you." You don't know how glad I was to hear that.

Later, we made our first communion in there, and we had to go to confession. That's like going to hell, too. Everything was a sin. Holy cats, everything, which was going too far. And we prayed, we prayed all the time. All the time. If there was a fire, if the grass wouldn't grow, if someone was bad, for any little thing, we prayed. Maybe that was good too, maybe that's what made us good, strong, and honest people. But, still, it was hard.

We did a lot of penance. Usually Sister would take away our syrup for our oatmeal, or we'd have to kneel on two pieces of wood in the middle of a floor for an hour and say five rosaries or so many Hail Marys or Our Fathers. We didn't really deserve to be punished that way.

And we were so homesick. I was allowed to go visit my brothers and sisters at times, but they would cry. My brother Steve had a problem; he was a bedwetter. And that sister beat him. In fact, both the priests broke his nose they hit him so hard. There were some that weren't mean; some of the nuns were not. But I suppose that was the way of the times. God, they were strict, strict, strict, strict.

My periods had started before we went to the orphanage, when I was eleven. My mother was sick, but we were home and she was at home. I got this period and the only time I'd ever seen blood in our house was when my mother had a baby. I thought I was gonna have a baby. I was so scared. I thought my mother's gonna kill me. You know what I did? I got my father's white shirt and cut the sleeves off and I bandaged myself. I didn't know what to do, and I was afraid to tell anybody or ask anybody, and every month I was waiting for this baby. That's the truth, so help me God. If you talked about sex or anything pertaining to sex, that was horrible. That's how they were.

Then, when we first went to the orphanage, I was in a room with thirty to forty young girls. Later, when I was twelve, I went in to the big girls dorm where there were about twelve beds in each room. One night Rose, the girl that was in the bed next to me, accidentally got blood on the sheet. And the sister came the next morning and saw that. She yelled, "Which dirty thing caused this?" It scared me so that when I got my period I didn't tell anybody.

I was working for Sister Clara up in the baby department. We used to cut off the sleepers for the little kids that were crawling, and I used the piece that was cut off as pads. I'd flush them down the toilet, and one time one got stuck. Sister Clarence said, "Now who threw this down?"

Do you think I'd own up to that? No way in hell would I. I said, "I don't know!" I felt like a freak and nobody tried to teach me.

When I had been in the orphanage for two years, a little Jewish couple, Mr. and Mrs. Arthur Stone, came from Nashwauk down to the St. James Orphanage and they took me out. They promised I'd go to church and that they'd continue to look over me. So we went to Nashwauk and I took care of their son, Arthur.

Mrs. Stone talked to me. When we got to her house, she says, "Helen, do you menstruate?"

I looked at her; I didn't know what the hell that meant. I says, "What do you mean, Mrs. Stone?"

"Well," she says, "when girls get to a certain age, every month they have blood come from where they urinate, down in the privates."

"Did you say every girl gets this?"

She says, "Every girl. If you don't have it then there's something wrong with you."

"Well, Mrs. Stone, I've had this from way before my mother died. I didn't know what it was and in the orphanage they made fun of a girl, so I never told anybody."

She says, "What did you wear for a pad?"

And I told her and even how I stuck up the toilet. She was good to me. She taught me a lot of things the two years I was with her. She would go and work with her husband after I'd come from school and I took care of Arthur. He was the cutest little kid. Then, after I'd been there about two years, my father wanted me to come to him to keep house for him.

Of course, every time I went to Duluth the kids would want me to take them out of the orphanage; they'd cry and beg me, so when I first went to keep house for my father I took Emil out. He was the first.

But things were bad with my father, and I ran away and my father put Emil back in the orphanage. I hitchhiked from Nashwauk at nine o'clock at night to Duluth when I was fourteen. I didn't know where to go, but there was a Polish family that was close friends of my people, so I went there and they took me in.

I was big, always big and buxom, so I went with the girl in the family, Mary Machowsky, to the Garon Knitting Mills, and we applied for a job knitting stockings. We said we were eighteen. We got the job and made 25¢ a bundle, and there were twenty-four stockings in a bundle. We'd made $2.50 a day, which was great big money. There were all us young women working there. God, you'd think we were a real big genius; we were so proud.

On weekends, Mary's father would get out the fiddle, and they had homebrew and then he'd play and us kids would dance. I can still see and hear him. [Sings.] He'd drink that homebrew and he'd play. And Mary's mother would make great big loaves of bread.

She'd take a brown bag and open it up and grease it and then mold these huge loaves and put them on her range so they would get just beautiful. And Sunday mornings we'd go to mass and would come from mass, and she'd have this fresh bread and homemade Polish sausage and boiled milk for breakfast. We were happy, happy, happy. Work was never hard, never.

My father didn't know where I was, but he kept looking and finally he found me. So I went back with him again, and we took Emil out again and I started keeping house again. But my father drank and he was generous-hearted to everyone else but hard on us kids. So one time I ran away again, and this time I stayed with a little old Serbian lady and helped her raise her grandsons, but then my father came and I went back again and we took Emil out again.

When I came back that time my father was staying at Mrs. Bozich's boardinghouse. Women would run boardinghouses where the mining men lived. So I stayed there also and worked for her for fifteen dollars a month, which was big money. Other girls worked too. She had forty boarders that she'd cook, clean, and wash clothes for. Would you believe that she got up at four in the morning and fired up that kitchen range and cooked? She fried potatoes, she made eggs, she fried pork chops for breakfast. That woman worked hard and she taught me a lot of this cooking. She and that little old lady that picked me up in Duluth. Our mainstay was bean 'n' barley soup.

And, because there were forty boarders, we had forty of those aluminum buckets they carried their food in to clean each night. The food would be cooked on, and I'd hate 'em with a passion. We would get an old rag and would put wood ashes in it and scrub. There was no Chore Girl or stainless steel.

And we had hardwood floors, and we washed them with the Gold Dust Twins. I'll never forget those Gold Dust Twins. [Laughs.] When you rung the rag eventually your skin peeled off because they were so powerful. That floor would be just white when we finished, and when the guys would come from work, and they'd step on my floor I could a just hit 'em one. Mrs. Bozich always had meals ready. That woman worked like a horse. She'd do all that and she had to carry water from a central pump that was about a block away.

And Mrs. Bozich had moonshine ready for the men when they came home from work and they'd each have two shots. Then on holidays they'd drink and they'd get drunk, but there was no ill effect. The men were always respectful towards me. Never, ever, did I have one of those men make a pass at me or any of the girls who were working there. And we were just young kids. Mrs. Bozich had us sleeping in a room next to hers so nobody got near us. She was smart.

By that time I had grown into a big, strong girl. When I was sixteen years old I weighed 200 pounds, but I was firm, like a bull moose. And I never stopped. Just go, go, go.

I'd go to Duluth to visit the kids from time to time. I'd bring them candy and big bags of fruit, but they always cried when I left, and they would beg me to take them out. And I remembered the last words my mother ever said to me, to take care of them.

Then Tony, the man I married, started coming to see my dad. He was born in the same time, same place as my dad. I was sixteen and he was fifty-one, about thirty-five years older than me. My father said he could marry me; first he had to have permission of the father, then me. I never went out with him, never, so help me God. I thought of the kids in the orphanage and said that I would marry him if he would take my brothers and sisters out of the orphanage. And he did. He gradually let me take all those kids out, and he never once complained. After I told him I'd marry him, he brought me an apple with gold coins. For engagement, that's what they do in the old country. I wasn't in love with him, and I never went out with him before the wedding.

We had the wedding at the Finn Hall, and the cooks, they barbecued lamb and pigs. They had moonshine; they had homebrew; they had cakes and patitzas, strudels, baked ham, all that. Then they played Yugoslavian wedding games and danced until five in the morning. I would have stayed there three more days 'cause I was afraid to go home. I didn't want to think I was the one dressed in bridal clothes and that it was my wedding.

By the time we got home I was very upset. We had two rooms that we shared with my father and Emil. My father had his room and my brother Emil slept with him, and Tony and I were sleeping in the front room. I wouldn't let him touch me I was so ashamed. What do you suppose happened? The next day we went out in the woods, and, believe me, it was no love act. Sex was "ish" from the first day to the last, ish, ish, ish. I was scared of men then, and I still don't have no trust in men. It's that guilt and fear that's put in you. If you get it when you're little, it never leaves. But I wouldn't trade those four boys I got for anything in the world. And they're beautiful husbands and fathers.

Yes, I was shamed by sex. So when I was pregnant with my first baby, I had no idea, may God strike me dead, how I got pregnant. You don't ask those questions then. That would be the worst sin in the world. So I'd be sick and I'd throw up and I didn't know what's wrong. We lived with my father and my father says, "You'd better go see Dr. Keasing to see what's wrong with you."

So I did. [Starts to laugh.] And I was scared of Dr. Keasing; he was a real gruff old doctor. He says, "Well, what's your trouble?"

And I says, "I don't know. I've been sick and throwing up."

"Well, you must be in the family way."

I says, "I can't be 'cause I'm taking all my brothers and sisters out of the orphanage, and I'm going to take care of them."

I can still see Dr. Keasing in that big leather chair. He says, "Helen, don't you know what family way means? You are going to have a baby."

"Have a baby! Oh, my God!" I said, "What am I going to tell my father?"

"Helen, you're married, aren't you?"

"Yes."

He says, "Did you have, ah, . . . When did you get married?"

"October."

"Well," he says, "did you ever go with your husband before you were married?"

"Oh, my God, no, Dr. Keasing. My husband never put a hand on me before we were married."

"So," he says, "you must be pregnant about four months. When you're with a man you get pregnant."

I was stunned and when I got home my father says, "What's the matter? What did the doc say?"

"Oh, he said that I got the stomach flu." And when I had to throw up I used to go out in the alley so he wouldn't hear me; I was so ashamed.

As time went on, they knew I was pregnant. It was a hard time; there was no work. And I went up to the mine to see one of the bosses, Mr. Whitney, to see if he would give my husband a job. And I was scared. I went up to him and said, "Mr. Whitney, I'm Mrs. Drazenovich, the Shebly girl. Could you give Tony a couple of days work so we could buy some baby clothes?" I was scared stiff.

He said, "Helen, by the time you get home, Henry Hughes will be there, and your man will be going to work." And Tony worked always after that, until he got too sick, and Mr. Whitney and I became friends.

I had a bad time with Tony early in that pregnancy. We were celebrating Serbian Christmas, which is celebrated on the seventh of January, and we were up at Mrs. Bozich and just had a beautiful, beautiful time. She made homemade chicken soup, with homemade noodles, barbecued lamb, barbecued pork, strudels, patitzas. You have no idea the food that that lady would put out.

My husband was extremely jealous and I never went nowhere, but this night when we were there, they had tamburitzas, string instruments, and they were playing them. A little old man, well, he wasn't so old then, maybe he was in his late thirties, but I was just a kid, he wanted me to dance, and I went once around with him and then I stopped. My father and my husband were there, and they just gave me awful looks. They were from the old country, and, God, they had awful ideas of what I might do.

Then my husband says to me in Yugoslav, "You whore." So I put my coat on and I went home. We lived about three blocks from there. Emil and my father stayed at the party, and about an hour later Tony came home. He had been drinking and he called me every name in the book. He just went too far, and I said, "Listen, Tony Drazenovich, you can go to hell. I am leaving this house right now, and you'll never see me again and this baby neither." And I went to get out of bed, and he grabbed me and tore my nightgown off. Of course, I was screaming and hollering.

Just then my brother Emil came home. I was sixteen and Emil was about fourteen. He said, "Ah, what's the matter? Tony, leave her alone. Don't hurt her!"

I says, "Emil, I'm going back. I'm leaving. I can't stand him. He's calling me dirty names just 'cause I danced once around with Old Steve, and you know that I'm not like he says."

Then Emil started to cry and he says, "Please, Helen, don't go, 'cause I'll have to go back to the orphanage." He had to go back to the orphanage three times already. [Crying hard.] So I didn't go. But any love I could have had for Tony was dead. We had our children but I was always in that sex bit without love, and I hate it to this day. Later, Tony quit trying to control me in terms of parties.

So, then I had my first baby. All my babies were born at home. And I had my first baby so dumb, so ignorant. I didn't know what to expect. I labored with that baby for three days. I was as green as grass and so young. My first son George was born the twenty-second of August, the day my brother Steve ran away from the orphanage.

Tony never worked with me with any child, 'cause, as I look back, I just think he didn't have the gumption. There's such a thing. But I didn't feel that way when I was a young person. I was looking for some moral support. So I learned to cover up my feelings. To this day I cover them up. Only thing is that I can't hide my emotions as easily as I used to.

My little George was colicky and he cried and I cried with him. Mrs. Balt, a sweet old midwife, took care of me. She had about ten or eleven children and was the midwife for many of us. She taught me most things that I ever knew. I had to stay in bed for ten days; you couldn't even breathe for ten days.

I had four boys; the first three were born very close together. I had George, Joe, John, and a little later, Tom. John, I had alone. Because my husband went to get the doctor and he got detoured. He had to have a little drink to calm his nerves. So the doctor wasn't coming and I was. That was my fastest labor, but my hardest labor. I didn't know what to do so I pounded on the wall, and the neighbor man came over. It was about midnight and I says, "Julius, will you go down and tell Dr. Keasing to come. Boy, I can hardly wait." And that poor man ran like crazy.

While Julius went, I had the baby by myself. So I left it just like that; I didn't know what to do with it. When Dr. Keasing came, the baby was laying there and I'm laying there. The doctor says, "What's going on here? I swear, it's in the water. I delivered twenty-three babies in this last week."

When Tony came home Dr. Keasing lit into him. He said, "What were you afraid of? You weren't having no baby."

So then I said to Dr. Keasing, "Dr. Keasing, could you advise me what to do not to have any more babies?"

He said, "Put your feet in a ten-gallon crock."

"My God, is that all the advice I can get from you?"

He said, "Helen, I would never advise any woman to use any preventative. Because if that preventative is strong enough to kill a live germ, it's strong enough to kill all your insides." So I didn't get any help.

When I was pregnant with my first baby it just got too close in the apartment with my father, and so I said, "Tony, we can't live like this," and we found an apartment in an alley about two blocks up from my father. Then I'd come down and I'd mix bread and bake bread and do the work for my father and Emil and the other kids as they came, and then I'd go home and do mine.

I worked hard, even when I was pregnant. I used to go out in the woods with my big belly and pull stumps out of the ground for firewood. I'd saw the wood out there, chop it, put it in the wagon, and bring it in. I had to because the men were in the mines working.

They worked hard too. They got up at four-thirty in the morning and walked five miles to work. In the winter, snow would be up to their waist. There was no insulated underwear, but they had all kinds of clothes on them so they could walk to work and back. And the winters were so cold back then. So cold that when you went to the outhouse the turd froze before it hit the ground.

My father and brother moved next door to us so I could take care of both homes, and, one by one, the kids came out of the orphanage. They lived with my father, and I cared for them all.

It wasn't exactly luxury living; it was tar paper shacks down in the alley that we lived in. There was two rooms. Everybody slept in one room and you ate and cooked in the other. The toilets were outside and the water was at a central pump. We didn't have a sewer and all of it was piped out into an open ditch. But, I'm telling you, nobody was sick. And rats the size of woodchucks. Oh, you should a seen that. They didn't come inside, though, cause there's all kinds of food we kept round the place for our pigs and cows and chickens. And everybody had big gardens.

I didn't buy much at the store. My bill would be like $4.80, for salt, sugar, flour, and coffee. That's all we bought. We even saved starters for the next batch of bread. If we lived like that, wouldn't we be rich today, and healthy?

We didn't have no electric stove; we had that old cook stove, but it was the most beautiful baker that you ever wanted to see. And on that cook stove we had one pot that had a handle on it. We used it for coffee. You just added water and coffee and it was so darn strong. [Laughs.] But it was the best-tasting coffee in the world. When it got about halfway up with grounds, you'd dump it and start over. Then we had a cow and we'd scald the milk from the cow and keep it warm on another part of the range. All the cream would come on top of it and was that good on bread. I made about fifty pounds of flour into bread every week for all of us.

We were healthy people and we ate healthy food and had remedies. Sauerkraut, it's full of penicillin, and I used goose grease for colds. When we'd cook a goose, we'd use two pie tins and put the goose on top of them so that when it roasted, all that fat would drip down. And I'd save all that grease so when the kids got a cold or any congestion, I could rub them with that goose grease. And I made a cough syrup out of that goose grease and Karo Syrup. You see, the Karo Syrup cuts the phlegm, and the goose grease oils it up and then all that phlegm slides out. I learned that from the old lady in Duluth and from Mrs. Bozich.

But one thing I couldn't do, and that was butcher. When the

kids were young, I tried to kill a chicken once and I couldn't. I got it on the chopping block and put the feet under one foot and the wings under another and I raised the ax. But I couldn't do it. I could never kill anything. I can see it so well, trying to kill that dumb chicken. I had already made my own homemade noodles, and we were going to have chicken soup that night, but they never got no chicken to eat that day, they got bean 'n' barley soup. So I told my father, "You'll have to kill the chickens, Pa, 'cause I can't kill 'em."

He said, "What kind a woman are you that you can't even kill chickens?" [Laughs.]

But it wasn't all funny, not at all. I remember about that time I had the first little boy, George, and my husband was sitting on the back porch. That's another time I was mad at him. I had just cooked slop for the pigs, and the slop was the big white cabbage leaves off of the cabbage and little potatoes and corn. We'd cook it and put the whole big container out on the back porch to cool so that we could feed it to the pigs.

My husband was sitting there and, geez, he was slower than molasses in January. He was one of those slow, steady, easygoing men, and I'm just the opposite, like a house afire. I said to him, "You watch that little boy so he don't fall in that hot slop." Wouldn't you know, I didn't come in the house than that baby tripped and went arm first in that slop. I dashed and grabbed him, Tony didn't.

George had burned his arm bad, and the skin felt terrible and he was screaming. I couldn't carry him up to the doctor's because I was so upset and was pregnant with my second baby, so my sister Ann grabbed him and ran him up to Dr. Keasing. Do you know what Dr. Keasing did? He told her to wait and come back for office hours.

Then I took that kid and went up there and says, "Listen, you old son of a bitch, this baby's hurt, and this baby's screaming all the time."

"Well, she didn't say he'd burned himself."

"Can't you hear that this child's in agony?" So he treated George right there and then.

I was mad at Tony and the doctor. There were some hard times between Tony and me. Once he hurt my feelings so bad I never again ate with him, never. When everybody was done eating, I ate. Sometimes the kids would leave a little meat on their bones, and I learned to love to chew on bones. So I'd gather all the bones up, and I'd chew on them and eat. I wasn't in nobody's way, and I'm not in nobody's way. I got this philosophy where I'll never be a burden.

I was never the quiet, sedate type person when I was young. After some years Tony quit trying to keep me from going out. Of course, I never went with other men, but I did have a good time. Once in awhile, we would go dancing. Tony would never go dancing, so I would go with two other couples and another widow. They'd give us a ride and we'd come to Hibbing and we'd dance and we'd come home. One night Emma Forest invited everybody who'd gone to a dance over to her house for chicken afterwards. She had two chickens and she had baked ten loaves of bread that day. Well, when they got to her house there must have been twenty people and two chickens. So my brother Emil said, "Helen, let's go down and get a couple of chickens from Pa. We'll kill 'em and bring 'em up."

So Emil and I go down in the dead of morning, at about three o'clock. We goes in the chicken coop, and Emil grabs some chickens and tears their heads off and throws them at me. They're squawking and I'm catching them and I'm all blood. Pretty soon the lights go on in my father's house. I says, "Emil, Pa's up!"

He says, "Get the hell out of here!" So he grabs two of those chickens and I have two, and we go up the dump, down the tracks, and way around on the back road to Emma's house. We cleaned those chickens, and we fried them, and we ate them; nice, fat, spring chickens.

Then the next morning at eight o'clock, I came up to Emma's to go to church with her, never missed church. When I got to Emma's house, there was blood all across the street. It left a trail right from Emma's to my father's coop. I went in her house and said, "Look out, there's blood from those chickens, and Pa will kill me 'cause he knows I was with you last night. I've got to get a pail of water, Emma, and wash that blood up." So I washed all that blood until it was outside someone else's door. My poor father died and we never told him about those chickens. We had a ball, those times. A lot of people would get the idea that we were out doing something wrong. But we weren't, except stealing chickens from my pa. When you're young you've gotta have some kind of outlet.

Tony and my father kept working in the mines all those years. There were things you needed to do to keep your job, like paying favors. We raised chickens and we usually killed them all at once and plucked them. I can't remember how in the hell we preserved those chickens. Oh yes, we canned them. And we butchered our hogs. We used to render the lard, and then we'd put the meat in the lard to preserve it. During the winter it never got spoiled; anyway nobody ever died. Then we'd smoke hams and bacon and sausage. But when we'd butcher, for appreciation, we would take maybe a pork loin or a chicken to one of the bosses, because if you didn't you just might not have your job. That's true. You always were paying favors.

The mining companies did some good things, though. When I was keeping house for my father, the company would give a Christmas party, and we came from all over the region to it. They had the nicest bags of candy, an orange, and a brand new dime for the kids. That was the biggest event of our life. It was outside under a great big Christmas tree, and blizzard or nothing, we'd walk the two miles out there. And at home with my father, Christmas was special. We didn't have gifts to exchange, but I would cook good, Yugoslavian, holiday food. And when I had my boys, on the holidays like Valentines Day or Christmas or Thanksgiving, there was always something for those kids. Always. No matter what.

But there were hard times in the mines. Men got killed in them. We had Mr. Manard working on the shovel and it caved in, and Mr. Hughes had to come and tell Mrs. Manard he got killed. She took it real bad and it scared us all. We tried to help her but there wasn't much we could do. The company didn't do anything for the widows or the men who got sick from working in the mines. Their lungs went bad from the work. Them days you didn't get anything. There was no social security or sick pay or help with a death.

When the unions first came to Nashwauk they started to organize. They'd have their meetings in the Finn Hall. Then the men would go out on strike. Now, I had plenty to eat because we had a garden and a cow and we raised pigs, but there were people there that never had this. One time at this union meeting, a Mr. Swanson gets up to speak. I'll never forget it. He says to the women, "I'm so glad to see you women are sticking behind your men."

And then I got up and says, "Well, they won't be able to stick behind their men very much longer. I'm not complaining about having nothing to eat because we've got food, but you've got to help these people. They have no food for their families." The next day there was two relief orders in the grocery store for me and orders for others too. 'Cause I had talked up.

Then Tony got sick from working in the mine. Other miners got sick like he did too. Them days, they didn't know what pulmonary emphysema was. So Dr. Keasing suggested we go to

Rochester. So we goes to Rochester. Tony couldn't breathe; he just had an awful time. We were down there about two weeks, and they decided that he couldn't work; that he was disabled due to his breathing. Then they told me that it was just a matter of time because these kinds of conditions cause high blood pressure and heart problems. So I was in shock. I didn't say nothing when we're coming home. What was I to do? There is no sick leave pay; there is no medicare; there is no nothing. The company didn't do anything for him, nothing. When he died they sent a big spray of flowers. Big deal. So I had to go to work. I couldn't be home with my boys.

I was criticized for doing that. A social worker came after me, and she wanted me to stay home and go on welfare. But no way. I said, "Miss Nelson, my boys are going to get an education no matter how. And they're not going to have you on the street corner counting their teeth!" Well, I was ridiculed and criticized and called every name, but after these four boys grew up and they were educated and they were God fearing and good husbands and good men, now I'm a big wheel.

I was afraid but I could never let the fear take over because then something would happen to me and my kids would have to go to the orphanage. That was the prime thing in my life; to keep them so they had a mother and didn't go to the orphanage. How strong that feeling was.

My first business was a nightclub and I worked hard. After quite awhile I moved us out of the alley where we had been living all those years and into a house with running water and heat. We bought that house for $600. God, you'd think we were millionaires. We were so proud.

Something bad happened, though, when I first started to work. I had an abortion. When I went with Tony to Rochester I got pregnant. We had intercourse just that one time. So I went to a doctor and said, "Doctor, you know that I cannot have a baby. Who's going to take care of it? Tony is dying; we have no money coming in except this money that I work and make."

"Well," he says, "Helen, I can't advise you where to go or what to do, and I cannot abort you."

"What can I do?"

"I don't know."

Some woman in Duluth, I can't even remember who it was, told me to come down there. So this girlfriend of mine drove me there. The woman put me in a taxicab, and we rode out to the middle of a woods. She put a blindfold on me so I couldn't see where I was going. Gee whiz, it was just like going to the electric chair. We came to an old house and she took me out. The lady that went there with me had to stay in the cab. An old woman was there alone in the house, and she said, "You got the $300?"

"Yes."

"Lay on this." She had a ironing board on the bed. So I laid on the ironing board, and she put a long, skinny, smooth piece of wood all the way up my vagina. I had no pain; I must be made of wood. The good Lord must have felt sorry for me so he gave me no pain. But I was terrified.

I didn't abort right away and they put me back in the car and away we went. I didn't have the miscarriage for a week. Then I was working behind the counter and, wooooooof, everything fell out. I hemorrhaged right there. I got some dish towels and went in the bathroom and put them on. Someone took me back to Nashwauk in a car.

I called up a doctor at the clinic, and I have a deep, man's voice and was kind of hysterical laughing, and I said, "Doc, I'm having a miscarriage. Can you come down? I'm bleeding like a stuck hog."

He thought I was one of his friends joking, and he said, "Yah, I'll be there, you big liar," and he hung up. I didn't pay no attention but he didn't come and he didn't come. I was bleeding so hard it was in gushes, and I kind of quit knowing what was happening. When my son and my husband come home I told them to lift the foot of the bed up onto the chair 'cause I was bleeding so bad, and I stayed in bed and finally I quit bleeding. I saved the embryo and put it in a nice, clean cloth, and the next afternoon I went down to see the doctor.

He says, "Hi, how are you?"

I says, "You, rag ass, how come you didn't come when I called you last night?"

"When did you call me?"

"Who do you suppose was having the miscarriage, your next-door neighbor?"

"I thought that was one of my buddies playing a joke. What did you do?"

"Well, I had my husband and son put the bed up on the chair, and I laid in the bed elevated. I thought, how do you stop a nosebleed; you put your head back, right. So that's what I did."

He said, "You probably saved your life."

And the next day I went to work. I can't tell you how horrible it all was. Gee whiz, it was just like dying. I wouldn't subject a dog to that. I never had sex again.

I worked in the nightclub for a long time following the abortion. A friend helped me start in the nightclub business. I was worrying about what I was going to do when a beer distributor I knew meets me and asks, "How is everything going?"

"Oh, it's all right but I don't know what to do now 'cause Tony's sick. He can never work and I don't know how I'm going to raise my family. I'm not going to go on welfare, though, and I'm not going to ask for relief. I don't care what happens."

"Helen, why don't you rent Club 65. The man who owns it hasn't been very well and he wants to rent it." So I rode with him in that beer truck out to Club 65 and we made a deal.

Then the distributor gave me $2,000 to start with, and I didn't even sign for it, and he filled my coolers with beer, pop, mixes. I got a beer license and a soft drink license and a cigarette license, but no liquor licenses were allowed out there. Well, in order to make a living, you had to sell liquor, not just sell beer and mixes. That's just the way it was, so I started bootlegging.

I had a business like you wouldn't believe. Oh my God, they came; all of them couldn't get in. I had a band and my boys would come out on Saturday and Sunday to clean and help me. That's the most fun I ever had in my life. Honest to God, we had the most beautiful fun. We danced and we told stories. Nobody got out of line. That's really true. And I met and made friends with people from the shit house to the White House. And I helped people; I'd talk to people about their problems. When the fellas would get drunk, I used to pile them up in the car like cordwood, and I'd drive them wherever they lived and then I'd take a taxi home. But, still, I lived in fear constantly 'cause I was bootlegging.

Tony would be home taking care of the boys, and I hitchhiked to and from work. I didn't even buy a car; I couldn't afford a car and pay payments on the house and still buy groceries. I rode with a milk truck at 5:00 in the morning from the nightclub to Nashwauk, and would be home by 5:30. That's the truth; you can ask anybody on the range. Then I'd catch the 11:30 A.M. bus back to the nightclub because there was no other buses going that way, and I needed to get my stuff prepared before people came that night. The owner was paying me $300 a month to manage the nightclub and I had to have it.

I'd probably sleep three or four hours a night, but my husband would help me with some of the housework. When I came home in the early morning, I'd knead the bread and set the alarm clock for an hour. Then I'd punch it down and set the alarm clock again. When it was time for the bread to be baked, I'd have it in the pans, and it would be raised and Tony could bake it. By then we had an electric stove, I'll have you know. I can't tell you now how I did the work all those years.

Then somebody squealed about my bootlegging. It was hunting season and two of the state agents came and posed as hunters. They had a ball and they drank with the rest of them for three days. Then those two hunters were standing by the bar when some of my hunters from Minneapolis came. They saw the agents and called me into a different room and said, "Helen, how come you're bootlegging with those two guys standing there?"

"What do you mean?"

"Those are two state liquor inspectors."

When I got back to the bar, they were gone, and then the sheriff came and said, "Helen, you broke the law."

"I know."

But he said to the others, "Helen will never run away and I'm not going to put her in jail." But I made the 10:00 news.

I had to go through a trial. Oh, I'll never forget it, I was so scared. I was charged $300 and supposed to pay a $1,000 fine. Holy cats, I was upset. That would take everything we had and more.

Then the federal agent who was supposed to deal with it came down to see me. He looked at me and said, "Helen, where did you come from? Where were you born?"

"Duluth."

"You're not Big Mary's daughter?"

"Yes, I am."

"Well, I'm not going to charge you this $1,000. Your mother did many favors for me. She was a good woman. I've got a $35 federal liquor stamp that's postdated and that will take care of you."

Oh, that was so beautiful; I had been so scared. You see, every time you're down something comes and brings you up. So after that the business was good, and I was paying my bills and taking care of my family and not having to ask for aid. But I started thinking; I have to set an example for my boys, and I cannot set an example by doing this. So I quit and rented a cafe, the Oreland, and I was there about eighteen years. I moved my father, my husband, and the boys from the house to the upstairs of the restaurant. I cooked downstairs and took the food upstairs. I loved the restaurant; I cooked and b.s.'ed. And I let people talk. When people are down, they've got to have some place to go to talk where they won't be blasted.

I had a morning cook come in, but at night I cooked my soups, made my noodles, marinated my roasts, and baked my caramel rolls. They were with pecans and I charged ten cents. Now they're seventy-five cents, outrageous, outrageous. People liked my cooking so much sometimes they waited on the sidewalk to get in.

I did all sorts of things for people in that cafe. I used to be the interpreter for all those old-timers in Nashwauk. They had come here as little guys and still could not read or write the language well. Those men died with lots of money, but still insecure 'cause of what they went through as boys.

Every Christmas Eve I closed at six o'clock, and I'd have a big Christmas party. I'd invite all my friends and my boys would invite their friends, and I would cook and bake and roast lamb, ham, pigs in a blanket. We'd have patitzas, whiskey, wine, beer. Then on Christmas Day I'd go down to the restaurant again because I had four or five bachelors that had no place to go, and I would make Christmas dinner and feed them.

My father was with us during that time, and even with his drinking he was a real generous person who loved people and the world. We had a lot of fun with him, but he also drove me up a tree. [Laughs.] I'd say, "Pop, when you got any friends, if you want to, you bring them here in the restaurant and treat them." Then he'd go and treat them all to porterhouses.

Another problem was that he'd go out with all kinds of women, young girls too. You know how girls are; they liked to be catered to and get candy. He'd buy jewelry and he'd buy candy and flowers. But I couldn't even smoke in front of him. We didn't even dare play solitaire; cards weren't allowed in our house. Oh, he was really strict and proper, but for him to go with a girl, that was a different story. One time I was walking in Hibbing right on Main Street, and my father was coming down the street with a young girl. I was so embarrassed I went in the first door that was handy to hide while they went by.

Tony lived for awhile after we moved to the restaurant. Then he got bad and we knew he was going to die real soon. He wanted me to sit on a chair where he could see me, but he didn't talk very much. But then he said to me, "Helen, I'm very sorry for how I hurt you. You gotta have somebody your own age if you gonna live a good life. I had no education; I had nothing. And you took care of all of us. [Helen begins to cry.] And you never said, 'Look at you. I have to take care of you and you're not working,' never. If you'd a hollered at me or swore or gave me hell, I'd probably would have felt better."

But I said, "Tony, how can you holler at somebody that's sick and dying? That work was good, Tony, 'cause I could take care of you and the kids."

Then he said he had a dream where God told him he would die on April fifth, so the night of April the fifth I stayed with him, and at three-thirty that night my husband died. He went peaceful, with no problems.

So, after Tony died, we went on living and working in the restaurant. I'm a lucky woman 'cause my boys are like they are. I couldn't be home with them until I got in the restaurant. Before that my job had to be number one, then the children, then me. I says to my sons, "You kids never really got any loving."

But they say, "Ma, you were so good to us, you don't know. We were always well fed."

I was always so afraid that something would happen to me, and my kids would have to go to the orphanage. It was almost an obsession that I might die. It's better for a child to lose ten fathers than to lose a mother. Men are not cut out to take care of little children. It's not in their nature, like it wasn't in my father's.

I had another obsession. I was determined that those boys were going to get an education so their wives wouldn't have to go out and work. That was the prime plot behind all those years of work. If they had good jobs, their wives could stay home and take care of their families and not have to be like me. And I did it; I got them all through college, and now they have good jobs as teachers.

I stayed close to most of my brothers and sisters all those years. Katherine, the baby, was in orphanages since she was born. The orphanage she was in is run by Catholic nuns, the St. Benedictine Order. The children and nuns prayed continually. Prayer don't hurt anybody but, I tell you, too much of anything is no good. All this religion got instilled in Katherine and she just loved the nuns. She also loved us and wanted to be with us, so when she got to be in the first year of high school, I finally took her out. I brought her home and she decided to go into a convent. So she did housework and went to high school until the last year and we got her ready.

She was a novice and started training as a nurse at St. Mary's Hospital in Duluth. One night there was a horrible rainstorm, and she had to run out in it to cross from the hospital to where she was living. The force of the rain had uncovered a manhole, and when she was running across the alley to the nurses' home, she fell in the manhole and hit the back of her head. She was in the hospital for weeks before she regained consciousness. For awhile she'd be rational and then she'd be irrational. I found out later that scar tissue was forming on her brain.

Finally, we had to commit Katherine to Mooselake, the mental hospital. She was in Mooselake several times. During her bad times they'd give her shock treatments and tie her down and restrain her. Then, at midnight, the day after Christmas, the hospital called me and told me she was dead. The next morning I went and brought her home. She supposedly had hung herself but I don't think she did. I think she was choked when they tried to restrain her. And, honest to God, I got a letter from Katherine on the day of her wake. She had written the letter just before she died. I'll read it to you.

"Dearest Helen, I got your card and gift and thanks so much. I'm so very sorry to disappoint you and not be with you for Christmas. My headaches got so bad, I just couldn't spoil it for the family. I do know you love me as I do love you dearly and I want you to pray for me. I tried taking my life once here but no more of that. That is the coward's way out. You were right about the doctor, he is a good man and knows what's best for me. I have more faith now than I ever did in him. Forgive me for disappointing you, won't you, but I'm not feeling good at all. All my love, your little sis, Kathy."

Poor little Katherine; she was such a good girl. [Begins crying hard.] May God rest her soul. I dressed her in her wedding gown, from when she started as a nun, and I put her veil on so she looked just beautiful for her burial. She was a virgin, that girl. My father had died ahead of her, so I buried her with my father.

And I lost my brother Emil, too. I was always so close to Emil that it was hard for me when he went. Emil was a rugged, honest man who worked in the mines and with the sheriff's department, and he used plenty of vulgar swearing. Men have their way, you know. Still, he had always been a God-fearing man, but when he got sick with bone cancer, he said that God came to him and he never swore again. Yet he died such a hard way. Almost every bone in his body broke.

We were all by his bed, his wife and children and me and he began fading away. Then we started crying and he came right back. Then he started slipping away again, and we cried again and he came back again. Then I said, "Oh, my God, we can't do this no more. We can't cry in front of him; he'll never let go."

He was in agony so while I was kneeling there I said to Emil in

Yugoslav, so his children wouldn't understand, "Emil, you just close your eyes and go. This is your time; you've suffered enough. [Helen cries again.] I know you can hear me but you can't answer. Emil, let go; we'll be fine." So we kneeled there and never breathed and never spoke a word and he went.

Life went on with the restaurant and I got involved with politics. Politicians used to come to my place to campaign and just sit around and b.s. They called it the "Tammany Hall of the range." Hubert Humphrey and Fritz Mondale came in, and I got to know them well. Fritz Mondale used to sit alongside of my fire while I cooked. Orville Freeman would come in there too, and I got real close to Congressman Blatnik. You meet everyone in the restaurant business. Those days were full of talk and laughing and food. It's not so much what you feed a person as how you feed him. If you're happy when you eat, anything tastes good.

Lots happened. I went to Washington, D.C., once and was talking with John Blatnik on the front steps of the capitol. He introduced me to Bella Abzug, and we stood and argued about liberated women. I said, "You know, Bella, this liberation of women is a pile of bullshit. I've been liberated all my life and I'm sick of it. I don't want to be a man, I want to be a woman, but I had no choice. Whenever you start putting women on a pedestal above men, you are not going to have happy people."

John Blatnik put his arms around us and had our picture taken. Then he said, "Well, I'm leaving you two girls to rough it out." And we did. She took me into the dining room and I had lunch with her and we argued steady. You'd like her; she's a clown.

I'm getting involved with politics again. I went to the caucus and said, "I could care less about the Democratic party or the Republican party. I am interested in the survival of people. The senior citizens are being punished; the wage earners are being punished; everybody's getting punished; but the rich are getting richer and the poor are getting poorer." I decided I'm not going to go hollering and screaming and swearing 'cause they might not listen, but I'm going to do what I can.

I kept my restaurant until my last son got married and then I went bumming. Did you ever feel like you wanted to run away? I always said that was what I was going to do. When my last son was gone I was going to sell the cafe and take off. So I did. I spent a whole year traveling around the United States, meeting all kinds of people and doing all kinds of things. But, let me tell you this, maybe you know it already, you can't run away. Finally, I went into a little, dark, quiet mission in California and sat there, and into my head came, "Go home, Helen, go home." So I did.

One of my great experiences was when I was asked to represent the Midwest as an ethnic cook in the World's Fair in Montreal. They asked me to come up, so I baked ten huge patitzas, a fancy, Yugoslav desert, and when I got up there they were all gone in the first day. Oh my God, I had thousands of people coming and nothing to feed them and no pans, no stoves, nothing to cook anything on. I stayed awake all night the first night, trying to figure out what to do, and I finally got places to donate equipment so I could cook bean 'n' barley soup. Served soup to 65,000 people! And, gee whiz, I made such good friends. Only slept a few hours a night, but it was some beautiful fun.

I also married one more time, to Joe Berklich. I jumped from the frying pan into the fire. I loved that man way before I was a widow, but that man was a God-fearing man, a good man and never did he put a finger on me or be intimate with me, before marriage, or after. When I first met him, I was working in the nightclub, and I was impressed because he was so respectful. I used to like to tell stories; in a nightclub you've got to know stories. He would say, "I don't like to hear you tell stories; ladies don't tell stories." So when he was around I never told them, but when he left I'd tell them. And he never used foul language and never made a pass or even suggested it. You don't find very many men like that, and I was attracted to him because he was real special and different from most men.

A while after Tony was dead I married Joe, and, I'll be honest, he couldn't be a man. We never had intimate relations. Yet he was the only man I ever really loved, and I loved him so deep. But his problem turned him mean, and he hurt me in many little ways. Later he got sick and I had to take care of him too. But for a while I still loved him.

Then, one time, when my brother Emil was still alive, I was leaving to go with Emil to Rochester. Joe was sitting in the living room chair. I had my sister here to take care of Joe. I said to Joe, "I am going with Emil. Don't feel bad because they need me."

But Joe was angry that I was going, and when I went to kiss him before I left, he snapped, "What's that for!"

I said, "Joe Berklich, look at me. Today is the last time that I will ever kiss you in my life." And I meant it. I never did kiss him again. I'm bullheaded too. And from that time on my love started just turning to hate.

It was just like he put a knife right deep down. After that, I wouldn't touch him with a fifty-foot pole. The poor thing would come and put his arm around me and I would just cringe. I said, "Joe, I don't love you. You killed it. I will take care of you as long as I live, but I can never love you again." But, I'll tell you, once you kill that kind of love I had, it kills a lot of things inside of you. That heart and that chemistry.

Later, when he was dying, Joe said, "Helen, you'll never know how much I love you."

I said, "Joe, if you'd have told me that last year I'd probably done cartwheels." But I never said no more 'cause why should I hurt him. He couldn't take the dying and cried to the end.

I was bitter over all that happened with Joe. I had lost a lot of people, my sister, three brothers by then, my mother, my father, my first husband, and I could handle those times with no problem, but it seemed like after I married Joe I lost hold of myself. The hurt just went so deep. I tried to bury the bitterness, but then I got so negative. I hated people; I hated everything; I barked like a dog.

One day my son John came home, and he crabbed, "Hi, how are ya, ya ole son of a bitch; What the hell's going on here!"

I said, "What's wrong with you, John?"

"Mom, that's how you sound. Do you like it? Ma, you're chasing everybody away from you. Look at the beautiful men you raised. Look at the people who love you. Ma, you've got to get out of that frame of mind, or nobody will come to see you."

I just sat there and looked at him, and he was right; it was true. I was like a bear, worse, a bear at least goes in a cave once in a while. And then I started to come out of it. I started to try and get more compassion so people wouldn't be frightened of me. So, that's what happened with Joe, and I haven't been with a man for, holy cats, thirty years. And so sex has stayed "ish" with me, all my life.

I still believe that if the man truly loves you and treats you with love and kindness and consideration and is gentle and isn't an animal, you will learn to love him. I taught my boys what I wanted to experience, so they could have normal, married lives. And their wives are beautiful, wonderful people, and these guys all came out of the alley. They're educated and they're God-fearing.

Now I'm an old lady and I'd be ashamed to go out with men. Guys come and ask me. They say, "Helen, how would you like to go for dinner?"

I say, "Oh, do I look hungry? Hell no, I don't want to go for dinner." I don't even offer to make them coffee because I want to discourage them. I don't need no one; my life is full. I've got nineteen grandchildren, two great-grandchildren, four sons, the people I take care of, and a lot of friends that I can help and who help me. So I need a man like I need another head. Joe Berklich fixed that up for me. I don't go out dancing anymore either. If some guy got smart and said anything to me, I'd knock him down.

When Joe was still alive, a social worker came and asked me if I could take care of two retarded people, and so I rented a bigger house so I could. Now I take care of four of them and they're just like my kids. We do all sorts of things together, like Gertie has two cats and two dogs, and we even have birthday parties for the cats and dogs. I've gone a little bit cuckoo now too. We've got lots of plans for Easter, and I got the cats and dogs these things they chew on to clean their teeth. We have a good togetherness. We holler at each other; we make each other mad and happy; we're like a family.

Do you know how much I get a month per person? Two hundred and eleven dollars! If I didn't use my social security to supplement it, we'd never make it. And I have to cook real good to spread the money out. And the forms we have to fill out for the government; it's just disgusting. It would even make the Blessed Virgin swear.

Although they're all old, they're like kids to me, like my kids, and I don't dare get back in the state I was in before John gave me hell. I've got to try and keep myself well so that I don't disrupt everything. I tell you, it's like when my own kids were little and I was afraid of them going to the orphanage; now I've got to keep these people away from the institutions. And they're God's chosen people, too, so innocent and so simple.

So I've accepted myself. I've lost like 2,500 pounds in my sixty-five years. Down to 180, up to 250. Down to 200, up to 260. Down to 210, up to 280. Back and forth I've gone. I buried my emotions and fed them. I should loose some more weight, but who wants to change at sixty-five? I don't want to change nothing no more. So, with all that's happened, I know that God doesn't want me to be handicapped or bedded down. I'm put here to do something, you see.

I've always been strong, like a bull, and only used eating as my crutch. But the last few years I've slowed down. In some ways, this has been the hardest time of my life because I'm idle and I'm blah. Nothing much interests me, so I need these people I care for more than they need me because I keep interested in them.

And when you get older you get to be more chicken. You can't cover up your emotions like you did when you were young. I used to go roaming the hospitals and hollering at everyone and telling them they're just pretending and to get out of those beds. They'd laugh and we'd have a ball. But I can't do that no more. And I don't want to go to the hospital and be a crepe hanger 'cause you don't help people like that, so I stay away. But I can say, I've been with the best and the worst in my life, and the secret is, they're all people. And so I have all these beautiful memories.

I never thought telling stories like this would cause so much emotion. And I never thought I could get so wore out just from talking. Telling it how it was is like going to confession. God, mine should be cleaned out now for the rest of my life. [Laughs.] Still, life isn't all peaches and cream, but I won't cover up. Maybe other people can, but I have to say what is true.

Last night the boys and I were reminiscing about all these different things, and, later, when I fell asleep, I dreamed. In my dream my husband Joe ran away, and I followed him and found him in somebody's barn. He was drunk and said, "What are you doing here? Are you looking for me?"

I said, "No, I'm running away." Then he fell down drunk on the floor, and I said, "You're drunk and I'm taking off." And I took off and I ran, and I got to a strange, old store. I stayed there and it was quiet and I was alone. Then my brother Emil came. I looked at Emil and said, "What are you doing here, Emil?"

"I'm looking for you. You ran away and everybody at home is worried about you. You must come back; we all need you, Helen." So I looked around the quiet store and said good-bye and went back to take care of them all.

*I tried to teach the fourth-generation
Japanese-American children, "You have
wonderful parents and wonderful roots,"
but the story always had to come out that
we were mistreated. We were
discriminated against and despised and
put into camps.*

—Mary Tsukamoto

During the first few days following the December 7, 1941, attack on Pearl Harbor thousands of Japanese immigrants living in the United States were arrested. Without benefit of trial, 110,000 men, women, and children of Japanese ancestry were taken from their homes on the West Coast, losing their possessions and livelihoods. They spent the remainder of the war surrounded by guards and barbed wire, confined in concentration camps in remote parts of California, Arkansas, Arizona, and elsewhere. This occurred even though many of these people were American citizens, and although no Japanese American person ever committed a recorded act of sabotage or spying.

Eventually, following about a decade of work, the Japanese American Citizens League pressured Congress into forming a Commission on Wartime Relocation and Internment of Civilians; in 1981 the commission held a series of hearings concerning the wartime experience. One of the hearings took place on August 12, 1981, at Golden Gate University in San Francisco. About 450 people were in the audience, and speakers were each given five minutes to state their views on the evacuation, recall memories of it, and make requests for redress.

Eighty-five-year-old Tom Nagasawa spoke of how he lost a grocery store in Oregon when he and his family were forced into the camp. Small, dark-haired Violet DeCristoford, aged sixty-one, wiped tears from her face as she told how her family was ordered to leave their Fresno home and go to the Tule Lake Camp. She then described how her husband was deported, leaving her alone with her three confused children who looked to her for an explaination of what had happened. She said, "I had no word of consolation. Mr. Chairman and members of the Commission, would you have had an answer for my children?" Tears rolled down from under her glasses as she told that when she too was deported, she found that her husband had married a Japanese woman, consequently breaking up her family.

Mary Tsukamoto, a small woman of sixty-six, moved stiffly forward. She spoke with much conviction, telling how many of her neighbors, working small grape and strawberry farms, were forced to move at harvest time: "They had struggled hard during the Depression to come out of it. Many of them had mortgages to pay. It would be hard to explain the sorrow that came to them. . . . I don't know how you could figure how that suffering could be repaid." She moved back to her seat and listened as the others, one by one, told of their sufferings.

A few days later I had an appointment to visit with Mary Tsukamoto in her home on the southwest edge of Sacramento, California. She was a small, lovely women with short, softly waved black hair that was edged with streaks of white around her face. Her brown eyes revealed her kindness, and she spoke with a gentle, young voice that nevertheless expressed much emotion and conviction. She moved stiffly and carefully; her hands were somewhat bent with rheumatoid arthritis, and I slowly realized that her left arm was totally immobile, stuck at a ninety-degree angle.

An antique tapestry showing life in the Japanese court in about A.D. 1,000 hung along one wall of the living room, and a Japanese doll collection was arranged carefully on a cabinet. One intricate doll dressed in a kimono was displayed in a glassed-in box. Books on Japanese art and history sat on shelves, and her home was filled with thriving plants. As she talked, a large long-haired cat purred, rubbed against our legs, and played with my tape recorder. During one of our visits, Mary showed me strings of many colored paper cranes folded by the schoolchildren to whom she taught the Japanese art of origami. She spoke passionately and cried unself-consciously as she described the sufferings of Japanese Americans, sometimes stopping for a minute to catch her breath. She would then sigh, regain her composure, and slowly start speaking again.

Mary T. My father came to the United States when he was only seventeen; he came from Okinawa. There were only two brothers and they both came, but his mother wanted to be sure he came back, so even though my father was young she insisted that he be married and she found him a bride. My mother was two years older than he and my father didn't like that, but, of course, he had to get married or his mother wouldn't let him go. That way she felt he would return to Japan. So my father married my mother and then left her in Japan and came to the United States.

He and his brother worked at many different jobs, as farm laborers, in laundries, as cooks. At one time a letter caught up to him announcing that he had become a father. My sister was born in Japan, Okinawa, after he left. My father was unable to send for my mother, though, and he and his brother continued to work. He picked up a few English words, but he was never really very good at English conversation.

He and his brother settled down in San Francisco in around 1910, and he finally called my mother to the United States. By then he and his brother and a few other boys were already established in a laundry business. The laundry became a sort of headquarters for all the young fellows that came from Okinawa that were lonely. They had many people helping and working for them and, I guess, staying in the rooms upstairs. It was kind of a laundry and boardinghouse; friends gathered there. All the people from Okinawa were very clannish, like the way those who came from Hiroshima got together more often. They were lonely for their village and their relatives and family and were all young people and very few had women yet in the United States.

My mother's coming to the United States was also a very sad story. She had to leave her daughter, my oldest sister, in Japan. My grandmother was a widow by then, and if my sister accompanied my mother, my grandmother would have been all alone. So my sister was about six when my mother had to leave her. And since my mother's husband wasn't with her, she couldn't argue with her mother-in-law and insist on bringing her daughter with her. So she finally consented to leave my sister. It was a sad thing. I often found her crying in the room when I came home from school because she was thinking about the sad time when she had to part from her daughter, and they missed each other.

It's a tragic story that happened during the immigration. Many families were like that; they would choose to send the children to look after the grandparents because they themselves couldn't be with their old parents, or they would send their children to school in Japan so they'd get a Japanese education. For many, many reasons the families were broken apart.

At that point they had what they called "picture brides." A young man who worked and labored around in the United States and needed a wife but couldn't afford to go back to Japan to get one, would send the money and a picture of himself and ask his relatives to find some maiden in the village for him. They would send him a couple of pictures and he would choose which one. Then they would have a wedding in Japan with the picture, and they would send the bride over here. Funny stories were told. Stories that he didn't have a good picture of himself or had one that was taken ten years before, and when the bride came she was shocked because he was so old. Things like that happened. Or the men were ashamed of themselves and borrowed a handsome young fellow's picture and mailed it. Or the girl knew she wasn't very beautiful, so she borrowed her sister's picture and sent it. Funny stories like that have come out of the picture bride story, but, whatever, it's an amazing thing.

Although there must have been a great deal of hardship because they didn't love each other or found out they weren't compatible or whatever, many of them endured and managed to start a family. Of course, we have heard that a few of them ran away or met someone else, but not so many. It's a remarkable thing that that's how they got their start. Many of them did manage to have good families and endured years of living together and grew to like each other or at least tolerate each other. I marvel at that kind of start. So I often think, when I teach the children, that it's marvelous to think their grandparents met like that and established a family and stayed here and survived.

I think that the girls left Japan because there was so much poverty and hardship. And in many families, where there were several girls, the girls felt it was their duty to go and help their family by being married and relieving their parents of this responsibility. So they would volunteer to go. There was courage and determination in every way to make this happen, and I imagine many were very lonely and nervous on the way over.

I guess the voyage over was long. They had to get to Yokohama and then come across the ocean, and my mother talked about being held at Angel Island for a week because she didn't pass her physical examination. All the Isseis,* all the immigrants that came over, were kept at Angel Island. We've taken the Japanese school children to visit it as a pilgrimage to a place where their ancestors arrived first in this land. Some of the immigrants waited and waited for a long time before someone came after them, and some of them never passed their physical examination and were sent home. They had some tragic experiences over there. There were many Chinese and Japanese immigrants that were kept together. For many of the Chinese women, either the ones who had sent for them had died in the meantime or something else happened so that no one came after them. They waited indefinitely; some of them committed suicide; and some of them were sent home. So some had tragic experiences.

My mother said that after she arrived, she worked as a housemaid in a home and learned some of the ways to run a house and cook in America. Then my sister was born in 1913 and I was

---

*Issei refers to first generation Japanese immigrants. Nisei refers to the Isseis' children, the second generation in the United States, and Sansei refers to the Niseis' children, the third generation of Japanese ancestry in the United States.

born in 1915 and I had another sister who was born in 1917 or 1918. The three of us were born in San Francisco while my parents were having the laundry business. I think they lived upstairs and then worked on the laundry business downstairs, so we were always close to my parents. Then a few years later they dissolved the partnership and different ones went in different directions; they found jobs as houseboys or cooks in private homes.

Around 1918 they had the influenza and many people got very sick. I remember our whole family was sick, but we survived. And I remember Father and Mother working on the farms. We would go out like migrant workers; we worked in different fields during the grape season, getting up early in the morning and then going to pick grapes. Then my parents settled in a place in Turlock where they started to raise cantaloupes and melons. My aunt and uncle moved in and lived with us for a while, and they all farmed together and raised cantaloupes and honeydew and watermelon.

My sister was the first to go to school, and I remember learning a lot of things from her when she came home, so it was a lot easier for me to first attend school than it was for her. But I imagine the language problem slowed us in our progress in school.

I remember that when my sister first enrolled she used to take her lunch and walk across the field, and then I was enrolled and we would walk with the other children in the neighborhood to school. And I do remember some of the embarrassing things that we started to notice. There were some children that would tease us and make fun of us and make us feel ashamed because of our ancestry. And maybe the principal never meant it in a bad way, but it kind of hurt us when they would always say, "Well, here comes the Japs." Those words meant a slap to us. But everybody used those words in referring to us. We'd always come in a bunch, all of us together because we were afraid to walk by ourselves. We came in a group and always huddled by ourselves in a group and we played by ourselves. And, of course, we were shy and maybe there were others that would have been nice to us if we weren't so scared, but I remember being singled out as a group.

But we do remember learning a lot of things, learning to read, learning a song, being in the Christmas program, going to the school picnic. Our neighbors were real kind and took us because our parents were too busy to take us. So they had a picnic lunch and shared it with us. My parents didn't go to PTA and knew nothing about school. So the neighbors would take us to the Christmas program.

But growing up we remember frightening things. My parents

read in the papers or heard their neighbors talk about the time when about fifty of the Japanese migrant laborers were forced at the point of a gun by a bunch of vigilantes to be put into a train freight car and told never to come back. So, there was a good deal of anti-Japanese sentiment expressed then, and we remember hearing our parents discuss it.

My father and uncle were always talking, and, although we didn't always understand what they were talking about, we sensed a kind of frightening insecurity. And I remember hearing my uncle and dad whispering about so many boys that they were expecting to have come to their farm to harvest the melon, but who were sent away, leaving my father and uncle short of workers. They couldn't often get the Japanese laborers they were hoping to have come to help make the crates and get ready for the harvest season. And if the laborers did sneak through and come, they were happy. And so it was a kind of surprising, joyous evening when these laborers drifted in one by one. But things like that I remember.

My uncle had found a farm a few miles away from us and they raised cantaloupes, but one year the crops were ruined by an invasion of some kind of cutworm. They were yellowish worms that had green and black stripes, and they were eating his cantaloupes and ruining his crops. I remember that we ran around with a can of kerosene and chopsticks and picked up these worms from the cantaloupes, but we couldn't save them. And my uncle just gave up farming and decided to do something else. There was a friend that had a boardinghouse in Fresno and so he decided to move there.

My father decided that Ruth and I should move with my uncle and aunt because the school in the city was better, and always they were aware of the importance of getting a good education. Aunt had been a schoolteacher in Japan in Okinawa, so she was willing to take us again. So we all piled into my uncle's and father's Model T car. I marveled at the real close friendship that my father and his brother had and the real bond they all had between each other and my aunt, who was a sister-in-law to my dad. They were real good to us, so that we were almost like one real big family. By then they had two children and the third one was coming. My aunt was big; she was expecting in a month or two when she piled us in the Ford with everything we owned. She had the four of us children and the fifth one on the way. So that's how we moved to Fresno and left our parents farming some more. My two younger sisters were with my parents, and my older sister and I were enrolled in the city schools. That was an experience, too.

My aunt and uncle had a boardinghouse that we lived in, and

there was a streetcar on F Street that came by. Uncle had to clean all the rooms and change the sheets and send things off to the laundry, and Auntie would cook for the people who came to board there. She used to cook for ten cents a meal and had a big boarding table. So we ran on errands for her, helped her with her washing, and on weekends helped her with her ironing. And they saw to it that we went to school. And they helped organize a Japanese language school so we could learn to read and write Japanese. That was important to the parents, that we could keep on talking to them. We were learning English during the regular school day.

Then, finally, in 1925 my father decided to move to Florin. We had a friend that encouraged him to come and farm strawberries, and so he decided to take the family and be together. I was ten by then and in the fifth grade when the family decided to move and be together. I remember in December we piled up our touring car full of belongings and moved. There were five girls and the last one was a son. That was very important to Father. And Mother. And so he was a little baby when we moved to Florin. We moved in December; in the fog and in the winter, we came to Florin.

By 1913 California had passed an antialien land law so that no Japanese who had been an immigrant could buy property. But there were arrangements that we could make with a white landowner where we could lease the property. The white landowners in this area found out that the Japanese were good at working on the land, and the landowners could make their hayfields productive by planting grapes. Then, in between the rows of grapes, the Japanese farmers could plant strawberries for a few years while they tended and took care of the grapes. It took four or five years before grapes could produce any harvest, enough to bring in any money. So during that time they would let the Japanese farmers use the land in between the rows of grapes to grow strawberries. The Japanese would harvest their own crop of strawberries and live on it while they cared for the grapes. So that was the arrangement my father found, and, without any money, he could start farming. That was a wonderful arrangement for many farmers who came without any funds to start with, and this is one of the reasons why I know many Japanese were attracted to come into this community.

And so we became a community. But the West Coast called us a problem and anti-Oriental sentiment grew because there was such a concentration of Japanese on the West Coast. And in Florin we became a notorious community. We were close to Sacramento and the legislators were in and out of Sacramento and often came running to see us. And they'd say, "Now look at that. They're living in dirty houses, like chicken coops, living in such a poor state and lowering our standard of living." Many women hadn't come yet and there were many men, so the legislators assumed we must have had some houses of prostitution, and they accused us of a lot of things that weren't true. So, that is what it was like when we moved to Florin.

My sister Ruth and I were at an impressionable age when we enrolled in the elementary school in Florin, and it was a shocking experience to see that every face in the school was Japanese. The elementary school had become segregated in 1923 when the whites decided to build a separate school building for their children. Many Japanese had wondered what that brick building being built up on the west side of the track was. Then suddenly they found out.

My husband was in the second grade, and he said that one day all the white children left the school. A white friend says, "I remember, I was in the third grade that year, and they gave us all American flags, and we marched away from the school. It had rained and there were some puddles here and there." So that's how it happened. There were many Japanese people in Florin, many Japanese stores, many Japanese farmers, and the schools were segregated.

After going through the Florin Elementary School with no Caucasian friends, it was really a shock when we attended the integrated high school. We were frightened and shy and stood in the corner and didn't volunteer for anything. They invited us to come to their socials but we were afraid to go, and we didn't volunteer to go be on committees in high school so we just sat back.

Like I said, the first generation Oriental immigrants were not allowed to be citizens and buy land, but the children born here were citizens and therefore could buy land. So when Ruth became old enough, father bought the land for Ruth. Then it was Ruth's land and we had to be very careful that we did it so that there wouldn't be anyone accusing us of breaking the law. There were some families that bought the land for their children but were taken to court and the land taken away. So we were always afraid that someone would try to take the land away, but we tried to do it by law, and by law the children were citizens and were entitled to buy land. My father waited until my sister was old enough to do her own business.

You see, we were accused of not being assimilated into our American life, but we were always kept in limbo because every time we turned around there was some group trying to agitate to send us back to Japan or send us away from California, so we never knew for sure whether we should sink our roots deeply. And we never knew for sure if we should spend our profits building a new home and living in nice homes like we wanted. So we endured living in shacks that weren't painted because any day we might be driven out.

There's a long, long story of discrimination when we were in high school, too, but I was fortunate enough to have a wonderful high school teacher that couldn't allow this discrimination to hurt me totally. She was a Caucasian public speaking teacher named Mabel Barron, and I took public speaking from her, so I was involved in an annual oratorical contest that they usually had the public speaking students participate in. We were required to write our oration and speak about California history, and we all tried out because it was part of our class assignment.

I had no idea that out of this experience they were really looking for the nine finalists in a community-wide oratorical contest that was sponsored by the Native Sons and Daughters of the Golden West, a group that had no Japanese. Evidently I was one of the nine that qualified, but I didn't know about it until one day when the principal called for me to come into his office and I found Mabel there. She looked very upset.

The principal and she were trying to tell me that there was an unwritten rule that no children who were not of Native Sons and Daughters, who were not Caucasian, could qualify in this competition. It was a community affair where the entire community would come out for it, and it wouldn't do for me to be one of the contestants. Well, Mabel was furious. She said, "Then they shouldn't have asked me to provide the competitors, because it was a class assignment and Mary was one of the students in the class."

She was real angry but they couldn't do anything about changing the rules, and I meekly said, "Well, it's OK, I don't want to stir any trouble." I wanted to just get out of there and forget about it.

Well, Mabel didn't forget about it. And at that time there were some Nisei students, second generation Japanese American students, at the University of California, and they organized a students' club and decided to start a project for high school students and sponsored an oratorical contest for high school students with the theme, "Is Higher Education Justifiable?"

So Mabel just got busy and sat me down and said, "You're

going to participate in that oratorical contest," and she helped me write the oration.

I knew nothing on writing orations on lofty ideas like that; I had never thought about higher education or anything like it. But she made me begin to see that my parents came from Japan and worked so hard and sacrificed to give me an education, and it was important that we begin to think about the cultural values that our parents brought. I knew nothing about that nor appreciated nothing about it, and I didn't even understand what American values were either. But Mabel began to pull these words into my mouth, and I began to learn the oration. I began to speak about the need for world friendship and world understanding and tried to think about being the bridge between two cultures and trying to establish some kind of future for us. [Begins to cry.] And so, that was the beginning of seeds that I needed to grow with. Mabel Barron gave me that, and, of course, I ended up bringing home an electric clock, the first prize.

But we were all damaged in many ways by the discrimination. We who were Christians in the Protestant churches often tried very quietly to hide those things that made us Japanese and tried very much to keep away from anything that was of the Japanese culture. We openly said we weren't going to adopt them, and we tried to adopt American ways. When we were younger we went to the additional Japanese language school, but we quit as soon as we could and told our parents we didn't want to continue to take the language. It was very sad for my father to think we wouldn't be willing to learn to speak Japanese, and, so, as the Niseis grew up, many of them didn't remember how to converse with their parents, which was a tragic thing, and the grandchildren became foreigners to their own grandparents! So we ended up becoming people without any roots because we were frightened of being pro-Japanese. And to be pro-Japanese meant even to be curious about our Japanese heritage.

Then, during those years, the Depression came. With living on the farm we managed to eat. My mother canned tomatoes in the summer, and we just had a lot of tomato soup and fried noodles which we dunked in the soup. That was our diet. It was probably the most economical thing for her. But it meant a great deal for Dad to at least be able to buy a few sacks of rice. At the end of the season when the money came in is when he bought as many sacks of rice as he could to last us through the winter.

The Depression was very hard but many of the people had big

families and their children helped on the farms. That's the only reason why they endured. Also, when their children were old enough, many of the families had begun to have their own land and then they could grow both grapes and strawberries. So they would have two harvests in one year. But that was hard work, running two crops. Strawberries were something that you stayed in the field with, year in and year out. If it wasn't hoeing the berries, it was weeding, and if it wasn't that, it was picking the crops. And there were runners to start, new patches to start, because with strawberry farming about two years is the best. Then about the third year, the crop wasn't good so then they would have to plow the plants up and start a new patch. So there was continual work with the strawberries. At the same time, they had to take care of the grapes and harvest the grapes, and the women had to care for the home and the children also. So it was a very hard kind of living here.

Many of the Japanese people had to borrow money on the land during the Depression, so the ten years from 1930 to 1940 were very difficult times for all the farmers here. And then we were just beginning to come out of it, just beginning to pay a little bit back on the mortgages, when the evacuation occurred.

I graduated from high school in 1933, but my father thought my older sister mattered most and needed to go to college. There were seven children that he was supporting because I had my older sister in Japan, and he felt that Ruth was important. If no one else was to get any education, she was the one. So she was going to Cal, and we just assumed that after I graduated from high school I would just go back to the farm and work.

But Mabel Barron had other ideas, and she got friends to give her old clothes and sewed them down so I'd have a wardrobe to wear to college. And she found another friend who committed herself to give me $10 a month for spending money, and then Mabel finally got the president of the college to consent to a $150 scholarship. That was a big amount of money at that time. And this was the way I got started to college, because of Mabel.

Once I got in there I worked in many different jobs to pay the $600 per semester tuition. I worked very hard and, finally, at the end of the year, after working all year and part of the summer, I started to get rheumatoid arthritis. I noticed that my fingers were swelling. I was nineteen when I got it, and it went into my hips and toes and all over and I was in much pain, but I kept working and made it through college.

Mabel was a really wonderful person, and all through my years, as I became a teacher, I remembered her and her great love for children. Of course, when I graduated from college, as a Japanese I was banned from many jobs and I couldn't teach. That was not allowed me.

I had known the man I married as we were growing up. We went through elementary and high school together and were in church together. So Al and I were married in 1936, and he farmed his family's farm that we are still on. We had only one child, our daughter, but my husband is an only son so that when I married him I came into a family that had his father and mother. His father was seventy-five years old that year and his mother was sixty-three, and then Al had an invalid sister who had tuberculosis who was also living with us.

Around 1935 Florin organized our own chapter of the Japanese American Citizens League, the JACL. It was an organization of young Japanese American citizens who tried to promote civic responsibility, and Al and I became active in it. We decided we could do something for Florin and looked around and said, "Well, why can't we decide to combine our elementary schools and make them a real American school and no longer have the children segregated." So then we contacted the trustees and the superintendents of schools and there was no opposition, so in the fall of 1939 all the children went to the combined school. I often felt how wonderful we thought of it before the war started. It would have been terrible to have had a segregated school and to try to have the children come back to it.

But still, before the war, we were very quiet about our heritage, and if we wanted to do anything about it, we were doing it almost under cover because it wasn't popular and it felt dangerous. We were criticized for being unassimilated, and hanging onto Japanese ways was another proof we were unassimilated.

Many of the people retained dual citizenship. That meant when children of immigrants were born here, Japan also had citizenship for us. But many of the parents around 1928 and 1930 began to say, "Our roots are here. We should, by rights, sever our ties with Japan." So my parents took away our Japanese citizenship. But many people kept theirs and this really caused trouble when the war started. Our enemies kept accusing us, saying, "Look there, they have citizenship in two countries." But they didn't realize that because of our precarious situation here, as immigrants or citizens, we never knew whether for sure we would be allowed to stay. And the evacuation and the war really proved it!

There were many reasons why we behaved the way we did, but

I can see that because we were all huddled in one community like we did, we were very conspicuous. There were many Japanese stores here and we spoke Japanese, and the Buddhist church here became very big and strong, and they had teachers come from Japan to teach flower arrangement and tea ceremony. But, today, look! Flower arrangement and tea ceremony is a very popular and appreciated kind of cultural activity. But then they pointed to us and said, "See, see, they want to keep their traditions. Why don't they go to Japan and do it."

Then, on a Sunday morning on December 7, 1941, we heard over the radio the news of Pearl Harbor. Because we knew of the long, ugly background of anti-Oriental sentiment in which we grew up, it was a frightening thing to realize that Japan was at war with the United States. We sensed something very, very foreboding and frightening. And immediately that night, the FBI was already at the doors of the Isseis and arrested many, many, and the rumors and news of all of this was frightening. Then one Issei committed suicide and real fear and terror and a great sense of helplessness came over us.

That night we had a young people's meeting at church, and I remember the young minister's sermon. It really was a dark world that night. We were afraid to even put the lights on because we were told that we needed to observe blackout, and the minister had just one candle lit in that darkness and said that we needed to remember that in the darkness in the world, if we light one candle, we will push the darkness away. And, somehow, I remember that sermon stayed with us through all of our grief and trial, realizing that we had a responsibility to be the light and to try to lean on our faith and know that God was with us.

But it wasn't easy to think of that and think why it was all happening to us and realizing and sensing the gnawing ache that it was always because of our face and our race. Somehow we felt terribly frustrated and helpless that it wasn't something you could take off and put away. We were born with it and there was no way to change that. Right away the pressure started against us.

There were people who wanted us out of the way for economic reasons and found the war was a good opportunity to do what they had been wanting to do for the last fifty years. They were upset because of our farming success. But many of the farms would never have produced as much if it hadn't been for the Isseis. They were willing to work hard, and where other people would never have thought of farming, the Japanese reclaimed the lands and changed them into productive estates. But, with the war, many were anxious to get our land and our flowers, fruit, vegetables, and fishing industry.

There were powerful people crying for our evacuation, but even at the time, some said it was not a military necessity. But people told President Roosevelt that it had to be done for military purposes, and he was running a war and was so busy that he had no time to pay more attention, and so he said, "If the military people think evacuation is a necessity, go ahead." So he signed Executive Order 9066 on February 19, 1942, and that's what decided the whole thing, the whole tragic, sordid affair. That we were to be taken from our homes and livelihoods and put into isolated camps surrounded by barbed wire and guarded by soldiers.

At first we couldn't really believe the evacuation was going to happen, but when President Roosevelt signed the order on February 19, we found out that the first group who had to leave were fishermen and their families from Terminal Island close to the naval stations. Many of the men were taken away first and the women were terrified. The evacuation was very hard for them all because they were unprepared for it and had great losses, their boats and everything. Also, they were told to leave, and they had no place to go. So they just moved from place to place, and they had very, very tragic experiences.

The very edge of the coast was the next to have to leave, and so we took a big truck and went after all of our family that lived there, thinking maybe we wouldn't have to leave because we lived in the rural community. Also, we thought, "Maybe the government is going to need our food, and they certainly will allow us to grow things for the war effort." So the others moved in with us.

Then eventually we found out we had to leave too. We were reading that the government was closing each area and sending the people all into camps, and, finally, by the middle of May, the sign went on the telephone posts. I became very busy. There were about 2,500 Japanese people living and farming in this area, and shortly before we evacuated, the WCCA, Wartime Civilian Control Administration, that was set up in Sacramento asked the representatives of Florin's Japanese American Citizens League to meet with them. They asked us to get the people ready to be evacuated. We knew there was no way of stopping the evacuation and thought that maybe by cooperating we could help the people as much as possible so they wouldn't be hurt too badly. So we agreed to do it, the Florin Japanese American Citizens League set up an executive office, and I became the secretary of it and ran the office.

Everybody else was working on the farms, working to try to get our crop in. We needed to get this crop in by May which would be the peak of our season. So the last two months I was terribly busy trying to take care of our family and all the families. And then we had curfew and had to be in our homes by eight o'clock at night and we couldn't meet at night, but all these people were busy on the farms during the day! Still, we had to have meetings to decide what to do, so we didn't get our work done on the farms because of it.

Then they started to issue a five mile travel restriction! And it was nine miles to Sacramento! It was really frustrating. And all the heartaches, the anguish and fear and fright that we went through, thinking that we would get caught by patrols because we were violating our travel restriction just to come to Florin to do our marketing. My sister went to get her driver's license because it expired. Well, it's terrible to be driving around without a driver's license, so she drove into Sacramento and had already violated her travel restriction. And they called me and reported her! So we knew that we were being watched and reported for anything.

Our friend was expecting a baby, and her husband had been taken away the day after Pearl Harbor. He happened to be someone who had dual citizenship and was over twenty-one. He had contributed money to Japan in lieu of being drafted. It was a frightening thing to be in the United States, have dual citizenship, and in order to be excluded from the draft in Japan, you had to contribute money. So that was a record and people could say, "Well, you're pro-Japan because you've been contributing to the military." So here she was; her husband was taken away and she was four or five months without her husband, and she had children and she was expecting. She was big and she was crying so I took her into the WCCA office, and I already violated my restriction to get her there to sit there for an hour or so to get her travel permit so she could go a few blocks to see her doctor.

That was only for one time, and there were people who needed to go to the dentist, to the lawyer; they were all in Sacramento, and so my office was busy just doing busywork like that, just frustrating, unnecessary things when there were other important things that had to be attended to to get us ready to go. People needed to see their lawyers; they needed to see their bankers to get prepared to leave their land. We were just running around like ants, busy, wasting a lot of our time and anguish over little things. So the fright and the fear; I could never explain to you all the terrible frustrating things that we went through. It made us sick and, to think, that after thirty-nine years, to realize it was all unnecessary. There never was any military need to move us. All our suffering and fears and all our boys volunteering and giving their lives; all of that was unnecessary. [Cries.]

When it was time to go they decided to split Florin into four parts to make it easy for the military. People who lived east of the Florin railroad track and north of the Florin road were one part. And then we found out that all four parts were not going to the same place. That was terrible because this community had been existing for so long. Al's father, who we called Grandpa, came and started farming in Florin in 1893 and had never left it, for fifty years.

And there were others who had come early and had stayed, so this community had gotten together and had become solidified and had social activities, religious activities. Economically, they were drawn together by the strawberry and grape business, and during the Depression they had stuck it out together. So there was a bond there, an unusual community bond where the people lived and breathed together.

It was a tragic thing then to suddenly find that we were going to be sent four different directions, and none of us may ever see each other again. We didn't know about this until the last minute when we were registering. And some people were related and they didn't want to be separated, and when they found out about it, at midnight they were moving across the tracks so they could sign up together. For some of them, it was too late when they found out. There was so much emotional strain and shock and anguish over things that the military was doing in the process of sending us away.

The last day was on May 29. Strawberries were red in the fields; in the peak of our season we left our berries to rot! [Cries.] And many farmers depended on that crop to pay back debts they had borrowed in the stores and shipping companies, because each year they had to borrow in advance to make it. That was the kind of life we were living; they were just poor farmers. And so they didn't get to harvest their strawberries and their grapes that year and they had debts they left, and the stores and the businesses had great losses they could never claim.

And some families had only two hours to get ready. The military came running over and said, "You were signed up for tomorrow but you've got to go today. You've got only two hours before you have to go." And the families were out in the fields picking berries at the time because the Farm Security Agency had said, "Keep picking berries until almost the last if you're able because every bit you pick now is for the war effort." So everybody tried their best to do that, and, of course, every cent meant more money for them anyhow. But here they were, out in the fields, when they were told to leave in two hours.

Some families were in the middle of their lunch, eating, when the military came running and said, "You've got two hours to catch that train."

I just thought, "Well, my gosh, I wonder what they had to leave in their house." We had time to sweep up our house and clean it before we left. That's something the Japanese people feel they must do. How terrible those families must have felt, leaving their dishes and running! Food half eaten, but that's what happened to some people. So it's a real sordid story.

Our family was very large. We had Al's parents and sister and our daughter, and then we were concerned about my father and mother and brother and sisters and married brothers and sisters. So we said, "Let's go together and register." But when we went to register I was busy at the Japanese American Citizens League office, and I couldn't get away until later. By the time I got there, it was near the end of the five hundredth number.

The military people had said, "Well, we are going to try to keep the families together." But when we went to sign up it was terrible. Already families had been sitting there and lining up who thought they were going to go together, but then they found out that there weren't enough seats all together so they were going to send certain ones to another place, to Manzahar. Families were split up at the moment of departure and there was such anguish. But our family of six remained together, and we left Florin on May 29 and went to the Fresno Assembly Center.

And when we arrived there all the ugliness came out. We were herded in together in terrible heat, and tar was dripping in from our barracks. So many feelings were hurt and some of us blamed us, and people were running around trying to come and tell me that it was my fault that families were split up. That I had betrayed them by helping with the evacuation. We were tearing at each other; when you get frightened, you do that. The ugliest part of us came out, and we were surprised that we were doing that to each other. We had been friends. [Cries.]

And the floor was asphalt and the beds were sinking, and they had a pile of straw and gave us a mattress to fill with the straw for our own mattresses. The first night that we got there, we got separated and we couldn't find our parents. We were supposed to stay together, as one family; we had our family number. But for some reason, they had put Grandpa and Grandma and Al's sister in another room way on the other end of the camp. Finally Al found them. We asked the military, "Please, we're one family. Put us together." So eventually they got us together. They had another family in with us in a small room for the first night. There were six of us and four more. It was Al's cousin and his wife and two little babies and the babies cried all night. So I never will forget that first night. We were hot and dusty and taken from our own homes, from our own lives, from our own security of farming, and we were thrown into that.

My daughter was five and I remember her crying for a whole week. You really never understood why the children were crying. They were just upset about the whole thing. They had left all they knew. I suppose when you're reporting to the federal government, little things like the disruptions we faced were unimportant, but they were very big things for human beings because we were a family. We each had our human lives. Each of us 110,000 have a different story to tell.

When we went to camp, I was in real pain from my arthritis, having gone through trying to get 2,500 people ready for evacuation and having wept so much all along the way. Then, when I arrived in Fresno Assembly Center, I was so much in pain that I went to the hospital to see a doctor, and he decided that maybe if I kept my arm immobile it would get better, and he put it in a plaster cast. Well, that's the way it stayed. So that was the wrong thing to have done. I've never been able to move my arm since.

Then we were slowly sent from the Fresno Assembly Center in California to Jerome, Arkansas, by train. We had to sleep sitting up, and life was going on on the train; babies were born and people died; and there was chicken pox and measles. We had to quarantine the people with chicken pox, and there was no place to quarantine but the women's restroom so the family had to sit in there. And some children who were very nervous were on the verge of nervous breakdowns; it was very hard for them because it was so confusing. I'm just surprised some of the children came out as well as they did. When we finally got to Jerome, Arkansas, the camp was crowded and in a hot, swampy lowland with water moccasins all around. But that's where we stayed.

It was such a hard time for all of us. We were surrounded by barbed wire fences and military guards, and people were confused about how to deal with all of it. Some family members turned against each other, and the government blundered in so many ways.

But, still, more than 2,500 boys volunteered from these camps to go into the Nisei combat unit and prove the Japanese American's loyalty, and they were sent to Camp Shelby and went overseas. They became the most decorated unit of that size in the history of the American military forces, the 442d of the Hundredth Infantry. But the boys came out to our camp, a concentration camp, on their furloughs because their parents were far away in Hawaii or they were in Manzanar or Tule Lake, and the soldiers weren't allowed to go to California to see their parents! So they just went to any one of the relocation centers where they could see other Japanese people because they were so lonely and so worried about their families. We realized that we needed to provide dances for them, to have the girls organized for when they came. I was the director of the camp YWCA and opened up a USO and organized the girls and tried to help the boys when they came. We ended up being invited to Camp Shelby before they shipped overseas. We took a bus load of girls over there for a dance and had our worship service with them the Sunday morning before they left. And many of the boys never came through the war experience. So many of them got hurt and died.

Many people lost their farms or stores or homes. Many of us still had mortgages on the land when we went into the camps, and the government said they were going to freeze the mortgages, but they didn't. So the banks wrote to the farmers and asked what they were going to do with the debt they owed when they couldn't pay it. Then the banks said, "Somebody wants to buy your property." Well, in the headlines at that time, the spring and summer of 1943, the American Legion was demanding that we be deported. All these headlines were sounding like we'd never get to come back to California, and so people decided maybe they should sell and they sold their property. They got very little money for it since they owed the money to the banks. So the banks made the money. During the war, grape prices were high, and people made a lot of money who stayed here. They just sent us away at the right time, so some people who drove us out must have surely known.

My husband had been working for the Florin Fruit Growers' Association, and he had seen the records during the First World War when the farmers all made big money. So he knew that people needed to somehow hang onto their farms if they could. But nobody would listen. By then they were so upset and so frustrated. They couldn't find anybody to look after the farms, and they didn't know who to trust. Some of them did trust people with their farms, but then they found out that those people had quit farming their land and moved away. So they didn't know what happened to their property, and there was no way of tracking who did what to it. So much was lost.

Al and I were lucky. Our farm was saved because my husband found a wonderful personal friend named Bob Fletcher who was willing to give up his inspector's job to come back to run our farm and our neighbor's and our cousin's farm. He made it by running night and day. He plowed and ran the tractor and kept our grapes. And when we came back, we had our farm. It was still all right.

But the evacuation destroyed so many. Many people were broken; they were never the same. They just mentally lost their minds, and some committed suicide and some never came back. Many of them got sick when they were young. They were old before they should have been. [Cries.]

The government or the people will never know the hardships these people went through. [Continues to cry.] Isseis were too old. At forty or fifty or sixty years old, they were too old; at that age they couldn't start over. But many of them had to because their children were so young. Many of the Isseis had children very late in their life. They had worked many years before they could afford to have a wife, and so many of them were grandparents' age when they had children. So after the camp experience, when they came back, they were old people, and the children were too little to help, many of them. Who's going to say what that loss was? There's no way to prove how much that loss was. In 1948, after we came back, we finally succeeded in passing a bill to claim some of the losses, but then they said that the only people who could claim losses were people who had papers to prove what they owned. Well, we didn't realize these were things we needed to be ready for. It was so chaotic when we left and very few had papers so very few got anything. Many people lost so much there was no way of claiming it.

But that was just financial, economic losses. That doesn't begin to count the psychological and emotional losses and hurt that belonged to each of us. So it's really a frustrating, disgusting thing that happened. And then, after thirty-nine years, we found out that it was all unnecessary. There never had been an act of sabotage and even the military people said it was not a military necessity! And all that loss!

Al and our daughter and I left Jerome, Arkansas, after about a year and a half. They let some people out early to work. We went out to a new community in Kalamazoo, Michigan, where my husband got a job at a bakery on the night shift. My father and mother came out too, but some of the older people, like Al's father who was over seventy-six by then, didn't feel they would want to move to a new place and a different climate. But they did go through traumatic experiences anyway. Jerome was sultry and hot and wet and different from what they were used to, and when Jerome closed, they were sent to Gila, Arizona, where it was dreadfully hot, there in the desert. There was no way to escape the hardships of the evacuees.

We came back to California from the camps in July, 1945, but some other people came back early in January, as soon as the ban was lifted. They came back then so they could prune their grapes and get the farm ready for harvesting by September. They told us later they were afraid and it was bad.

A friend said that a few days after they arrived, their neighbor's house was burned. Also, they had stored a lot of their belongings in the Japanese social hall, and it had been burned while we were away. And there was a family where bombs were thrown in their house. One-third of Florin was burned and gone by the time we got home, and nobody would say how the fires got started. And so we came back to the community with fear. Our family came back in July. We drove in early in the morning and didn't go anyplace, but gradually we had to go out and so we saw people. Then the minister of the Florin Methodist church called, and before long, we were active in the church and had some friends in the church, which was good.

As more people came back they had no place to go, so those of us with homes opened our homes to them and it was like a hostel; we had ten or fifteen people sleeping all over the floor. The people who returned to nothing had to find a house and find a job and find a way to make a living again. They didn't have their own farms anymore, and some of them lived in the chicken coops of their neighbors. But, with all of our social halls, as soon as the boxes and crates of things that the evacuees had stored in them could be moved, the families moved into the halls. So that ten, fifteen, twenty families had to live in those places until they could find a way to get their new homes established. It was a very frightening, unwritten part of our story.

A friend was telling me how her old father and mother, who were way over sixty, had to get up early in the morning to go work in the hops ranch after they returned. And how they came home dusty and dirty because the work in the hops ranch is very, very hard. They had to work like that, and she felt, gee, at a time when their life should have been easier, when they were at retirement age, they had to struggle again to get themselves established. Also, with everyone in the camps as they had been, the economy of Florin had changed and the community died. When the Japanese farmers were sent away, there was nothing here to keep the community alive.

When we had been home a month and were trying to clean up our old house, which wasn't occupied for three years, and when Grandpa and Grandma had just come back from Gila, Arizona, we heard the news of the atomic bombing of Hiroshima. Grandma and Grandpa both came from Hiroshima so immediately the shock and the hurt was very deep. They had accepted the fact that Japan had attacked and was responsible for starting the war, so they realized that maybe they deserved some punishment, but not like that. Their thoughts were immediately about their own relatives; they were all in Hiroshima.

There were many lost. Some we don't know really what happened to. But, of course, some had been in the country at the time or visiting someone else or working somewhere else, and we gradually discovered some were still alive. We're not sure of a lot of them; nobody seems to know, and we just assume that they must have been killed. In later years we visited Hiroshima several times and even invited some of our relatives to visit us, and in 1977 seven of them came. In the course of all these contacts, gradually the story has been coming out. But it hasn't been easy for them to tell us of the whole experience. But still Grandpa and Grandma did not die with too much bitterness. They had developed a deep faith and learned to accept what life had, and they had a strength that was deep.

Grandpa had always wanted American citizenship, and the only reason why he was technically an alien during World War II was there was a law that kept him from taking out citizenship. Finally, in 1953, the Japanese American Citizens League pushed for and received the citizenship. So we had Americanization classes, of American history and such, that we conducted all over the United States so the Isseis could learn what they needed to pass their test. But many of them were eighty and ninety years old and too old to hear, too old to see, too old to remember. Grandpa, who was eighty-six, went for one week. He sat and tried to remember what was said, and a lot of it had to be by rote because they couldn't read and write; they had to memorize it. Then he just gave up; he couldn't learn, but it was a tragic thing for him to finally realize that after all these years, it was too late for him. It was too late for many of them. My father had a stroke and it was too late for him too, but he would have wanted it, too.

Al and I had some hard times financially after the war, when we realized that we couldn't make a living on the farm with grapes. The prices were so bad that all of the people started to pull their grapes out and had to plant something else. We realized that both Al and I needed to get a job if we were going to support our family of six. Grandpa and Grandma were old and Al's sister was sick. When I was first going to college, Japanese Americans were not hired to teach, but later my daughter's school principal helped me go into teaching, and I then taught elementary school for twenty-six years. My underlying theme in teaching social studies to the children was learning to be concerned about every person's feelings and respecting everyone and loving them and caring, and I used United Nations materials in the classroom before it was popular. During the last years of teaching I began to share some of the things from my own culture with the children and adult groups, and that sharing brought a great deal of appreciation. In the meantime, Al was a fruit produce salesman and then a quality control inspector of radar equipment at the army depot, so life gradually got better for us financially.

As the years passed our parents grew older and Al's parents died, and after my father died my mother lived by herself for nine years. She had always quietly worked hard, and she wanted to be independent and be responsible for her own needs, and so she endured as long as she could. And finally, when she didn't feel physically up to living alone anymore, she moved over with my sister in Concord because my sister did domestic work and was available, in and out, during the day. I was out teaching school and wasn't home. She lived with my sister for about a year before she died at the age of ninety-one. She had lived a long, hard life, working out in the fields and raising seven children.

We continued to live on our farm here, the twenty acres that we came back to after the evacuation, but we don't grow anything on it now. We are deeply involved with our church, and our daughter is an adult now, a teacher, and we are close. I've always had to keep my courage going during the pain from my rheumatoid arthritis, but my husband has been a support.

Also, I've kept involved in education since my retirement from teaching in the public schools. I ended my teaching career by directing the Jan Ken Po Gakka, a private cultural heritage school for fourth-generation Japanese American children. We meet in the summer and try to give the children an in-depth understanding of what went on and also try to build up their confidence and self-image. We have events like taking the children on a trip to Angel Island as a pilgrimage to a place where their ancestors first arrived.

When I was still teaching in the public schools, I had started to teach the children about the events in Hiroshima, and then I taught about them in my Japanese cultural school. Each year the children folded a thousand paper cranes and sent them to a school in Hiroshima, as a memorial to the children who died there and as a prayer for peace. This year some of the children and I carried the cranes and participated in a vigil marking the anniversary of the bombing of Hiroshima, and I told the story of one of the girls who had died of radiation sickness. It took me a long time to learn to speak out like that. I directed Jan Ken Po Gakka for the last time this summer, and it's been a very special way to end my teaching career.

But when I was director of the school, I felt great pain teaching about the bombings and great pain teaching about the evacuation. I tried to teach the fourth-generation Japanese American children, "You have wonderful parents and wonderful roots," but the story always had to come out that we were mistreated. We were discriminated against and despised and put into camps.

Recently the Japanese American Citizens League got the movement going for redress. It's been about a ten-year effort, hoping to get the government to admit they were wrong and to pay us all compensation for what we went through. There has been opposition to it by some Japanese Americans. Some still can't bring themselves to confront the government. The evacuation was so painful that they just want to forget it and just let well enough alone. But other young Japanese Americans are saying, "How come you took so long? Why did you let it happen?" So people are upset on both sides.

In asking for redress we are asking the government to admit it was wrong and to give a redress of $25,000 for each person who was in the camps. The government responded by appointing a commission that is holding hearings throughout the country where each of us can talk five minutes about the experience, and when the hearings are done, the commission will make a recommendation to Congress about redress. There is so much pressure to try and tell all that we went through in just five minutes in front of the commission.

But it is so important. I learned through teaching at the Jan Ken Po Gakka that children need the government to admit the truth. It's important for the fourth-generation children to know there is nothing to be ashamed of. In public schools other children tease them and say, "Your great-grandparents must have been spies or something or the government wouldn't have put them in camps. They must have committed a crime or they wouldn't have put them behind barbed wire fences and had soldiers watch over them."

So the children need the truth, because if they don't get that, they don't have anything. Then there's nothing to be proud of, really, being an American. It makes me upset when people say it never could have happened in America, that they never heard about it and so it didn't happen. This is why I've been telling my children at Jan Ken Po Gakka, "It did happen and you learn what happened and tell everybody what happened so it can never happen to anybody else again." That's my terrible fear; that we won't speak up; that we'll get old and die, and it will happen to somebody else.

I shudder to think that in the years after we returned from the evacuation, I was asked to give speeches on it, and, at first, I didn't realize all of the terrible suffering connected with it, and mainly I spoke of the fact that it was not all tears. After a while I learned the details of one of the camps we weren't in and learned of the terrible turmoil and pain and suffering those people went through. I am ashamed to think that in my talks I did not assume my complete responsibility for the whole experience, not just for me, but for the whole Japanese American people.

So we Japanese Americans must fight to make it right. We don't want to be pointed out as a model minority group so people can say, "Oh, they made it so it's OK. Let's forget the wrong we did to them and the wrong we do to others." That's not the way it should be. If they wronged us and others, we all need to clean it up. If the Constitution is going to be interpreted the way it was with the evacuation, another group might be mistreated. Because America did do a wrong. And it was a terrible wrong. [Cries hard.] If our story is not heard by Americans, and they're not aware of what happened, then many other people could be treated in the same way, and America is going to continue in this sordid history. We don't want that to happen in this country.

Now, many of our third generation are turning against those of us who were interred and are saying, "How come? Why didn't you have the courage to oppose and speak up?" Well, during 1940 and '41, nobody did. The whole society was meekly following our country and leaders. Whether they were right or wrong, we supported our country. And at that time, when war was declared, we felt the only patriotic thing we could do was to obey and cooperate. So we did.

But our third-generation children are saying, "You're crazy to have done that. You were U.S. citizens!" It's true. Those of us who were second generation were citizens, but we didn't feel as though we had very many rights as citizens. We were treated so badly that we always felt we were still visiting as guests. And I still sort of sense that, even today.

For all those years, I felt as though we needed to be at our party-best behavior. "It is poor etiquette," my father used to say, "to hurt other people. So don't shame the family. Don't rock the boat." That was the way we were raised. And so we were quiet and meek, and we were agreeable, never wanted to criticize other people and never opposed them even though we disagreed with them.

With that training, it made me feel ashamed to think we were suing the government, and I felt ashamed to think we would dare to say, "You were wrong and you need to be sued." At first, I just couldn't do that; it was just like pointing my finger at my father for making a mistake. I felt that this was wrong for us to do.

So seeking redress is a very difficult thing for me to do because I'm breaking through a cultural background that is different and that taught me to be meek. But I'm finally learning that as an American I need to speak out. And I'm finally beginning to realize, after I'm sixty-six years old and maybe don't have that many years ahead, I'm suddenly realizing that I've wasted a lot of my time just being afraid and just being polite and just holding back and just letting people do just what they want with us. And that's what happened. We let them do everything.

And I know that I have to let our fourth-generation children know that I'm proud of being an American citizen, and I believe that in America we have rights, that we have power as a citizen and our individual voices can be heard. [Cries.] If I'm really going to ring true and prove that this is so, I need to show them that I believe in it enough to move ahead with this redress. To prove to them that there are Americans in this country who have the heart and ears to hear us, and they are for justice and fair play too. And, if we were wronged, they're going to want us to ask for redress and be sure that the American government that made the mistake admits it. I want the children to believe in America and love it and want to do for it and serve it and grow in it. This is why I feel it's important that we ask for redress.

So I feel that there are many unfinished things that have to be done after forty years. I feel that if I'm not willing to show this and do this, to prove that I am proud of being a citizen of America and that I have pride and belief and faith and confidence in her democratic ways, I'm really lying to my kids.

*But, I tell you one thing. I've just
been straight all my days. If I don't like
you, I just don't like you, and I tell you I
don't like you. People just don't mess with
me.*

—Sarah Jones

The old woman, Sarah Jones, shuffled out of her apartment on the ninth floor of a public low-income senior citizens' apartment building in the inner city of Milwaukee. She was a frail-looking black woman of seventy-two with dark brown skin, hair twisted into a rubber band on one side of her head, and large, dark, weary eyes that looked out from a face bearing the wrinkles of all of her years. She muttered to herself and kept pushing the button of the elevator impatiently, stabbing at it with the index finger of her long, gnarled, but still lovely hands.

It was a day in November, and despite a cold wind outside, Sarah was dressed to go to the store in shoes that were little more than tattered bedroom slippers, and her bare legs were poorly covered by an old lightweight coat. Her cotton dress was torn and hung loosely on her body, and she clutched a white plastic pocketbook in her left hand.

At last the elevator came and we took it down to the orderly ground-floor lobby, where many old people, mostly women, sat talking with each other or staring out at the desolate weather. Sarah walked stiffly past them, mumbling one- or two-word responses when several tenants said hello; she stared straight ahead, continuing with frail steps to the door and into the cold.

We walked several blocks through the primarily black urban neighborhood, past old apartments, three-story houses, a church where children enrolled in Project Head Start were leaving for the day, and debris-filled lots where buildings had been razed. The wind blew hard against Sarah's coat, and several pieces of trash were hurled against her bare ankles and nearly bare feet.

There was something fierce as well as frail about her, and several times she swore beneath her breath and muttered about the chicken wings and potatoes she planned to get at the store. A child, out of school, came riding toward her on his bike; he swerved and just missed hitting her when he drew near. He glanced at her face for a second, then went on his way. Sarah passed a parked car filled with teenagers, rock music blasting out of its windows, as she slowly worked her way to the store.

Sarah Jones first came in contact with the Milwaukee Housing Authority when, as part of an urban renewal project, the city razed the building she lived in. For years she had managed to survive with her few belongings in a couple of roach- and rat-infested rooms, fighting the rats off at night with a broom handle, but then she was forced to relocate to the Housing Authority's apartment building for the elderly. When she entered the building, she entered a new and complex social environment for which she had not been prepared during her childhood and young womanhood in rural Mississippi. Neither had her experiences during the years when she had eked out a living washing dishes in the North prepared her for the new life-style of her neighbors.

As a result, she was not always popular with the housing project's tenants. Most residents wanted to project an image of a certain respectability that was at odds with Sarah's character. She no longer spit tobacco in the elevator or came downstairs in her bathrobe, but she did cause a small fire on the ninth floor because of her inexperience with a gas or electric stove; several times she was censured by the other residents because of her drinking in the lobby, and her possessions harbored roaches that periodically spread to the neighboring apartments, causing the need for repeated fumigation.

Sarah was completely illiterate, signing her name with a double X; while she had a fierce sense of independence, she was frequently tricked out of her small monthly income and exploited due to her inability to protect herself in a literate world. But her initial appearance of fragility was offset somewhat by her deep, energetic voice, a voice with which she swore without self-censure and muttered her expressions of independence to anyone within hearing range, another attribute that did not always make her popular with her neighbors.

During our visits she drifted around her apartment, talking softly to herself and then at times saying a few words in response to her own questions or ideas. She frequently echoed comments she'd heard from other people, repeating the phrase several times, often from her bedroom, chewing the idea over and chuckling to herself about the turn of the phrase. She gradually revealed a wry sense of humor that displayed itself in her inflections and curious repetitions of parts of sentences, rather than in the actual words she spoke. It took a number of interviews before I could put her story together, since she spoke briefly and then would drift away to her private thoughts and amusements.

Sarah came to project a growing warmth to me while at the same time emphatically stating her independence of all emotional attachments. She was quite close to a younger woman, a Catholic nun who helped her manage her world and often smoothed out problems with the other residents for her. Her great caring, however, was reserved for her brother, now dead. She had been the youngest girl in the family of twenty-one children and he was the youngest boy, and throughout his life she called him her "baby brother." She also softened visibly when speaking of her mother. Through most of our talks she vehemently asserted her independence, with her voice becoming somewhat more gentle when she spoke of her father, her mother's roses, and the plants she grew in her apartment. She stated many times that by remaining the "cussedest one" in her family, by staying mean and independent, she had carved a place for herself and protected herself against a crowded home life and a hostile outside world.

And the world in which Sarah Jones grew up and lived as a young adult was cruel and dangerous. The Mississippi county of her childhood was flat, rich, and alluvial, and cotton was the major crop. The land had few trees and was built up by the waters of the Mississippi, Yazoo, and Sunflower rivers, whose overflowings caused a major flood at least every five years. At the time of Sarah's childhood, blacks outnumbered whites in the county two to one, but the whole social structure was still based on the plantation system. Whites owned the land and most blacks worked as sharecroppers. Sharecroppers such as Sarah's parents had no capital, owned nothing, and worked under a system based largely on credit where living expenses were given in advance. The parents and children, who were often ill and hungry, worked in the cotton fields from sunup to sundown, ending each year's work with nothing left for themselves. Even today the blacks in the area are deeply poor and often hungry. Abandoned sharecropper shacks dot the landscape, and many such shacks are still inhabited by hungry, impoverished people.

Sarah grew up in an area with rigid and dangerous racial prejudices, with absolute segregation in churches and schools and no voting rights for blacks. Lynching was used as a weapon of terror against blacks; Sarah recalled that the cemeteries were full of hanged people and traced her extreme fear of the dead to the terror expressed by her mother over the experience of seeing a lynching victim. Sarah moved to Indiana as an adult, and despite her poverty and years of toil in the North, does not regret leaving Mississippi, recalling hatred for it.

Life in the North was not easy for Sarah, and she suffered on a number of levels. Open to exploitation as an illiterate in a literate world and as a displaced person coming from a rural background into the inner city, Sarah also suffered as a poor person, as a woman, and as a black. In addition, when I knew her, she was faced with enduring the special vulnerabilities of the old. Yet, Sarah survived with a vision of personal independence and, undoubtedly, will keep this sense of unique stubbornness to the end.

 Grew up in Indianola, Mississippi. In the Delta. I was there all my days, until I come up here. Been up here forty years. There was twenty-one kids, twelve girls and nine boys, in the family. Me and my brother who died here; he was the baby boy and I was the baby girl.

I was the cussedest one in the family. Sure were. And I ain't played with nobody; don't do nothing with nobody. Still don't. When you see me you see my daddy. Look like him and got his ways, too. Hatefulness. He'd have nothing to do with you, just like I didn't. Not other people. He played with his kids, though. House is full of good kids, so I's the bad one. Only way they know I be there. I was bad, just like my dad. I figure, best way for me is to be mean. Keep the kids from getting me when I's little and other folks away from me when I'm big.

Mother said I was like my dad. Said I ain't like her. My brother were like her. I'm a Cherokee Indian, some, like my daddy. But she was darker than any of us. My brother looked just like her and was like her. He was more friendlier than I am. He knew seven dozen people, but, land, I don't know three. Couldn't take no time with people and don't now. But couldn't get no better parents than we did.

Didn't play with no other kids, except my baby brother. Always take care of myself and the baby boy. He's younger than me. When I played, I just sit out there on the trussel. They called it a trussel 'cause it just a bridge across the train track. I'd sit there and catch crawfish and run the hell out of my brother. He's scared of crawfish. He'd sic his dog on me and make me mad, and I'd go there and catch the crawfish and chase him. He'd flop and howl and laugh. Them dogs would bite me; he'd raised them from a puppy. But we be play-fighting. We'd have good times and play together, but I just the very devil, me.

My mother go fishing but I don't fish. They don't want me on no river, no lake, nohow. 'Cause I was clumsy. I could fall in. And I don't want to go there. Jenkins Lake is loaded with snakes. It's got a lot of trees and bushes and those damn snakes and turtles and crawfishes laying on those bushes. When I little, I don't do nothing to play but cook mudcakes and climb a tree. That's all. It was fun to me. I didn't even play with cat or dog. Always been by myself. Except for my baby brother.

I remember everything, when I was small. After I got to be nine or ten and eleven, twelve. I feel just like I twelve now. All the kids left or dead from down there now. Lots of people dead. Mr. Archie and them folks too. Ain't but two of us living. The baby girl and the oldest. My sister down there, she's ninety-nine years old.

My daddy's other wives died. Miss Julia and Miss Sarah both died. My mother's name's Annie. She's dead now too. She only had one girl and two boys. Mother took care of all the kids; it weren't bad, though. All of us worked in the cotton, and the bigger girls took care of the little ones. They didn't forget me; the oldest one'd say, "Where's so-and-so? Where's so-and-so?" They remember me 'cause I was so mean.

I remember what it like down there, down by our farm. We have trees, oak and cypress and pecan trees and thorn trees. All the leaves done fall off them in the fall, and they rake them and burn them. And then there was moss, moss hanging in the trees. Got lots of birds too. Black birds, pepper birds, buzzards, and crows.

In Mississippi some of the dirt black and some clay. Ain't too much sand. Where you make cotton and corn, the land is black. You don't grow cotton and corn in clay; you grow it in rich ground.

By fall, cotton been done over and dead and gone. Winter don't kill things down there. Cold, but it don't kill things. Some flowers could sit out there all day, all night, all year. I don't like the spring down there, 'cause you got to go to work in the spring. Don't like the winter either. I just don't like it down there, nowhere.

Rains a lot in Mississippi. All our rain come from the north. Get a tornado out of the east. Have storms as bad as tornados; storms that tore down houses. We had hurricanes when I growing. Same thing as tornados. You see a big black cloud rising over there, and you better be getting out of the way. Tear down houses and everything. Houses blow down on a lot and kill them. You don't have no basements. And it'd hail and beat the devil out of you if you outdoors. Hail be as big as hen eggs. When I see it making up I come in the house.

We had the Sunflower River down near us. Full of moss. Crawfish, fish, snakes. Snakes, oh God, yes. Snakes down there longer than I am tall. Didn't scare me 'cause I get me a stick and kill them. Ain't nothing bother you in the southern states but rattlesnakes and he will get you.

We right on the Sunflower River, about twelve miles from the Mississippi River. The Mississippi runs into it and when the high water come, it backs up in the Sunflower River and that makes it go all over the place. Then it floods us. Didn't flood the house, just in the yard, but we not scared. What we going to be scared of, born and raised down there. I didn't go in the boat when the high water up. They did, but not me. I just stayed in my mama's house.

We had a town with a courthouse and everything, but I don't like town. Couldn't understand them things down there. The people all called me funny names. Called me "Mother" in a hateful way. That's what my daddy used to call me and my baby brother. His "Mammy" and his "Daddy." So I don't go to town. My mother and my sisters, they'd buy things. I don't feel bad about not going places then, just like I don't here.

I start working in the cotton fields when I was nine. See, every people put you in the fields, down there. You don't run up and down the street, up and down the highway. Yes, sir, when you get nine years old, you got to hoe and pick. Wore a dress or pants when I hoed, no hat, but the sun didn't bother me.

Sometimes when I'd go out a worm'd get on my hoe and I'd have a fit. Oh, Lordie, I couldn't stand them worms. When they got on my hoe, I'd scream and knock them off. Then my people would let me go in. They didn't like to hear me cry or holler or nothing. Didn't like me to be in the field then.

I don't like the fields, no way. Don't like to pick cotton. Spent lots of time doing it, though. I'd pick 200 pounds a day, a sack longer than me, and I'd stuff it from the top to the bottom.

When I was little and we're done in the fields that day, I played mudcakes. But it's evening time when you get done and it's dark. You don't do hardly nothing but go in the house and eat your supper. But I didn't eat with the family, no way. I eat by myself. I'm like that.

Sometimes I lived good at home. Times were, you had everything you want there. You have green beans, peas, corn, and you don't have to buy meal, and you don't have to buy flour. You made your own flour. And I didn't drink coffee so I didn't need it. Still don't drink it. And we had soda water stuff on the stove. Anything we wanted, meat and bread. We raised corn, peaches, pears, apples, potatoes, hogs, chickens, gooses, ducks, turkeys. Everybody raised it; lot of the food you all get here is from there.

Oh God, did we have a garden. And I had one for me, a little bitty one. I growed cabbage, mustard, turnips, onion, peas, beans, and corn. Mother, but mostly the girls, canned. We had sugarcane and ribboncane. Ribboncane is larger, longer than my arm. We go out and break it off and carry it home, and we sit on the porch and eat it. Sweet as honey, it was.

They make molasses out there and had a mule going round and round, round and round, squeezing the juice out. Then it go in a pot and they cook it. And people thrash the pecan trees down there. They take a stick and jar the pecans, so the pecans fall off. And knock you in the head, if you be out there under them. My daddy had three trees shaked and the pecans picked up. Then we have a couple of bushels in the house. All those he didn't sell, we eat.

Good times, my daddy had pigs, but I scared of them. They bite you. Had cows too. Those good times. We didn't have to buy nothing like meat and milk and bread. I was eating butter and bread. And if it wasn't that, I was eating meat. I could go out there into the store my daddy worked with or into the smokehouse and get me meat and cook it. I was the funniest one of the bunch about eating. Always eat alone.

'Course, bad times, we don't got nothing much to eat. Those times, we're hungry. Time goes slow and my stomach hurt. Those times we got to give all we got to the man. Those long, hard times.

Lots of animals down there. Wild cats, mad dogs. Dog would go mad and he just bite the devil out of you and you go mad too. The mad dogs might come to your house at night to catch a chicken or turkey or duck or goose. Day time, you don't see them. So we stay in the house at night and we don't be near them. Rats in Mississippi too. Had great big rats but they didn't go in your house. They stay outdoors, in the cotton and in the cotton houses. I didn't have no pets. I scared of cats and dogs. They had too many damn dogs there for me. Never liked them and never will.

We'd stay home at night when I'm little. You better not go no where at night. My mama beat the shit out of you if you do. We just sit out there on the front, sit on the porch. Had old wooden chairs on the porch. We had kerosene lamps. I didn't light them; was too small to fool with them. But no electric down there, then. Got it down there now, though. We see electric when we go to town. We just see the lights on the streets and in the stores. Part of the stores had kerosene and part electric.

Wasn't too hard for me to get along down there. See, 'cause the older ones worked lots. The oldest girls washed, washed with a wash bowl in a tub, and they cooked too. Way my mother raised, the boys and girls both cooked. One cook one day, the other cook the next; one cook breakfast and the other dinner. That's the way she raised us.

My mother took care of all the kids. Raised them all. And they all just as crazy about my mother as I am. All them. They didn't treat me special 'cause I's the youngest girl. I didn't give them a chance. 'Cause I's mean. I'd fight them. I didn't like nobody. They treat the baby boy better than me. They just loved him to death. I were mean and always have been. I got funny ways.

I wouldn't eat their cookin'. I cook my own self, for me. I was

stubborn. Made them look at me. Notice I's there. And I don't care
for tomatoes, I like okra. I like greens, don't like peas. No. Ever
since I been big enough to know how to cook, I always fix my own.
And our table for eating was only little. All us couldn't get there.
We sit on the floor. Have to sit on the floor if you want to eat with
the rest of them. So, I could eat by myself.

And sometimes if they had chicken up there on the table, I
didn't want to see up there. 'Cause I didn't like chickens and I's
scared of them when I was little. Before I was born, my mother was
scared of chickens out in the yard, feeding the hens, and that's why
I scared of them. When you're carrying a baby, you don't supposed
to get scared of nothing, and she was and that's what made me
scared. But I eat them now.

My sisters mind my mama. They didn't get mad at having to do
the work. Kids didn't know what mad is then. See, you don't play
with your mother down there the way these kids play with you-all
here; my mother beat the shit out of you if you did.

The kids didn't whop me though. Nobody whop you down
there but your ma. Kids don't whop each other. Ma did, though.
Lord, she'd take a limb off a peach tree and tear you apart. She
didn't play with you. I always mind my ma. My ma had trouble
being mean to me, though. 'Cause I'm hateful. I don't go in with a
lot of folks, don't fool with them. Only me and my baby brother
got along.

Don't know too much about writing, reading. You didn't have
but two months in school. It's like, school starts today, and next
month, it's time we's in the field. I could have went to school some
but I dodged school. Oh, the teacher'd beat the hell out of you if
you go to school. They don't play with you there; the teachers don't
either. Miss your lesson, you better not miss it.

I stayed out of school, just didn't go. Dodged it. They didn't
know no where I was. Out there in the field somewhere laying
down where they couldn't see me. And, then, the school wasn't too
good there, no way. They didn't teach you nothing but junk. They
didn't teach you how to read or how to write. Or nothing. Most
school I got was up here.

I only think about one good teacher down there. That was Miss
Raspberry. Tall, brown-skinned lady. She's good; she's nice. She get
out in the yard and play, but I didn't play. I just didn't like it; I'd
ruther sit down and be by myself. Been that way all my days.

Went to school up here; better believe I went here. I went to
the county general school. Taught me writing and I didn't like it
but I had to take it. Then after I got it, I like it. 'Cause I can write

my name but I just don't do it. I just put my number [XX.] down. Sometimes the sister here gives me some writing and reading too.

Sometimes, when I's older, we'd go to the Mississippi River in my daddy's car, old T Model. All of them kids didn't go, just a few. The schoolteacher went with us a lot. She'd say, "Sarah, why don't you just put your foot in?"

I say, "I ain't going to put nothing in that river; I can't swim and I ain't going to put nothing in it." See, the Sunflower River ain't all that big but the Mississippi River is.

Except when we went to the river, all we did was work and play and go to church. We didn't miss no Sunday school. Not with my mama living, but my daddy didn't go. That's where I get my cussing, from him.

Joined the Baptist church when I was about twelve years old. They baptized me in the Sunflower River. It was OK with me. You had to put on a white gown. About ten of us baptized at the same time. Scared me when I had my head in that river. Belonged to the Missionary Baptist church. No white people came; they don't mix together in Mississippi, but everyone in the house come to the baptizing. The church full. After they baptize you, you come to the church, and they have the prayer meeting. Thursday night you got to go to the prayer meeting. And then you go home and eat your dinner and get ready for the night service. And hear that man preach again. He didn't preach for a long time, though. He wouldn't have nobody there. Doggone right, we'd go home. Ain't going to go back there that night and stay all night.

We had holidays, just like here. Christmas, Easter, go to church. At Christmas we had toys, dolls, but I never played. I never played nothing. The hatefulest one in the family.

Most of all, when I was little, I was scared of the cemetery. And the cemetery right at us, outside our door. It was hard for them to get me to go to church 'cause you had to go by the cemetery. So they didn't worry about my going no where; it's too close. Been scared of dead folks all my days.

Nobody scared but me and I always been scared of them. I ain't never been to a burial. You're dead and you're done, done with me and I done with you. That's the way it goes for me. Here and everywhere else.

But my mother ain't scared of no dead folks. My mother bath them, put the clothes on them, everything else. But they won't get buried, if I have to bury them. I was born scared like that, I guess.

My mother said she made me scared. She say that when she was carrying me, she went to see a dead man, and his eyes and mouth be open and awful. He'd got hung and she got scared of him, and it made me like I am. And, I ain't playing. I'm real scared of dead folks. I ain't never been to a funeral or burial in my life. My father wasn't scared but didn't have nothing to do with the dead either.

Nobody scared of dead folks but me. They'd say, "Put your hands on them dead folks."

But, I'd say, "I ain't putting my hand on nothing."

"Then you won't be scared of them."

"Shit, I'd be more scared of them."

And, them folks, they're cold as ice. And it don't take them no time to get cold. When the breath leave their body, they're cold. When I saw my baby brother die, his toes and hands they jerk and stretch out. He breathe hard and was gone. I can't stand dead folks, even him.

Looks like the church buries somebody every day. I hear the bells. They had bells in Mississippi too. Big ones and I'd hear them when someone died. Could hear them ten miles down the road, and down there the church is right in front of our door.

I'd hear them bells. See, they'd ring so long. Then they'd stop and then they'd start the toning. If you're eighty or sixty or seventy, they'd tone it that many times. If you nine or ten, they'd tone it ten times. They'd ring and that's the reason I'd know when somebody was dead.

People were hung down there and everything else. And I know they're hung, 'cause I seen them. Tongue out real long, eyes real big and popping. Them son of a bitches awful down there. They don't like blacks. I seen them walk right up and yell at me.

When they hang you, they put a rope around your neck with a knot bigger than my fist, and then they drop you and you jerk up there and back down, and it breaks your neck and you turn around. That's it. And they bring you out there to the cemetery and bury you. I knew all of them. Black folks don't do nothing in Mississippi and get away with it.

My sister, she's ninety-nine; she wants me to come down to see her there. She wants me to go down so she can worry the hell out of me about staying, but I'm not staying. I'm scared of the cemetery and the dead, and all of them are out there at the cemetery now, but her.

They say they can't see spirits, but I can. I can see something. I don't know what they is, spirits or dogs, but I see them. They say, I wasn't born to see them spirits, but, shit, I see them.

Me and my sister were sitting on the porch one evening, just about nine o'clock, and I see a big, black dog coming, a spirit dog, and before he got to the house, he went off, down into the ditch. I ran into the house and my sister said to me, "It ain't no use of running, he can come into the house."

But I said, "God dammit, and I'll give it to him too if he does." See, I got a lot of people dead. If there was any way in the world for them to see me, they'd come. You know, they ain't nothing but a shadow in the wind.

That dog, he was a ghost. One of my dead brothers or sisters. Or my niece or nephew. I went in the house. I didn't sit out there on the porch. She sat out there and wasn't scared. Ain't nobody scared of dead folks but me.

Here I have a little light by my bed all night long; I don't want to sleep in the dark. I don't know who died in here. You see, they won't tell me. They got a man from up here; a man died up here on the next floor. And they took him on the elevator and I got right off. The undertaker was carrying him down.

They say to me, "Come look at so-and-so. He died. She died." But she done with me and I'm done with her, and I ain't never going to go to a funeral.

They tell me, "You got to die and they can come to yours."

I say, "They can do anything to me. They can burn me up if they want."

I don't think about dying. I know one of these days I got to die, but I don't think about it. We don't be getting very sick in my family, just like I'm sitting here, talking to you. That's the way they die. All of my people. Just breathe and fall dead. No sickness. We all have the same thing. High blood pressure.

When I'm grown I worked for white people. Tend to babies. Took care of Mr. Hulio's babies, Bobbi, Susie, and Jean. They crazy about me and I crazy about them. All them about dead now. We sleep in the same room with the babies. Get up and bathe them in the morning, put their clothes on, and we gone. School or somewhere. I'd take them to school, the ones who are big enough.

I go to my church on Sunday, but they'd go with me, the kids. They'd say, "I want to go with her. I love Sarah; I ain't going no where but where she goes." And that's all they said.

Didn't get time off. Mr. Hulio say, "Why'd you need it?"

Them children's mama knows me since she was a girl. Me and her come up together. So she married McCoy, and when she had children, she wanted me to take care of them. We played together and fight too when we little. Me and her fight like hell. Mr. Hulio come out there and whop us all. See, Mississippi is not like it is here; white people whop your black ass there.

And that's the way the white people is. They ain't like they is here. Don't allow none to fight. Me. You. Nobody else. When I jump on her, they whop me; when she jump on me, they whop the hell out of her. Ain't not like these folks here.

Mr. Hulio would tell my daddy, "Wes, I whopped Sarah."

My daddy say, "Was she fighting?"

"Yes."

"Well, don't tell me about it."

None of the kids could whop me. Just like I am now. I can fight the hell out of a person if they bother me. I don't bother them.

Every time I was married, I was married in Mississippi. William Johnson was in the army. Steve, I quit. John Thomas, I quit him too. And William, he died. First got married when I was eighteen. Wasn't excited, just married to get away from home. So I can have my way. It was good to have my way then. It's good now. Better to have your own way than to have somebody boss you.

Husbands didn't mess with me. If they did I would have cut the shit out of them. I'll tell you, I didn't stay with them very long. When they found out the way I was, I be gone. Just like you walk in, I walk out that door. I weren't scared. I ain't never been scared of them. Ain't no man going to beat on me. No. I am got too old for that mess. I don't need one and I don't want one. No man. They want you to feed 'em, and I'm not going to feed nobody but me. Got to be tough to get by.

'Bout eighteen when my father died. I lived right there when he fell off the bed, and he just breathed and were gone. That's the way them go; they don't be sick. My mother was but my dad ain't. My mother's a young woman when she died, 'round forty-one or forty-two. She got the sugar diabetes.

When I left Mississippi, I left by car. I came with my baby brother. He left first and then he had wrote me and I had wrote him. He came and picked me up. I didn't want to stay in Mississippi if he wasn't there. Didn't want to stay nowhere he ain't.

I ain't never missed Mississippi. I didn't like it. When I real little and didn't know much about it, I might have liked it. But I got to coming up to Indiana and to see my brother's kids, and I didn't like it down there anymore. It tickled me to move. Lots different there in St. Louis.

I don't have but two kids. Two girls and they're twins. When I had my daughters, I had a midwife. They be born in South Bend, Indiana. Didn't know I going to have twins. Knowed when I married the man, something was coming. I was surprised, two girls.

Stayed home with them. And my auntie too and my mother too. We do fine when we were there. Then I brought them up here and they start getting in trouble. I don't know why they get in trouble. I guess 'cause of their dad.

I raised all my brother's kids. Six kids. My baby brother died and then his youngest son died too. He didn't live no time. He's smoking that dope and then got hit by a train. He knows better than to be on the railroad tracks. He shouldn't smoke that mess. I don't see what the world smokes for.

I know about raising kids. Been around them all my days. Don't miss kids now. Glad I ain't around them. They worried me to death. I ain't kidding. "Auntie, this; Auntie, that; Auntie, this."

My daughter has a kid, just one. Bad little girl. She worse than I was when I was little. Well, they don't allow children to live here and I don't keep her. That's OK. I been by myself all my days, and I don't want to be worried with children.

'Bout forty years ago, I's in Milwaukee, and when I couldn't find no job, they sent me over there to the county. See, it was welfare, but you just didn't get nothing for nothing, like a lot of them do now. You had to work for it. Do something. Had us all making some old dolls. Making dolls and all this fur going up your lungs and nose. So I got off it. I wasn't there but two days. They didn't know what come of me; I was gone. I went down to the YWCA and that's where I worked. That's where I stayed.

Worked there a hell of a long time, forty years. I was cooking but mostly washing dishes. I was hired to wash pots and pans. Then, you know how it is, they get new bosses, they get new bosses, they get new bosses. This old Mexican boss comes by, and he says, "I want you to go upstairs and wait on the parties." He wants me to work downstairs, upstairs, wash pots and pans, and then wait on the parties and I won't do it. Didn't like it up there with all them people.

I said, "Goddamn. Is that so? I ain't going up there." I say, "I hired down there in that kitchen."

He told me he'd give me five dollars a week more, but what do I want with that old five dollars.

I told him, "You give me back my money. My money you been taking, my social security money. Who wants that old five dollars." So, that's what I did, and that's what I be getting now. And the SSI. The government give me that.

All those years when I be working for the YWCA, I don't do much else. When you come home from the YWCA you don't want to do nothing. You just so tired that you sit down or lay down and relax so you be there the next morning. I ain't never liked to do nothing. I didn't watch TV. Don't now. Would rather listen to the radio, I'm going to sleep anyway. And I don't like no ball games and that's all these folks watch. But I quilt. My mother learned me. I don't like crocheting. Been doing quilts all my days. I piece quilt when I was little 'cause I didn't like to work in the fields.

Used to live in apartment over on Fourteenth Street, but they [the Housing Authority] tear them houses down. Had to sleep with a broom handle over there. Used the broom handle to fight off them rats. Don't see no rats and roaches here, do you? When they tear it down they bring me here, to the apartments for the old.

Put me on the ninth floor. I didn't like it up here, too high. But when I got here I stayed. I walk down the stairs, every one of them, 'cause I say, "If someone going to get a fire, he ain't going to get any elevator." I walk down and get my groceries. I go get them and then rest and take the elevator up. I get busy. I ain't going to sit here and get stiff.

These folks will run you to death. But you got to go, never know when you be down yourself. A lot of them gets mad with me, "I wouldn't go, I wouldn't do this, and I wouldn't do that."

But I say, "You don't know what you going to come to. You never know when you going to get down. That's why I don't mind going out for them. How in the world is she supposed to go herself?"

Yet, they say, "Get Sarah to go, she'll go."

Well, I don't mind going. It don't kill me. So, I goes for them.

They tried to get me to a meeting down there, downstairs. But I am stubborn and ain't going. They know I'm quick to get mad and they don't fool with me. If you can't get along with people, best to stay away. Don't none of them mess with me. But one man is nice. When I get ahold of something and can't read it, I take it there and ring the doorbell and he'll come and read it.

Had some neck bones on the stove here once. Left them on and when I come back, they done burned up, and they smoked up the ceiling and halls and everybody gets mad at me. A gas stove it was. Had a wood stove in Mississippi. Just leave a little bit of fire in them to keep it warm. Electric and gas, you're afraid you'll set the house afire. Have to know how to set it. You can't leave this stove. Folks all get mad at you.

Fixed my place up nice, though. Bought me some plants.

Always liked plants. We had them down home, lots of flowers, everywhere. My mother liked them too. We had rosebushes. Pink ones, white ones, yellow ones, red ones. All kinds.

My brother died when I be living in that other place. You know, whatever you believe, you believe that, don't you. And I believe that if he and his old lady didn't have that other man living with them, my brother'd be alive now. 'Cause she take that man to be her new old man just as soon as my brother died. Living in that house, with her. She called me that morning, "I believe we're losing Joe."

He died that day and I moved that day, and I ain't never been back down there since. She wouldn't have been living with the man, if she didn't have something to do with it. 'Course, it could have been that his time's up. He had the high blood pressure. And asthma.

Didn't go to his funeral, no. But he had some grown-up kids, and they come and got his body and take him to Indiana. I loved my baby brother. More than anybody. He was the only baby brother I had. Missed my mother too. Miss her still yet. And miss my baby brother.

Used to drink, lots some. But had to give the drinking up. Can't drink no more, just now and then. It runs my blood pressure up. And the folks round here hateful to me when I do. Don't smoke either. Just chew a little.

Was large before, 210 pounds. But the doctor made me lose. Said so 'cause of the high blood. I could show you some of my dresses, if I could get to them, you wouldn't believe it was me. I'm smaller now than I ever been. I'm telling you, I'm no little person. I look little but I ain't little.

Lose weight too 'cause I can't eat too good 'cause I don't have no teeth. I don't ever wear them. They hurt. And when I don't have my teeth, I can't chew my food. Still, I don't worry about being sick. Fact, I don't worry about nothing. I always was headstrong and hardy.

Welfare won't help me now. Ain't nothing that help me but my social security and my SSI. That's the reason I don't ever have no money. Got to pay rent, telephone bill, buy some meat or some lard. I buys neck bones, potatoes, stuff like that. Wanted some potatoes this morning but I didn't have no money. Won't have none until the first.

I'd work now if I could find me a babysitting job, but those folks don't allow me to work. They think $300 should go for all. Ain't go nowhere. You got to know how to take care yourself. And it don't be many people that know. I keep having to borrow and paying back and I ain't got nothing. I have to keep paying on that damn TV, paying and paying. But they say, "You owe it to them, you got to give it to them."

Government doesn't help the people. You know that old president, old president, what's-his-name. Carter. I despise him. I just never did like him. He wasn't nothing but an old farmer, down there, and he comes to be a talking proud president. He don't help nobody here. He goes out of town, all across the ocean somewhere. No help here.

Things be different now than they used to be. They didn't treat the girls in Mississippi like these folks up here do. Didn't try to rape them. No, that stuff wasn't done near our home. We could be out there naked and they wouldn't bother us. They ain't like these people here. Nobody's safe here. Take us right now. We don't have no night watch, nor nothing here. They took 'em off. Things ain't right for these old folks here. You had to mind any old folk down there. Anybody, old person. They don't do it now, not here.

See, if you raised down in Mississippi, you know how to handle it. I know more about how to handle there than I do up here. Still, I don't think about none of them down there. Thinking don't bring them back. I don't think about them and I don't think about what's going on here, either. To hell with it. I don't think about nothing.

But, I tell you one thing. I've just been straight all my days. If I don't like you, I just don't like you, and I tell you I don't like you. People just don't mess with me.

It's been a really rough life in many ways, but it has helped me to see things. Now I've learned a lot about myself and other women. It's been hard, but in a way, it was worth it. It's like the song. We want the bread, but we want the roses too.

—Darlene Leache

A pretty but thin and tired-looking young woman named Darlene Leache stood up to speak in front of about sixty women gathered high in the Appalachian Mountains of northern Tennessee. She spoke in a quiet and reserved voice.

"For me and my family, as far back as I can remember, women have worked as hard as the men. My grandmother had nine children and went out working for other families. She would work all day for a gallon of milk or a dozen eggs. She had to do these things because of the lack of education.

"I quit school and married at fifteen. But things were not easier. If anything, they seemed harder. I hauled coal when I was pregnant, and my sister and I have loaded and unloaded coal with a shovel with a six-month-old baby lying asleep between us. I have cut paper wood to buy the baby the medicine she needed and sold berries to buy clothes for an unborn baby. There wasn't enough money for these extras we needed. I didn't have the education I needed. But I am determined to educate myself. Several of us have got our G.E.D., and now we are taking bookkeeping classes.

"I have come to this meeting without my husband's approval. He doesn't approve of the education I have worked hard for. Many of the men in our community feel that a woman doesn't need an education. They want us to live with the old traditions. But we want to feel like we can support ourselves if it were necessary. We want pride; we want dignity. We don't want to be on welfare. I love my mountain land, but it is so hard to earn a living.

"Still, I have worked at our community action center for several years, and I know that the efforts of all of us women together have worked wonders for each of us as individuals and for the mountain community where we live."

She quietly sat down, and the main speaker continued to show slides of the area: of the coal mines and small towns consisting of clusters of battered houses along the riverbeds and up in the hills, as well as of the handicraft projects various women were working on. She told the history of local community and craft centers, the mountain women who ran them, and the formation of a group called Mountain Women's Exchange, a coordinating group that, two years earlier, had been organized to improve women's lives by developing joint programs and forming a power base for political action. It was for this meeting of the Exchange that this group of women had gathered. They were both young and old, and many showed the strains of poor health care and impoverished living. Many had small children with them.

I met with Darlene for several days following this Exchange meeting. We talked in the Crazy Quilt Friendship Center where Darlene worked part time as a bookkeeper, and as women chatted and quilted in another room, she talked quietly of her past and the role the Center and Mountain Women's Exchange had played in her life.

Darlene was a thin woman who looked much younger than her thirty-three years. She dressed carefully and had soft, dark shoulder-length hair; clear blue expressive eyes set against pale skin. It seemed amazing that the painful experiences of her life had not touched her more visibly; they had left their marks, though, in her reserved manner, her air of tiredness, and her poor health. Her voice was soft and gentle, and she asked me to use her real name when telling her story, saying she thought it was important that others should know.

Darlene's story is the story of exploitation and survival. But it is also the story of women attempting to change the complex forces of oppression through individual endeavors and common struggle.

Darlene

There were five of us kids in the family and we never did have much. When I was about thirteen, I'd already quit school because I didn't have clothes or shoes to wear. About that time Daddy went to New Jersey to try to find work up there. But Daddy had a hard time and he didn't send money home. He just sent twenty-five dollars home one time.

We were so poor we couldn't pay our bills, and a man came to our house to turn off the meter for electricity. He told us he was going to do it, and Mama said, "No, you can't cut it off."

He said, "Yes, I'm going to have to."

"No, I can't let you. Just me and these children are here; you can't."

"Well, I'm gonna have to climb the pole to cut it off."

"No, I've got a gun." She had a shotgun. She said, "You climb the pole and you're gonna come down faster than you got up. I can't let you do that. I told you I'd pay when I got the money. But we don't have it."

And he got scared and wouldn't climb the pole then and went off and left. She talked him out of it, the rough way, but she did it.

And we didn't have anything to eat. You've heard of poke salad. It's a wild salad that grows. We would go out and get it and fry the stalks sometimes for breakfast because there was nothing else. We'd also try to gather wild strawberries. We'd have those and we heard that they were giving commodities out. We didn't have any way to go get the commodities, though, and, while Daddy had a car sitting there, none of us knew much about driving. But Mama said, "Darlene, we have to go."

"Yes, we do."

"You'll have to drive it."

"Well, I'll try, Mama."

It was winter and we lived way up on this mountain, but I did it. We went and we got the commodities and came back home. And we would use the commodities. I've heard people say, "We couldn't use the flour; we couldn't use the meal," but we used every bit of it. I learned to bake cakes out of it and to make biscuits in order to make do. We lived in a little house my great-grandmother owned, and we carried water about a mile to cook with and a half mile to wash clothes with. It was just so hard that life was, having nothing.

Then, when I was fifteen, I met Virgil. He was twenty-two and wanted to marry me. I didn't love him but I listened to him, and I thought that if I left home, Mama and the other kids could have more. That it would make life easier, not knowing that me marrying and getting in the situation I did was going to make it harder. I hadn't known him that long and didn't know him at all, not really. I also didn't know the facts of life. I thought I did, but I didn't. I thought it was just people being together; I didn't know there was the sexual part of it. Mom never had talked to me about it. But, then, after the marriage I learnt.

We were married by a justice of the peace. Mom and my sister-in-law were with me. I was so scared when I was standing up there in front of the justice of the peace, I wanted to run. I wanted to run back out and not get married. But I thought that if I got out from home things would be easier for Mom and for us. And I thought, "Oh, I can't run away, he's spent all that money for blood tests and the license. I can't do that." But if I knew then what I know now, I would have run.

But I had hopes then. I thought, "It's going to be easy now." You know how children dream. I thought, "Oh, I'm gonna have the things I never had; it will just be a bed of roses." Well, I was wrong.

I was pregnant in just a very few months. It wasn't too hard until after the first child was born. I loved that baby but I was up day and night with him 'cause his formula didn't agree with him. Virgil didn't want anything to do with the baby. He told me one time, "You have terrible patience to sit there and rock that kid, day and night. I'd bust his rear and put him to bed." That was before the baby was six weeks old. And Virgil starting drinking right after that and started in beating me.

My childhood wasn't like the bad times with Virgil. There was always plenty of love there when I was a child. Seemed like there was just enough love to go around to everybody; nobody was ever out in the cold for love.

I remember my great-grandmother and my grandmother. They lived right near us. My great-grandmother drew her check each month, and my grandma would go out and work for people. She didn't have any education at all. The poor old soul couldn't even write her own name. She'd work all day, doing people's washing and ironing, cleaning their house, and they would give her one dozen eggs or maybe a gallon of milk for all the day's work.

Mom used to tell me that when she was growing up, they had these mines, and they would go way up there to the mines and gather coal to burn. Then they would carry coal on their back in a sack all the way home. Mom said that one time, while Grandma was way pregnant with Mom's sister, she was out there helping to kill a cow so they could have some meat. Also, they went out and gathered wood, and Mom said that when she was a little child, she would just follow along behind because she was too small to help. There were nine kids. My grandmother was a hard worker; she never gave up. She always kept everything spotless and I remember the tables full of pies and cake. She was up at daybreak and she'd walk the ten miles to church.

My great-grandma delivered me. She was a midwife and delivered plenty of children. She was short but not real fat, just plump, like a grandma. And she was on the go constantly. I remember that when I was expecting one of my own babies and my aunt was also pregnant, my aunt came up to my grandma's house. She had a bedspread doubled up between her legs, and she said, "My baby's being born." Grandma took her in and fixed the bed, put her in it, and delivered that child.

One of my earliest memories was when I was three years old and my sister Bertha was born. We lived in a log house and there was a door that closed off the living room from this one bedroom. I was in the other room; they were trying to keep little nosy out. But I went and peeked through the door because I wanted to watch and see what was happening. After she was born, Grandma said, "Did you see the baby that somebody brought you?"

"Yes, I seen that baby. But they didn't bring it. I know where that baby come from." Then I said, "I want to name her." Berthy holds that against me today.

Mama said, "What do you want to name her?"

"Bertha Frances." And she let me name her.

I remember going in and the baby was propped up. Berthy was a huge baby. She weighed about ten and a half pounds. And, oh, I loved her. Seemed like I always did love her just like that. And they couldn't tell me she'd come from under a cabbage or a stork brought her. I knew where she'd come from.

Later, when I was older, I learnt what pregnant was. I was traveling with my aunt and uncle and mom, and I was playing like I was asleep in the back of the car. They were talking about somebody being pregnant. I thought, pregnant, pregnant, what does pregnant mean? Then, when I got back home, I went around asking everybody what pregnant means. And I finally found out that pregnant means you were going to have a baby. Oh, I was so nosy; I had to know everything. Even if I had to eavesdrop to do it. Mom always said I was too nosy, but that's how I learnt a lot of things.

Bertha and I have always been real close. And you wouldn't believe the things that child could do. Lots of times she got in trouble when we were little. I remember one time when I didn't have hardly any clothes. This was after I quit school. Bertha had gone up to New York with my aunt and uncle. I guess you could consider them wealthy; it seemed like they really had a lot. And when she was up there, they bought her all kinds of clothes, little suits, gloves, purses, and hats to match. I was always smaller than her. And when she came home, I had on a pair of her jeans. She had told me I could wear them. But then she said, "Get my jeans off!"

"No. You said I could wear them."

"Get them off!" Then she picked up a pop bottle and said, "You better have them off by the time I count to three." She held the bottle back to throw it and started counting, one, two. And as she said "Three!" and let it go, I ducked, and Mom came through the door and it hit Mom. And my grandmother was there, too. Bertha said later that she just turned cold with fear, and then she shot out from behind that table and went through that door running. She knew to get away.

As she got to the bridge, she screamed back, "You're not my mommy. No old nigger woman's my mommy!" But Grandma ran her down and caught her, and, oh, did she give her a good whipping. She was rotten mean, Bertha was. She had real black hair and her eyes were real dark and she was dark complected. She took after Daddy and she looked like a little Indian running.

But Bertha's turned out all right. She turned into a really

wonderful person, with love for everyone. And she does everything she can for people. I've seen her take the shoes off her feet if she's seen someone that needed a pair. And we still have a special relationship. It's like she knows what I'm doing and thinking, and I know what she's doing and thinking all of the time.

I have happy memories of growing up with Daddy. He would always take us if we needed to go places and he'd play games with us. He got me my first bicycle and put me up on a hill and said, "Now, you've got to ride it."

I thought, well, I've got to ride this bicycle: Daddy's depending on it. And I learned and from then on I learned every child in the neighborhood how to ride it. Daddy said that was the best bicycle that ever was 'cause every child around us learned to ride on it.

When I was real small, about three or four years old, I cut my leg bad and Daddy didn't have no car at the time. He was working in the coal mines. And Daddy bundled it up in towels, and he went out to the road and caught the mail truck into town to get it sewn up. He really cared. Daddy was just there if you needed him. Later, he was the first one to buy the private things that a girl wears. He was a really considerate person and Mom was real loving too. She likes to joke and cut up with you.

And my grandma would play with us when we were little. Over on Stinking Creek there was a big haystack, and we would play in the haystack with Grandma, and she would go swimming in the creek with us. We lived in the same house with her for a long time when we were small and Daddy was in the Navy. Then, after we moved a little off from her house, I'd go and stay with her. Last night Bertha and I were sitting and remembering all those years and we really had a ball.

I can think of us going to those fairs and carnivals where Daddy would take us. The memories just come flooding back. I remember the family reunions where the house and yard would all fill up. I used to go to this one's house and that one's, visiting with relations. But after we married, Virgil didn't want me to do things like that. So I stayed at home.

One time when I was young we moved to Michigan for about five years so Daddy could find work. We had good times there but I always missed it here. But Daddy got laid off up there, and we couldn't afford to stay so we moved back here. Then the hard times hit when Daddy was gone to New Jersey to look for work and Mom and us kids were left at home.

After a while my grandma got cancer and she took real bad. She was about ten miles away from us when some people called one day and said that she was really ill and we needed to come right away. It was February and there was a real bad snow, but we started walking the ten miles. When we got there she was desperately ill and I told them, "Call a cab." The cab wouldn't take her to the hospital unless we had the money, but I had some babysitting money so they took her. Then mother and I would walk to the hospital in Little Elk where we'd sit with her all night, and then we'd walk home during the day and back that night. She died not too long after that. We were there with her when she died. It still hurts to think that she's gone, since we were so close.

So then Virgil and I got married and we had the first baby, and he started in drinking and being mean and lots of the time he couldn't work. He wouldn't let me take birth control pills, and he wouldn't do anything to keep me from getting pregnant, so I got pregnant again and again and again. My first baby was seventeen months old when the second was born. Before she was born, I didn't have no clothes for her to wear, 'cause someone had stole the other baby's clothes. So when I was about seven months pregnant with my little girl, I'd take my baby boy out and sit him on a blanket in a big prairie field and I'd pick berries. Then we would walk to town and sell them berries for the new baby's clothes.

The cord was wrapped around my second baby's neck when she was born and she was real dark. But the doctor said, "It's a girl," and I remember raising up my eyes and just laughing. I wanted my little girl so bad. I was absolutely tickled it was a girl, but a couple of months later I was pregnant again.

Before Bobby was born, I would haul coal. We'd have to wade out in the water up to our waist to get the coal to haul to sale. My sister and I hauled it. We got it with a shovel and unloaded it with a shovel and drove the truck. And I tumbled paper wood when I was six months pregnant with my little girl. My other girl was sick and I had to do enough to buy her medicine. The logs would be about six foot long, and my little brother and I would tumble them off the mountains. Then we would cut the paper wood with a crosscut saw. It's just been altogether a real hard life.

I knew how bad things were with Virgil, but I didn't think I could get out of it, not when the babies kept coming. And I thought the husband had to agree with it for you to take birth control pills. I tried an IUD but it went wrong. So I had six children and I lost one when I was pregnant. I was carrying coal and I was carrying water about a half mile to our house when I lost that child. I wasn't as strong as I thought I was. It took me about two weeks to lose the baby. It just hurt me to lose a child, but then, later on, I realized it was better this way because I didn't have the money for the child.

I was so worried that something would be wrong with my last baby because Virgil had got really cruel to me when I was pregnant with the baby and had hurt me bad. I was absolutely tickled when the baby was born without any defects. It just seemed like that child was more precious to me because of it.

Virgil got so he was drinking up his payday. Sometimes I would go pick up his check and would buy food before he would have a chance to get the money, but then he would come home and if I refused to give him the rest, there would be a fight. We would fight constantly over money and over the children. The children were right near looking on, so it was hard on them.

Then Virgil got to where he couldn't work at all because the alcohol just got his system down so bad that he couldn't do it. And I went to work in a restaurant. I worked in different places, in a factory and at different restaurants cooking and washing dishes, and they always praised my work. I worked real hard for them. But then Virgil'd take the money out of my purse, and he got so he couldn't do anything. One day a flood came while I was at work and just completely destroyed the furniture and the house, and Virgil was in such a shape that he wasn't able to get anything out. By the time I got home it was already up to the porch. All I could get was a few of the children's clothes.

Things were so bad at home. I've always hated fighting and was one to hide in an argument, and when Virgil and I would fight I'd just sit and cry. I wouldn't say anything back. But through the years, I got to where I would speak up if I thought he was wrong. I'd tell him, "No, I don't think you're right."

I got to where I felt like I was absolutely nothing. I didn't want to face people or talk with them because I was so ashamed. I just mainly wanted to be left alone and to be off by myself. I didn't think I had any brains at all and that I was completely alone in the world. But then, when I felt the worse, one of the children would come up and put their arms around my neck and whisper, "Mommy, I love you." And that would help me over the next hill.

But I had a kind of pride and I guess that pride stood in my way 'cause I didn't go to welfare for help. When you go to the welfare department, you have to tell different things, and I just didn't want other people to know. So I didn't get any help.

I can't really understand Virgil, and I don't guess I ever will. You can't predict the way he's going to be; it's a fear that I have to live with. I don't know whether to try to talk to him or just go off and be quiet. He's unpredictable, like a grenade. And he was hard on the children, both mental and physical. The children were afraid of him, and they would try to run and hide when he came in.

When the baby was about a year and a half old, Virgil was still drinking, drinking, drinking and getting worse and worse. I started feeling real funny and could hardly stand up. I saw my sister and she said, "Darlene, what's wrong?"

"Nothing."

"Yes, there's something. Move your hand."

And when I couldn't, she said, "Oh, my God, you're having a stroke. Go to the doctor."

I said, "I can't. I got all these kids and no money."

So she went and got Mom and Dad and they took me to a doctor. Then they all put me in the hospital 'cause I couldn't hardly walk. I was in for a long time but the doctor there finally told me it wasn't a stroke. I'd got hit on the head by Virgil several years back, and I had a blood clot where he'd hit me. Then they gave me some medication that I was supposed to take for quite a while. When I got to come home Virgil had just kept a drinking and the house was full of cans.

Sometimes when Virgil would get real rowdy with his drinking and maybe go on a spree for a week, we would just go up to my mom's house and stay for a while. And one time we didn't have anywhere to go, and I took the kids and said, "Come on." It was raining and the children and I walked down the railroad tracks and went to the police department, and I said, "It's your responsibility to help me. I need somewhere to stay tonight with my kids."

The man said, "We don't have any place for you to stay."

"I'll stay here." And he put me in a cell and kept us there all night. It was better than being home.

My sister came to the house one time when he was drinking, and he had just beat me to where I couldn't move. I couldn't walk and she took me to the hospital and took care of me. She would help me by just talking to me and being there with me. She would take care of me but she wouldn't interfere. She never wanted to get involved in it. She was just something special in my life.

Daddy and Mom didn't like how Virgil treated me. One time Daddy told him, "I'd rather you just leave, Virgil, than to do these things. I'm gonna have to do something about it. I'll have to do something because she's mine."

That scared me and I didn't want them to know if there was trouble or nothing. I always tried to keep it hidden from Daddy and from Mom. Oh, Mom was real hot tempered. She came in the kitchen one time when Virgil was drinking real bad and had hit me against the wall and was choking me and she started beating on him. He got real mad and I thought he was going to hit her but he left. I knew that if he ever hit my mother, I wouldn't put up with it. Mom was very loyal and stood by us no matter what. She was just there to be with us if we needed her and she never put us down.

But I still felt so alone sometimes. I thought, "Why not just go on and do something to finish it, to get out of the way." Because sometimes I felt like I was standing in the way of people. I'd often think on my way to work, "Well, why not just drive over something and hit a big tree." But I had five children at that time, and then I'd get to thinking, "What will happen to my kids? What will they do? I don't want them separated. I want them to grow up together."

I started to go ahead and do it once, and then I thought, "Oh, Lord, what am I doing! What am I doing? I've got these children, what can I do? Lord, help me over this. Just help me to get over this, and I won't attempt something like this again." And I came through it. I made it over.

But I'd sit up many nights and cry. Cry a lot, "Lord, help me. Help me, Lord." When he would be out drinking, I'd be desperately afraid and I'd think, "What am I gonna do when he comes home? What can I do?" But I think my faith helped me to survive.

And my great-grandmother, she would help me because she was really religious. She believed in God. And I would run to her when problems got real bad. She'd pray for me and it wouldn't be long till I got what seemed like new strength. My great-grandma lived according to strict religious beliefs but didn't say anything against other people who didn't believe like she did. Still, she didn't believe in divorce and I was raised not believing in it either.

But even she said, "Darlene, sit down. You need to divorce him. You can have a better life."

"But, Grandma, the Bible says no divorce."

And she said, "Honey, under certain circumstances, you can divorce." But still it didn't seem right according to what I'd been taught and I went on and on.

What really hurt the worst, I guess, was when I would be at work and Virgil would be with the children and then they would tell me Virgil would say bad things about me. I could hardly believe that he would tell things like he would. One day one of the kids said, "Mom, I'm gonna show you what he does say."

So I came home from work one day, and I went upstairs to straighten up the bedroom, and we had got a little tape recorder when things had been better, and the tape player was sitting there. I don't know why I turned it on but I did, and there he was on the tape. He was drunk and telling the kids that I wasn't working, that I was meeting other men and staying in a motel with them. Oh, I was so hurt I couldn't stand it.

I guess I told Virgil about it at the wrong time because he was drinking but I said, "You have no right to tell the kids that."

He said, "I didn't tell the kids. That's a lie they made up. They'll do anything to get you to leave me."

I said, "No, Virgil, the kids didn't lie this time. I heard it."

"How did you hear it? You was at work."

"Well, I just went upstairs and got the tape recorder and it was on it."

Oh, he flew so mad. He broke the tape recorder and everything. It went on and he got really, really bad. Finally, I just got him out and locked the doors so he couldn't get back in.

I started thinking, "Well, maybe it's me." He made me feel that it was really me that was doing all the wrong. I was thinking that I was the cause of him drinking; that if it wasn't for me, he wouldn't drink. So I decided to go to see a psychiatrist through the Regional Health. It was a place for low income people. I went there and they asked me what kind of dreams I had. I'd think and most of my dreams were that I was closed in a room and I could see my kids fighting to survive. So they encouraged me to get a divorce. They said, "You are working and can support your kids."

So I went and talked to the judge to get a divorce. Virgil begged me not to do it, but I said, "No, Virgil. I can't let you come back."

He said, "I won't drink no more, I promise."

"You've gotta do something about it first. Prove to me that you won't drink."

When I got the divorce I had to move off from where we'd been staying, and when I moved I couldn't find no work. We started a bad time because we didn't have any money, but at least some things got better with my kids. My son had been getting into a lot of trouble, and after Virgil left he changed so much. And my daughter, who'll be sixteen pretty soon, was great. They would help me in every way they could.

And after the divorce, Virgil quit drinking. It's been close to two or three years now since he drank. At first I didn't believe it; I looked for it to start again just about anytime. But he started going back to church too which has been helping him.

But where I was living after the divorce I had no way to get to work. My baby was still young and I didn't know hardly any of the people to where I could get someone to watch the baby. We had no money to live on and things got worse and worse. I'd had a station wagon but when we had no food, I had to sell it for thirty dollars. And then I sold my television to buy more food for the kids. And I sold just practically everything I could sell just so we could eat.

And Virgil would come over to the house and beg and cry for me to take him back. He'd just keep hanging around and hanging around, and I didn't think it was right when we weren't married. Also, he'd stopped drinking which is what I'd said I wanted and my religion said I should take him back. Plus, we were desperate for money, and he was working, so, finally, I said I would take him back and we remarried. I was definitely scared when we remarried; I didn't really want to. And I know now I could have done something else. I realize that now, but then I didn't. Deep down there is fear that he might start drinking again. I get to thinking, "Oh, what if he were to go back to drinking, what would I do?"

Virgil has not drank or hurt me or the children physically since I remarried him, but he has hurt us emotionally and he definitely didn't want me to take the work I'm doing. Now we live on Calico Mountain in my mother's house. She's got two houses up there and it's comfortable. It's pretty and mostly we see trees, and we have water in the house, which sure is easier. Also, I can have myself a garden. But I guess living there is what has helped the marriage the second time. Dad and Mom live close by, and Virgil is afraid to beat me because of their closeness.

As I said, now that Virgil has religion he has lots of beliefs. He says, "Women are not supposed to work."

But I told him, "You can't show me that in the Bible. Because if it hadn't been meant for women to work, the Lord wouldn't of give them the knowledge to do it."

And he believes that if people are living good lives, they shouldn't have to go to the doctor. He doesn't believe in taking medicine. But still he takes it. And he believes that you can't work a picture puzzle; you can't read a book; that women shouldn't wear pants; they shouldn't wear shorts; that people shouldn't watch television. But he watches television. There's just a whole lot of beliefs he has.

But I don't believe that way. I think that as long as you believe that there is a God and you feel that he is in your life, that's all that matters.

The children are real good now, though. They care about

people and animals. Right now we have a little baby groundhog that's a pet. When I got up this morning I was hunting for it 'cause it wasn't in its box, and Bobby had it in bed with him. Young Virgil is bad for strays. Anything that is out, he picks up, including snakes. He had an old black snake that would wrap itself around him, and that's the way young Virgil would walk. Then he would tie it in an old pillowcase for the night.

I told him, "Virgil, I'm gonna get up some morning to put on the light in the kitchen and step on it and have a heart attack."

It went up in the cherry tree the other day, and Laura Ann was reaching up to get some cherries, and she thought it was a limb. She reached to move it and felt that it was the snake and just screamed and ran. We finally talked young Virgil into letting it go, but he is really great for all kinds of animals. He's a quiet turned boy, but a real good one. I feel sad, though, 'cause he quit school.

Mostly, I live for my children, but maybe I just want to be too protective of them. I don't want them to see the hard things in life. I know they're going to face them someday, but I'd like life to be easier for them than I had it. I keep praying they will grow up to have an education, that they will try to make something out of theirselves. And, hopefully, that they don't turn to drink. Hopefully, none of them will drink.

I worry about my children getting married too young. My daughter Tribbie is fifteen and she is wanting to get married now. I don't want her to marry, not this young, but her boyfriend is considerate and doesn't drink and has a good job. He's a real thoughtful person. For Mother's Day, he brought me six red roses, the first roses I've ever received in my life. She's been going out with this boy for three years and has been wanting to get married for over a year. I wonder, "Will I be making a mistake by letting her marry, or will I be making one by not letting her?"

Virgil, the older boy, said, "Mom, I think you should let Tribbie go ahead and marry him. She'll have a good life. She'll have the things that she's not had at home and he'll be good to her." So, I don't know which way to turn. His parents are all for the marriage. If they do marry, I'd like them to have a nice wedding. I always wanted my girls to be married in church with wedding gowns and all. Maybe I want too much for them, but I would really enjoy it.

I've discussed birth control with her because I think it is important to talk about it with your children. Mom was always too backwards and would never talk about sex or nothing. Tribbie said,

"Oh, Mom, if we get married, we're not gonna have any babies right away."

"What form of birth control do you plan to use?"

"Well, not birth control pills. They have side effects."

"Yes, a lot of it does."

"So we decided to use Norforms."

I said, "Norforms! Tribbie, that's a deodorant!"

"I didn't know that."

So I said, "I think if you're planning on marrying, you're gonna have to see a doctor so they can tell you these things. Because I don't know that much about it." I think she probably will marry. She's very young but she probably will.

Some things have happened in the last few years that have helped me change myself. About six years ago some Catholic sisters came here to work with us women, and they helped to start a craft co-op. It's called Crazy Quilt Friendship Center, and we sell used clothes and have other programs and make quilts and other crafts together. Then we sell them and share the money. I've known Sister Yvonne since she has been here and she has really helped. She's helped us with food. She gave Virgil some money to see a specialist about the drinking. And she helped me get some furniture after the flood. I was scared but started to volunteer to work at the Crazy Quilt about five years ago, and she would just give me a little more to do each time.

I have never considered myself intelligent. I always thought that I was just some dumb person, really. Then Yvonne came along and gave classes for the G.E.D. and here I passed it with a real high percentage. I was really shocked. Then she helped me get the eight dollars for the certificate and I was so proud. Virgil didn't want me to get my education. He didn't have much education, and he felt that if I got one, that I would be above him, but I had a real strong desire to learn, to really be able to support myself if I needed to.

Then Yvonne got the bookkeeping class set up, and it just seemed as though it was meant for me to take it. I had to walk a long ways to the test, but I passed the test with a hundred and I was tickled. When I opened up the book, it just seemed like I knew what was going to be there, that I could do it.

And one time I was worrying and praying about having no money for food, and then the next morning Yvonne called and said, "How would you like to be the bookkeeper at Crazy Quilt? It's part time and we can't pay you very high, but we'd like to have you." I had to walk to and from work, but I loved to do it, and still do. I work as hard as I can and now even go to the craft fairs. It used to be that I wouldn't have been seen out in public like that, but now I can do it. Now I feel that I am doing some good somewhere. I'm helping other women, and then the men and children, to see that they are somebody.

They've really helped me build my self-confidence, but there's still a ways to go. I had lots of years of feeling bad about myself, and it's going to take some time to get out of it, but I'm coming. It seems that there's things that people are born to do. Like the Lord has a calling for each one of us and bookkeeping feels that way for me.

And now we've got the Mountain Women's Exchange. It's just a bunch of women who got together that thought they could come out from under just the directions of men, that they could do other things besides sit at home and have babies, that they could help themselves and other people. The main thing about Mountain Women's Exchange is helping people, helping other women with the needs that they have.

It is like helping battered women. Battered women always thought that you had to sit and you had to take, that there was nothing that you could do about it. But there is a shelter now so there is a place where women can go with their children, where they all can be cared for. It's women working together to find peace of mind and to help bring other women together.

I think that Mountain Women's Exchange is one of the greatest things that could have happened. We spread the word that there is help for anyone, but mainly it's for the women. It will help women get the education they need, or if they need food or money, they will be helped with it. It's to help women to not be pushed back into the corner like some kind of animal that's afraid to move or a little mouse that is afraid to stick its head out from under.

I guess that's how I saw myself and other women, too, like little mice. We look out to see what's going on, but then we want to crawl back in; we are afraid to come out. But we shouldn't be. Because the world was made for the women as well as the men. We have a place here too.

Now we have a group of women that builds and repairs houses. They get trained as carpenters and rebuild and fix up houses for low income people. I think it is great that the women can do that. The funny thing about this is that you take the men, they don't approve of these things that these women do. But, like years ago, I'd help Virgil get paper wood and I'd help him to roll it, and I'd help him get coal and everything. That was heavy work for women, but there was nothing wrong with that to him. It was perfectly all right. But if a woman goes out on her own to do it, it's wrong. Why? I don't feel that it should be that way. You can't limit the kind of work a person can do. That's what's so wonderful about Mountain Women's Exchange; we can come together and we can talk about these things. And if the men want to come, they're invited to come and listen. But it's our time to talk things over.

It's been a really rough life in many ways, but it has helped me to see things. Now I've learned a lot about myself and other women. It's been hard, but in a way, it was worth it. It's like the song. We want the bread, but we want the roses too.

My grandmother was a tough, little old woman, but a good one. She taught me a lot of things, and the first thing she taught me was not to be afraid of the white man. She said, "God gave you a big mouth, and I'm going to teach you how to use it."

—Irene Mack Pyawasit

The first time I visited Irene Mack Pyawasit was in the early evening of one of the first days of spring. I drove into the alley of the old inner-city neighborhood where she lived, turning where a large church stood. The alley was filled with children playing ball. Irene's gray shingled cottage stood behind an old two-story house from whose open windows came the shouts of children. The houses were separated from each other only by narrow sidewalks, and so the sounds of several families could be heard from the alley.

I parked the car and walked to the cottage door. Early stalks of tulips and crocuses lined the walk, and soft pussy willows bloomed across from the door. I knocked on the door, heard the bark of several dogs, and was greeted by a sign:

"Kev—

Open the door with ease,
I've let the snake run loose.

Gram"

Irene was a Menominee, a Native American woman in her late sixties; she chose to use her real name for her story. She had light brown skin, a wide strong-chinned face, and gray and white hair pulled back in a bun and decorated with stick jewelry. Her hands were heavy with turquoise and silver rings and bracelets, and she wore several necklaces and long earrings as well as decorated large-framed eyeglasses. She was wearing shorts during one of our first visits, and her legs were muscular and tight, showing her strength. Her face was intelligent and alert, and she had a mischievous smile and a deep, firm voice. Her total presence was of competency, strength, keen aware-ness, and a shrewd sense of humor.

Irene's small, crowded house in Milwaukee had been burglarized recently, and thousands of dollars' worth of objects collected during her long and active life were taken. She grieved deeply for a large tapestry once belonging to her grandmother, depicting deer in a forest, and for the boxes of cassette tapes containing the stories and history she had carefully told of her tribe. In addition, her husband's dog was stolen and was deeply mourned. Months later Irene was still grieving the loss of articles associated with so many memories, and while she and her husband had another dog, two cats, and the six-foot-long snake, they still spoke sadly of the small dog that was gone.

Irene's husband, Wallace Pyawasit, was a stocky man in his early sixties, who had deep creases in his brown face, and black, white, and gray hair to his shoulders. He was a quiet, gentle man with a low voice and was a leader of the Big Drum, a traditional Menominee religion. Irene traveled with him across the country as he performed his religious role, and they sometimes taught together, Wallace teaching Native American crafts, Irene teaching Native American history.

Irene's understanding of history and tradition was deeply rooted in the Menominee reservation of her childhood. The reservation, located in Northern Wisconsin, is a watery labyrinth of lakes and forests where the loon calls, bears still roam, and there is an abundance of deer. Ferns grow tall and thick in the deep woods, and the earth is soft with pine needles and leaves. In the evening, mist descends on the multitude of lakes formed by ancient glaciers, and vast forests of pine, spruce, hardwood, hemlock, and other trees grow dark. It is from these forests that the Menominee have derived and continue to derive their livelihood.

The early Menominee ranged along the shores of Lake Michigan and over to the Mississippi. Following contact with the French, they began to depend on fur trading in addition to their traditional reliance for food on fish, wild rice, maple sugar, and forest animals. The United States government gradually took control of their lands and forced the Menominee to relinquish their lakes, forests, and streams. Finally, more than a century ago, ten heavily forested townships were set aside as the Menominee reservation.

At that time the religion and education of whites was held up as the key to the Menominee's self-improvement and social acceptance, and children especially were compelled to move away from the ways of their ancestors. A large number of these children were wrenched away from their heritage and forced to live at government or religious boarding schools. Part of this legacy is that, today, 80 percent of Menominees profess Catholicism, and only a minority continue traditional Native American religious beliefs and rituals.

A number of the Menominee remained on the reservation, living intimately with the land they so deeply loved, but frequently suffering from poverty, ill health, and unemployment. Many others moved from the reservation to Milwaukee and other urban centers in an attempt to improve their conditions. This urban population is highly mobile, and many of the Menominees return to the reservation for weekends or the summer. However, their poverty persists in the cities, and the statistics paint a grim picture of life for Native Americans living in our nation's cities. For example, about 33 percent of urban Native American households are below the national poverty level; the death rate of urban Native American infants is seven times the national average; and Native Americans are seventeen times as likely to commit suicide as the average American.

Irene attempted to fight these trends, especially in the realm of education. She urged students to complete their education, taught young Native Americans more of their cultural background, and encouraged the people she worked with to fight for their rights. When I met with her, she was working as a recruiter of Native American students for the University of Wisconsin at Milwaukee. She spoke to several students as we talked, and showed me an intricate, traditional beading pattern for a ceremonial belt which she was working on during quiet times.

Her office was made colorful by posters portraying aspects of Native American life; one carried a boldly stated message: "You were here first. Don't finish last. Stay in school." The office also contained a number of photographs of family and friends, including one of her grandmother from the early 1900s. The thin woman in the photograph wore a dress carefully chosen for the occasion of having to come in contact with whites; her hair was pulled back into a bun, and her serene and sober eyes stared straight ahead.

Irene   I grew up back in horse-and-buggy times on the Menominee Reservation in Wisconsin. It is heavily forested and there were a lot of tall pine trees there. Nothing is nicer than walking through the woods with a carpet of pine needles on the ground. I remember a place we used to call Paradise. A bunch of us kids used to go back there. It was such a beautiful place that we'd just sit. Sometimes we'd take a lunch or we'd take our beadwork with us or our sewing or whatever we were doing. Or sometimes we'd just go back there and play. We'd have to cross a swamp first, not a very big swamp, but it was awful sticky if you fell in. The rocks were so beautiful back there and there was a tiny creek, a little rippling stream maybe a yard wide at the most. There was also another stream that had a little waterfall. I've always remembered it.

We used to go berry picking a lot. My grandmother taught me how to pick strawberries with a snake coiled around the berries. The snake would be sleeping and you'd pick the berries without disturbing it. We'd pick blackberries, raspberries, blueberries, gooseberries, you name it. We had any kind of berry that was edible and my grandmother would can them. Any vegetable we grew in the garden we'd gather, clean, and can. We'd do the same with fruits in the trees. We had anything that nature would provide, including the highbush cranberry which you very seldom see today.

It was God's country. We still have the beautiful, tall pine trees. We have twenty-odd species of trees on our reservation; a variety of pine, hemlock, maple, oak, poplar, green walnut, beech, birch, elm, ash, both black and white, and conifers of all kinds. It's wonderful just walking through the woods. We have a lot of little tiny streams with plenty of fish that no outsiders have ever found, and we have many lakes where a boat has never been.

Porcupine are plentiful up there and they're very good to eat. It's not hard to skin them. There again, it's just in knowing how. There are so many different animals up there, small and large, and I can't think of one that isn't edible.

Not too many years ago I worked watching for fires in a fire tower on the reservation. I worked there for three years and had 169 steps to climb a day. I got to see nature come to life each year. I went up in the spring when there was still snow on the ground and I watched the trees bud. I was alone but there was no possible way to get bored because I had a lot of company. There were birds flying around and I had nosey squirrels that came to visit and looked for a handout. There used to be an eagle come by every day. About five in the evening, he'd swoop by there and say his hello and then fly off into the distance. And I used to watch a mother bear with her cubs. It was quite some distance but I could see the cubs gambolling out there in the field, off the highway, where they couldn't be seen. I really know our land; from the roots of the trees to above the treetops, I know it.

My mother died young and my father was not around, so I was raised by my grandmother. My grandmother was a tough, little old woman, but a good one. She taught me a lot of things, and the first thing she taught me was not to be afraid of the white man. She said, "God gave you a big mouth, and I'm going to teach you how to use it."

She could speak English and understand everything that was said, but when she went outside she spoke our own language. When I was just a little kid I'd act as interpreter when we went to see the agent. She always told me what to say, and I never varied from what she said, because I was more afraid of her than I was of that ugly agent. She was a little toughie, all right. I don't think she ever weighed more than a hundred pounds in her lifetime. I have a picture of her in what she called her Sunday-go-to-meeting-white-people dress. Sometimes she wore her hair in braids down her back, and when she went out, she wore a great big bun on the nape of her neck.

My grandmother had eighteen children, although some of those were multiple births. I don't know how many lived; the only ones I know anything about were my uncle and my mother. She had a great deal of strength. It's surprising how many people she assisted in her lifetime. People used to come to her, telling their stories and crying on her shoulder. She taught many people how to cook and how to do many things.

She died in 1929 when she was ninety-six years old. She used to talk an awful lot about the silver war—the Civil War; she never could say that name. And she used to talk about the black slaves and how many times the Indians hid the slaves from their persecutors. She even spoke about Jesse James. She said, "Jesse James was a good friend to Indian people; when he was around, Indians ate good." She described him like a Robin Hood, where he robbed the rich to help the poor. He could go to any Indian reservation or Indian settlement and find shelter.

My grandmother was a good hunter, a good fisherman, a good gatherer. And she did the most exquisite needlework that you ever saw in your life. She would do a lot of sewing for the government employees 'cause her stitches were always so tight and so perfect. She had a sewing machine but her stitching was better than the machine. She also did cleaning for people and took in laundry from the government employees on the reservation. She was a good woman and knew all about the herbs, the berries, the roots, the barks, and the medicine. She knew what was edible, which was poisonous, so a lot of our food came from the land. We always had rabbits and squirrels to eat. We were poor but we lived good.

I don't know anything that she couldn't do, really. Anything that I see people do today, I think she could have done better. And she was a tough little old lady; I was more afraid of her than I was of some of those government agents, and they were ferocious-looking critters. But she never licked me much. She corrected me but she believed that if you did wrong too often, there was a way to punish without hurting me physically. I would be deprived of something that I really liked, a pleasure, a food. In those days, when I was growing up, the allowance for me was a nickel a week. There were lots of weeks when I didn't have the allowance because she didn't have the money, but when she had the money, she gave it to me. When there was a shortage of money, she would try to make it up in many other little ways.

So when I got my nickel in the rich days, I'd go to the store where a lot of other kids would be buying a bottle of pop or an ice cream and spending their whole nickel for that. I'd look with longing and get, maybe, a lick of an ice cream cone or a sip of somebody's pop, but I never would invest my nickel that way. I would look at the candies that you could get the most of for a penny. Whatever there was ten or more of for a penny, that's what I got. So my nickel went a long ways. I knew that we were very poor, and if I didn't take care of my little bit of change, nobody else would do it.

Today I'm a sucker for kids and a bug on education. My grandmother believed in education and she taught me the importance of it. She always said, "Without education you'll get nowhere. You got to be smart as that man out there in the world so that not only can you live side by side, but make sure that he don't cheat you or rob you." So I didn't have much choice when it came to going to school; I had to go. I remember one time when I was in the day school on the reservation, several of us kids tried to skip school, and every one of us got a good licking for it. I never tried it again.

Later, when I was in boarding school, they tried to break me down, but I never did break. My grandmother taught me too well. She told me, "I'm going to teach you not to be afraid," and she did a pretty good job of it.

I was in a day school at the reservation for awhile, and then the government had a habit of picking up kids and deciding who was going to the mission boarding schools and who was going to the government boarding schools. Parents really didn't have too much choice. First, I was sent to a mission school and my grandmother didn't like it. She felt the devil about it. My grandmother had no transportation and it was far away so I didn't see her often. Even if your parents brought your clothing you might not get a chance to wear it except when they came. You had to wear the school uniform all the time.

My grandmother knew they were going to whitewash us. She knew the methods they employ, and she knew that we were going to have to learn to speak nothing but English because they were not going to let us speak our own language, and they would try to take our religion away. She said, "You have to keep our religion inside of you, in your heart." They wouldn't let us practice our religion because to the government employees, we were just a bunch of pagans, uncivilized savages. So I had to keep within me all that I had learned from her.

We were so homesick at the schools. We'd sit and look out the windows at night and listen to the trains going by and just wish we were on those trains. Sometimes kids got sick from loneliness and were sent home. A lot of them couldn't hack it. Also, a lot of kids ran away. Sometimes they were caught; sometimes they weren't. But if they were caught and brought back they were always punished with severe whippings. Sometimes the boys had their heads shaved. They'd cut all of our hair. None of us had long hair in the government school.

The mission schools and then the government boarding schools were horror stories. At the mission school, which I attended first, we had a certain number of hours a day when we attended classes, and the rest of the time we were put to doing various chores because they were civilizing the savage. We spent an awful lot of our time on our knees in church were we spent hours, it seemed, at prayer. We had to get up awfully early, make our beds and do that work, and then went downstairs to church. After that we went to breakfast and classes.

There were probably some pleasurable things, but I just don't remember too many of the pleasant things. I remember that they did waste an awful lot of Holy Water on me because it seemed like I was getting in trouble all the time. They tried to embarrass us girls or humiliate us if we were committing what they thought a wrongful act. Then the nuns would call the priest who would take us over to the boys' building. Then the priest had the pleasure of pouring Holy Water over our head in front of the entire male student body. Well, that got to be a habit for me. In fact, it was the only way I got to see some of my own relatives and my cousins. It got to be a pleasure. I had a chance to see the boys because the boys and girls were always kept separated.

The boys had to work out in the fields, and the girls had to do a lot of sewing, patching, and mending and had our duties in the laundry. One thing I must give the nuns credit for, they did teach us how to do beautiful needlework, embroidering and crocheting. But, at the time, I couldn't figure out how that was going to serve me in the future. We also had kitchen duties. Some of us wourrd up in the kitchen as clean-up girls and kitchen helpers. Some had the dining rooms and then, of course, there were those who had to clean the buildings, the dormitories, and hallways, the classrooms. But still, we spent too much time on our knees praying, and it seemed like with the smallest infraction we were being punished.

It was not unusual for them to put kerosene on our heads for punishment. If we were caught speaking our language, we had a bar of soap shoved into our mouths. We would get demerits and we weren't allowed to go home during vacation time like other kids if we had broken too many rules. We'd have to work in the fields for them. A lot of the kids spent the year round at the mission school because the priests and the nuns ruled the roost, along with the agent. The idea was to Christianize us and to civilize us, at whatever cost it might have been.

Then they decided to send me to the Bureau of Indian Affairs school across Lake Michigan. I remember we crossed Lake Michigan in one hell of a storm. I thought any minute that the old boat, the freighter or whatever it was we crossed in, was going to go under. The waves were high and that boat was rocking something fierce. Everybody was sick but I didn't get sick because I was just too mean and rebellious and curious, I guess. When we reached the other side of the lake sometime before morning, it was dark and it was raining. I don't remember where they took us but we had to wait in that waiting room for someone to pick us up, and it seemed like hours before we ever got to that school. We looked like a bunch of water-logged ducks.

In the boarding schools, after we were awakened in the morning, we had to make our beds right away, get dressed, then line up for drill. In the wintertime we lined up in the basement of one of the buildings. When the weather was warm we all lined up outside and we had drill, marching, early in the morning before breakfast. Then we'd all be herded into the dining rooms like a bunch of cattle. And there again, like at the mission school, you couldn't talk at the table. You had to remain silent. If you asked for something to be passed you had to ask quietly. It was one of the rules, "silence in the dining room."

In the Catholic schools the nuns read stories from the lives of the saints during our meal, and in the B.I.A. the old witches read something else. It was supposed to be enlightening and an education for us, but I can't recall one instance where it was interesting enough for me to remember. We had classes in the mornings. I remember one time, one of the teachers came in and she said that she was going to tell us a little about communism and that was going to be the end of it. We were not supposed to mention it or even talk about it any more after that time. Karl Marx and whoever were all to go. According to her, they were crazy in the head or something. I couldn't tell what the hell was the use of telling us about it to begin with if we could never talk about it.

After our classes were over in the morning, we had to go to our various duties. Some of us worked in the fields picking grapes, sugar beets; some of us were assigned to the dairy barns; some of us were assigned to the homes of the government employees. And that's where they thought they were going to have a lot of fun with us because we were a bunch of dumb Indian girls. I was twelve but I taught one of the men a lesson that I'm sure if he's still alive, he's never forgotten. His wife wasn't in the house at the time, and he came in from the dairy barn and thought he was going to have some fun with me. He tried to push me into a corner between the door and the refrigerator, but I gave him a good example of what a knee was built for. I had him walking like a camel.

They took his word against mine and figured I was disobedient and unruly. Of course, I was punished, but I never went back to that house to do any more work. For punishment, I had scrubbing duty on my hands and knees, and I had what seemed like miles to do. I had stairways, hallways, and dormitory floors. I had no privileges to go downtown, no recreation privileges at any time. I had to scrub and scrub and clean and clean and clean. I had about three or four months of just scrubbing duty to do, but still I got him away from me.

The government employees that they put into the schools had families but still there were an awful lot of Indian girls turning up pregnant. Because the employees were having a lot of fun, and they would force a girl into a situation, and the girl wouldn't always be believed. Then, because she came up pregnant, she would be sent home in disgrace. Some boy would be blamed for it, never the government employee. He was always scot-free. And no matter what the girl said, she was never believed.

Earlier, in the same household where I taught the man a good lesson, there were two kids walking and one in diapers, and the wife was a loafer and lazy old thing. I not only had to dust and sweep the house and keep it clean, but I had to do all the dishes she piled up all day long and all over the night. And I had to scrub the floors in the house, upstairs and down. I had to clean the basement, I had to wash the walls and the ceilings, do the laundry and the ironing. So I was kept busy all the time.

Of course, by then they had washing machines, but she didn't like washing machines. She claimed they ruined her clothes, so she enjoyed watching me over a scrub board. And she didn't always soak the baby's diapers when the baby soiled them. So I'd have to scrub those darn things till they were white. But there was a turning point. One day I got there and she said, "There are some things in the bathroom in a bucket to be washed, and I want you to get at them right away. Clean them good."

I thought they were diapers so I went and took a look. When I saw what they were I came back out, and I told her, "No. I won't." I flatly refused because they were women's personal laundry. In those days women didn't wear Kotex, they wore pieces of cloth, and she wanted me to wash that bucket full of dirty rags of hers.

I told her, "My grandmother taught me that I should never wash anybody's but my own because there are germs and diseases coming from a woman's body and I should not touch anybody else's personal things like that."

So then I was punished for that. She reported me to the matron. And besides working for her I still had more scrubbing duty after I got through there in the evenings and when I got back to our building for supper.

I've seen them punish kids so bad. I have even seen them wrap girls up in canvas sheets, put them in a bathtub with cold water and let them lay there unable to move and soaking in the cold. That's how mean some of those people were.

The teachers we got were the dregs of society, outcasts from other schools. They weren't allowed to teach the kids of the dominant society; they were either drunks or immoral or they just had a lot of bad habits. They weren't intelligent; they couldn't pass an exam. If they had to take the exams that are required today they could never have made it to first base, much less all the way around to home plate.

I was punished for so many things when I didn't think I was guilty of anything that I thought as long as I was going to get punished, I'd get punished for something worthwhile. There was a bat in our girls' dorm and everyone was screaming, so I got a ladder and I climbed up with a bath towel and caught the bat. Then I saw a nun's bed. She was our supervisor and also head of the laundry. So I took that bat and I shoved it between her sheets. Boy, when she got to bed that night, you talk about unholy screaming! Somebody snitched on me and I got punished, but it was worth it. It was really worth it.

As part of the punishment, they shoved me into the eaves of the dormitory. There was a section there, like a closet, where they stored old linen and furniture. It was dark and there wasn't any standing room, only bending room. I was tucked away in there for a whole day. There were mice and rats in the eaves and I was scared to death. I could hear and feel them moving. The only animal that scares me today is a mouse or a rat, and they will make me vacate a building quicker than anything.

But I got even in various ways with those people who punished me so. It took me a while but I did it. On a May Day one of the matrons who punished me a lot took us along the Chippewa River for an outing. I was relieved of being punished just for that day because everybody was going to go out. She was going to teach us all about the birds and the bees and the flowers and the trees, as if we didn't already know about them. As Indians, we knew all the birds; we knew all the different kinds of bees and wasps, all the different kinds of flowers and plant life. So she wasn't going to teach us anything new, but she was just delighted that she was going to teach these uneducated savages, that she was going to enlighten our minds.

It was a hot, miserable day, and the only nice thing was that there was a slight breeze, and there were a lot of trees out there. The matron was a five-by-five. She was about five feet tall and five feet in any direction you looked at her. She had a habit of wearing very plunging necklines with big ruffles exposing what she had. She had plenty but it wasn't that pretty to look at, and her upper body was full of freckles. She was the ugliest thing. Way back in those days, I thought it was horrible for her to expose herself like that.

She found a rock, just high enough where she could lean back and flop right on to it, no problem because it just fit her perfectly. It must have been built by nature just for her. Then she had one of the girls reach down and pick a flower which happened to be an anemone, and she was going through all the phases of life and different stages of growth and how one plant helped feed another plant. Of course, I was in the back. I didn't want to sit in front of her where I could look at her ugly face, so I moved away with some other kids and found me a shady spot. As I was sitting back there I saw something moving on the ground, a pretty little green snake about twelve inches long. Boy, an idea hit me in the head! I reached down and grabbed that poor little critter and I put him in my pocket. The girls who were sitting with me there knew I was up to something but they didn't know just what.

Because it was so hot, the matron kept pulling her blouse away from her body, both back and in front, opening it up and getting air. Finally, she reached the proper stage for me. She was holding her blouse open in the back, so I just snuck up there and dropped the snake down her back. Somebody snitched on me again and I had some more floors to scrub and more stairwells to clean. But that time I didn't mind scrubbing; it was worth it. I finally got even with the old witch.

She wasn't immune to using the whip on us, or she would have us drill for hours at a time. We had to get out and drill in the mornings no matter how cold it was. A lot of those kids were little, bitty things, first and second graders who had been removed from their homes and put in these schools. They didn't even know what it was all about, and those poor little fellows were freezing out there, both girls and boys.

See, we weren't considered human; we were just savages, and because we were still in an uncivilized state they thought they could do as they pleased and get by with it. All our mail was read. If we wrote a letter home it was read by the matron before it went out, so any complaints we had never reached the outside. And any mail we got from home was censored. If we received a package from home, they went through it first, just like a prison. That's why I'm bitter in so many ways.

Somehow the years passed and I left school. There wasn't much of anything to do on the reservation but work in the government homes as somebody's housekeeper. If you were a man, you could work in the woods or the mill, but there was nothing really for women to do. Finally, you got married and all of a sudden, you decide to leave and explore the outside world. Once I got out here I found out it was a competitive world, a rat race, really a dog-eat-dog world. They say only the strong shall survive in the animal world; I think it's the same in the human world. You've got to learn how to exist with the animal on two legs out here.

I had a dream when I was young. It was my grandmother's for me too, but we never could accomplish it. It was my going to college. At that time, Indians were lucky to get into and out of high school. Colleges were remote and few and far between, but all my life I wanted to go. Finally, I made the dream come true. In 1974 I became a full-time student and I graduated May of 1978. By then I had my kids, my grandchildren, and my great-grandchildren.

While I was still a young woman I had five children, four who are still alive. During that time my grandmother died. It took her just three days to leave us. She had ached off and on but not of any serious consequences. However, she had always talked about what needed to be done in the event of her demise. She had her grave clothes, as she called them, in a trunk. Still, her death was quite a shock and it took some adjusting. But I always remember her saying, "What has to be done must be done," and the fact that when relatives would die, she was always so strong-willed and not one to shed a great deal of tears. So I tried to act as she would expect me to.

After her death, the Depression came, and I was a single parent and caring for my children and working in Milwaukee where I got thirty-two cents an hour in a dress factory. With those wages, it was hard to get along with five children. I went to visit a snake show in a circus, and they had an opening for a performer and the pay was good. Like I said, I had learned to handle snakes from my grandmother. When we were picking strawberries, she taught me how to pick berries with the snake coiled on the plants. Then, when I was still very young, she taught me how to pick snakes up and handle them. She taught me much so I wouldn't be afraid of animals that girls are usually afraid of. Snakes are trustworthy. They're more safe than most men.

The offer with the circus was so good that I couldn't turn it down. It was better than I was getting with two jobs in Milwaukee. The kids weren't really too excited about it. It was too foreign to them at the beginning. Later on they adjusted. We always traveled from place to place. Nowadays, the circus is nothing to people. With TV the excitement and thrill to the kids isn't there. But the performances in a circus take skill and an awful lot of practice.

I bought my snakes from an importer in New York. I'd get them green and I'd do my own breaking. That way they're accustomed to me and my voice and my hands. I don't like to get a snake that somebody else has been working with because there is a conflict. Today, I've only got one little one, about six foot long.

I was in show business for twenty-three years. I handled snakes and I lectured. I made my living talking, using that big mouth my grandmother told me I had. I took my kids with me out on the road and raised them there, and they got a darn good education. They all went on for higher education and are doing real well.

I taught the kids when we traveled. They would have much preferred regular school because Mama was too tough a teacher but they had me. In between shows, out came the books and the blackboard and it was time for classes and lessons. I worked with the board of education in Chicago, and they used to send me the framework of the lessons the kids had to do.

Then a grandchild became involved and other people in the show were watching and decided they would like to have their kids learn. So, where I had just four or five to begin with, I went up to forty-three students, from kindergarten through college level. A lot of the adults were getting into my classes there to take what they call refresher courses.

I taught under the circus tent. They sure did learn an awful lot of geography! They got their basic three R's and learned much about human relations. Every now and then I run into someone who remembers that I taught them their ABC's. They'll say, "Don't you remember me? I was in such and such a show and you taught me." It was just something that had to be done and my kids needed an education. Since I never had a chance to go to college, I was going to prepare them for it.

As time went on, I was not only a participant in the show, but we owned our own unit, a sideshow. So I was not only the booking agent, but I was a bookkeeper, a manager, a porter, a teacher, and a housemaker, constantly on the move. We had to worry about those gas stamps during the rationing, trying to determine our itinerary for the next six months so that we'd have the right number of stamps to cover our gas and the right amount of food stamps. Money was short at times, but I enjoyed that life very much.

I also worked in the big show. I was a trapeze flier for a while. It wasn't really scary because I used to climb a lot of trees when I was a kid. It's just a matter of coordination, of being able to time yourself. I didn't do a great deal of that, but I could pinch-hit if there was a shortage of people in the big top. I also was a dancer and I used to do a lot of singing. And I worked with the animals. To me my favorite animals were snakes and elephants.

We used to have a nosey camel in the show. I made the mistake one time of feeding this critter some candy. He watched when I went to our trailer, and he made a practice of coming over there every day. If I happened to have the window open and I was sitting at the table doing my bookwork, all of a sudden I'd have his head shoved through the window. He would push my hair and nibble on the back of my neck or my pug. I used to wear a big pug in those days. Then I knew that I better get out the lemon drops 'cause this camel loved lemon drops. So I'd keep a big bag of them for him.

My kids did their part, too. Some of them rode horses or other animals. They were always part of things. My youngest son was drinking coffee pretty heavily by the time he was three and a half years old. After the show was over, we'd walk around, and we'd go to what we called the grease joint, that was the hamburger stand on the show. All carnivals and all circuses have what they call a grease joint. People would go get their after-work snack there. I used to get a cup of coffee, and my son would sit next to me with his chocolate milk. He'd take a sip of my coffee, and he began to like it so I got him coffee too. He even got so he drank it black, and the people on the show used to be amazed at how much coffee that little fellow could consume. They'd say to him, "Come on, I'll buy you a cup," just to see that little bitty kid drink a cup of black coffee.

It was good for the kids to be a part of the circus, and I think it gives the kids a brighter outlook on life and teaches them that they are not the only ones in the world, that there are other people out there. When you're working on a show, you're separate from the rest of the world, and you've got to conduct yourself in such a fashion that you don't bring disgrace. People automatically believe that those who work with shows, circuses, carnivals, any kind of show, have low morals, but they don't. Rules are very strict on shows, and if anybody gets loose, it's not the fault of the management. Most of the shows are family affairs.

The circus community and the carnival community are different than living in a neighborhood. Because you're living together, you're working together, you're traveling together. For so many months out of the year, you're in constant contact with each other, so you learn how to coexist so there'll be harmony. We try to weed out the troublemakers, try to avoid any problems that they might create. It's being on the alert, being cautious, and being sensitive to the other person's needs. That's very important. Out there you don't go and slam the door shut because you have to go outside in the next few minutes for the next act.

Of course, the hardest part was getting up and loading for the next move. We lived in a trailer and a car, but we got used to it all. I've traveled everywhere. I haven't been to Japan or Russia or India, but that's about the only places I haven't been. I'd say, I've had a chance to bum around a little bit.

The only time I really noticed any tension in circus life was during storms. Storms can be very frightening under canvas, not so much for yourself, but you worry about that audience out there. Hopefully, the wind won't blow hard enough to knock the tent down or cause a pole to fall.

Also, during a storm I used to worry if a lot of animals were performing, say the cats, the lions and tigers. I used to worry about a sudden burst or crash of thunder that would be so powerful it would frighten them and would cause them to jump out of those high cages. When the cats are in their own cages, they're very secure, but the thought was always there if there was a little bit of wind. I used to worry about what would happen if those animals ever got loose.

The other thing that used to worry me a lot was fire. What if somebody carelessly threw a cigarette down where the grass was dry or they threw it against the canvas and it went up in smoke? All the canvas was treated to be waterproof, but it was a waxy solution which would be horrifying in case of fire. So I used to worry about it, especially if I knew somebody in the audience was drinking. On weekends you get a lot of drunks. Other than that, there was no tension.

My kids still talk about their life in the circus. Every so often they get together, and they have a rap session about all the different places we've been and the different kinds of people we've known. I lost one son. He'd been in the service and was injured and came back to the states. He had four children and was out buying tires for us when there was a holdup and he was shot. He died and it was hard to deal with the pain.

Along with being in show business, I've been involved in tribal politics since the early thirties. Because of that I did a lot of research about problems for Indians. I was the first woman in our tribe to ever represent them in Washington as an official delegate. I am a registered lobbyist for the federal House and the Senate. Since then the doors have opened, and other women are in there now.

The senators and congressmen paid attention to me. I don't know whether it was tolerance or shock. But, after a while, it got to be respect because I had always done my homework before I went into those offices. And I learned that many ways to a congressman or senator's heart is by observation. When I would walk in the door of their office, I would look around and would try to find something there that would tell me what his hobby or his personal delight was. It might only be a pine cone or rocks displayed. I would comment on those items so that he would rise his eyebrows and open his ears, and we would have a common ground to stand on.

It was always quite a shock to them when they found out a woman was there instead of all males. During the time I was there I never allowed the men to even carry my briefcase. I carried my own weight and when we got through in the evening, we used to go to my room where I'd type up and get material organized for the next day's meeting.

I used to know every foot of those halls in the Capitol. I would carry a big purse with a pair of mocassins in it. So it was not unusual for people to see me stop in the hallway and take off my high-heeled shoes and get into my mocassins. That way I'd make better time going down the halls. Those marble and tile floors are killers.

They had a little chapel there, for all denominations, and every once in a while I'd go in and just sit there and relax and pray. If a bill came up that we were really interested in or something very serious, I'd stop in there and ask for help from the Creator. I'd ask the Creator to guide my feet and especially put the right words in my mouth. I'd also ask that I wouldn't flip my lid or blow my stack. I'd ask him to help me keep my temper and help me be a pacifist instead of a militant so we'd be more successful.

There are a lot of people I know through politics, and I've also been with a lot of people because of my religion. My present husband, Wallace, is a leader in the Indian religion we have, the Big Drum. We travel an awful lot and we visit prisons too because of the Indian inmates who are there. We conduct services for them and then we have visitation with them. They give us three or four hours instead of half an hour or forty-five minutes to be with the prisoners. It means a lot to the prisoners and they look forward to it. We get a great deal of response from them.

We don't talk much about our religion, and the reason is that in the translation, it gets distorted. Sometimes the meaning is lost. It's really hard to speak about it in depth, to explain it so that if it's written on a piece of paper people could understand it. When there's the written word people immediately begin to imagine things other than what is down there because they don't have that in-depth perception; they have illusion. Very rarely do we invite outsiders into our services, because unless we have known them a long time, we know that they aren't going to understand.

My children and grandchildren already have knowledge of it. My grandchild, just six years old, knows what it's all about. He knows that when it's time for the Big Drum services, it's time for silence and careful listening and praying and singing, and, for the men and boys, it means dancing, but not the type of dancing that you see out in these fun powwows. It's a different type altogether. These are prayer dances.

I have great-grandchildren who I hope will be able to pick it up too. I've been doing a little bit of writing, as I think about it, trying to recall the stories. I give them to my son up north so he and his wife can take care of them. They are the stories I recall, the creation stories, the legends, the myths as white society calls them. Some might be just humorous stories, and humorous stories told in our language are really funny. But if you try to translate them into English, they're the driest damn things. There is no way to describe the meaning in English because with the gestures, the tone of voice, and the words we use, we just don't know how to put them in the right sequence in English. But when the old folks get together and start telling stories, they have all of us rocking with laughter. It means a lot to me that I can carry down what I learned from my grandmother to my grandchildren and my great-grandchildren.

My husband and I were talking a short time ago about the possibility that someday we could have a small classroom where he could teach the language and legends, and while he was doing that, in another classroom, I could teach our Indian history. Wallace also teaches Indian crafts of all kinds. Wallace and I share a great deal. We like nothing better on a weekend than to go hunting or fishing or just walk through the woods together. The land means much to both of us.

I work now recruiting Indian students for the University of Wisconsin here in Milwaukee. But I do a lot more with the students than just recruit them. The students come in to me when they have problems, and they know that I have big ears and wide shoulders and they can talk and I'll listen. I have a variety of students come in here, not only Indians. A lot of times, students don't want to talk to advisors of their own age. They would rather talk to an older person. By listening and understanding, I can help a student talk himself out of a problem. And I try to help teachers throughout the city. People will call me and ask me questions. I also do a lot of public speaking. I'm on the Commission on Human Relations and on the Commission on Aging. You have to study your audience before you open your big trap. I learned very early not to be scared in front of groups.

Sometimes it's uncomfortable to be the first Indian or the first woman in a group. Because all of a sudden, you're considered a Wonder Woman, but they don't realize that you first have to learn all the steps that go along with the group. You've got to learn the rules and the ropes.

I've been alone many times on different things, and I have to make others respect me. Sometimes I have to fight alone for an issue, but, there again, it requires me to do a lot of homework so that I know when I open my mouth the words coming out are the right ones. I need to know that the others will understand what I'm saying and so that I know what I'm talking about.

I also care about the young Indian leaders that are developing. Dennis Banks and I are friends. We don't see each other much but each of us understands the other. He understands the role that he has to play as a rising leader, and I understand mine as an elder. He hasn't reached the stage of being an elder yet but he will in time. The understanding that I helped somewhere along the line gives me a good feeling, and if I can continue to help, I'll even feel better.

But I always remember my relationship to the land. My term at the University of Wisconsin expires in February, which coincides with the time that sugarbush opens. Sugarbush is the tapping of trees to get maple sugar. At that time I'm going to go to the woods for at least six weeks to take care of the maple trees. That will give me a good breather.

It will be good to have a rest. I get very involved with the problems of Indians today. Registration and enrollment of Indians in universities and high schools has dropped considerably in the last few years. A lot of that is due to the attitudes in the high schools themselves. They aren't giving the Indian students any incentive to continue. The students are being constantly harassed, and a lot of times they don't know if they're going to graduate until maybe a week or two before graduation. That way, they can't register or apply for college because they don't know until almost too late. And some high schools make no bones about telling the Indians that when you're sixteen you don't have to go back to school. It is discouraging because when I go home I see those things happening and the kids tell me about it. Maybe the people are afraid that if the Indian kids get too well educated they might try to take this land back. We don't want it after all the damage that has been done to it. All we want is the part that's undamaged and that belongs to us.

Right now we're trying to deal with a mining problem in terms of our reservation. Exxon apparently found a large deposit of copper up in the Crandon area. It's right next to the Potawatomi Reservation, right next to the Mole Lake Reservation, and very close to the Menominee Reservation. We feel that the tailings and waste could hurt the rice beds that we depend on and could hurt the water, as well as making big, ugly holes in the ground. We are also really worried about the drugs and drinking that comes along with the influx of people connected with mining. We just don't want a mining town there.

We've had meetings and conferences, trying to block Exxon with proposals and resolutions that are being submitted to the government through the proper channels. We want to prevent them from digging out their first shovelful of dirt. We've watched what's happened in the other parts of the country with mines. We don't want our place stripped out and our water destroyed like with the Navajos. The same things apply in Montana and Wyoming, parts of Idaho, Utah, and the Dakotas. We don't need that situation here. But the problem is that Exxon has so much money and we're just so few. They have so many lawyers to employ that we might be exhausted before we can beat them, but at least we'll try.

It's similar to what is happening with the Sioux in the Dakotas now. The government has found that their land has oil, uranium, copper, and many other minerals under it, and the government now wants to start mining those areas. They are trying to make the Sioux allow them to do it, but all Indians regard the earth as their mother, and you don't cut out your mother's heart. So the Sioux are raising hell, and they have refused the government's offer of money time and again, and the courts just keep on saying that they must take this money. I don't know what the final outcome will be, but the courts tend to close their ears to Indians and their problems.

There are many problems for the Menominee today. Employment is a terrific problem. Although we own our own mills and control them ourselves, there isn't enough work there to employ the entire population. Therefore many of the people have to commute. They work in the cities and come home on the weekend. They might have to drive to Chicago or Gary, Indiana, to work because there isn't enough industry on our reservation to support the entire population. Also, alcohol is a big problem, and there has been a sudden influx of drugs among the young. There are many problems to deal with.

I've worked on those problems and tried to preserve our history. So personally I'd say I've had a good life, a full life. I don't have any regrets. The only problem I'd say is that I've always had that nose problem. I'm snooping and looking for something else to get into. I was always curious and still have an insatiable curiosity for what life has to offer, the things to be learned. Because life is fun but you have to make it that way. If you think that life is a drag, it will be. You have to have enough curiosity to get out from under the shadows and find out what's cooking. I want to be involved with life; I can't see no reason yet for dying.

But it is hard sometimes, when I think of how Indians have been treated and remember experiences like at the boarding schools, to not let bitterness come through. When that happens, I think about my children, my grandchildren, the effect that it's going to have on them if I allow my bitterness to overcome my willingness to work. If I would become so bitter that I couldn't function properly, it would cause injury to my kids and my grandkids. So I think of future generations and work towards their benefit. We've had our day, they've yet to get theirs. We've enjoyed our land, our heritage; we want to preserve it so they can enjoy them, too. So I bottle up the bitterness and do a lot of praying. I ask that man upstairs to give me strength and courage and allow me to work hand in hand with other people, to fight the situation no matter what the odds are or how long it might take. I'm sure many other Indians would say the same.

And my grandmother taught me an important lesson about all forms of grief and not letting it hurt you too much. She taught it to me with a story, a different story that I've never heard anybody else tell. There's a lot of wisdom in it about learning how to cope.

She believed that tears wasted weren't good. She said, "In a person's lifetime, each one is given so many tears to shed and if you shed them too soon, when it comes time of real need, you won't have any left, and the hurt will be too deep because your eyes won't spill them out.

"According to the old legends, there are little containers, like pint jars, and there was created a storehouse of these jars, one for everybody in the universe. Each jar is a container for just one person's tears, and when that jar is filled to capacity so it will contain no more, the Creator puts a lid on it and your tear ducts dry out. Then, when you really need to cry, the solace that you get from shedding a few tears won't be there. It's harder to have a dry cry than a wet one, and the hurt will be too deep."

Then she would say, "Let the children cry because there's an allowance in the jar for children to cry, but once you reach an age of semimaturity, then you have to learn how to control all these things and not waste all the tears that are given to you." My grandmother taught me many good lessons. I remember them and try to share them with those coming after me.

*I couldn't do for all of them. I don't
hardly ever remember reading to them. I
did encourage them to read to each other.
And I know a lot of times, when the kids
needed a hug or affection, I was too wiped
out to give it, even a small gesture. And I
think back on all the things, the
deprivation. When people say, "I'd like
another child but we can't afford one," I'd
say, "Forget that. It isn't the money. You
just can't stretch yourself."*

—Lee

I stayed with Lee for some time one summer in her small duplex, part of the public projects for low-income people in a town in northern New Mexico. It was a time of peace for me as we drank iced tea and talked for hours. We had no transportation for reaching the nearby mountains, but the gigantic and changing western sky was our continual companion, giving us bright warmth and sunshine in the morning, brief tumultuous thundershowers in the afternoon, and long evenings of deepening dusk which were accented by the sounds of children playing. Through those long, gentle hours, Lee told me her story.

Lee is a heavy, sensuous Anglo woman in her early fifties, of medium height, with quiet and tolerant blue eyes and arched eyebrows. She has an attractive face with high cheekbones and fair skin. Her blond and gray hair is short and stylishly curled and she often dresses in draped blouses and pants. She has the strong air of sexual attractiveness, despite her size. During the years that I have known Lee, I have seen numerous people turn to her for help and comfort and have heard her respond with a wisdom based on her intimate understanding of the struggles of life and a belief in the renewing possibilities of hope.

Her two-bedroom unit was crowded and cluttered by the mementos and possessions of her six children. She had a number of drawings, prints, and embroideries on the wall, and her house was filled with green plants. Her nineteen-year-old daughter Lynn watched television frequently; the living room's focus was the TV set. The housing project's managers were slow to make repairs, and for many months she had to get hot water from the bathroom sink. Lee had recently finished both her work as a counselor in a community crisis center and her education, after years of attending the university part time. Her time of child rearing was nearly over. That summer she was slowly clearing away the accumulated possessions of a lifetime and preparing to move to another New Mexican city where she would look for work.

When I next visited her in New Mexico, she had moved to that other community, a small city with Hispanic, Native American, and Anglo populations. The plaza was crowded in the summer, with tall trees and white benches; the high blue-gray mountains stood in the background. The winding streets were narrow and crowded and were bordered by log and adobe fences with arches over the gates. Bright red strings of chilies hung on adobe homes, and green aspen and cacti gave the yards touches of life.

Lee had raised her children in that mountainous area, living in a rural and sometimes harsh impoverished county, where grass often grew on the flat adobe roofs and animals grazed, running nearly free through the rural villages and towns. Few government social services were available to the residents, and families aided each other and handled their own needs as best they could; Lee struggled without real assistance as she raised her large family in this setting.

Lee is now head of a program for parents with problems, primarily child abuse, and works mostly with mothers of young children. The program she runs was formerly part of a national program for child abusers, fashioned after the Alcoholics Anonymous model; because of funding requirements, the program had to break off and operate on its own. Lee works extensively with these women, taking calls at any time of the night, meeting with women individually, searching out the social services that they need, and running groups in which the members help each other. These people, in turn, respond warmly to her intense acceptance, empathy, and care. Lee's name, the names of her children, and some other details have been changed to protect the privacy of her family.

Lee   I never played with girls as I grew, only with boys, and I just grew up knowing any girl that hangs around boys like I did has to be twice as capable as they are in order to con membership. I honestly thought I was just as strong as anybody, and if I wasn't as strong, I was tricky. One way or the other I had the knowledge that I could do anything I really wanted to do. I could climb trees or ride horses bareback, faster than most of the kids, and I would do almost anything on a dare.

One Halloween night, the three boys I was with dared me to go into the back of a dark cave and leave confetti in there to prove I was in the back. It was an old coal test place where miners dug in to see about coal, and we played in there off and on. The boys searched me for matches before I went in, and it was scary because it did have bats and they made noises. It was really narrow and I had to slide through on my belly, and later I could stand up half way. At the end there was like a room with a ledge where we put candles, and there were a couple of gunnysacks full of pine needles to sit on. It was a place we went when we were feeling particularly Huckleberry Finnish, but that one Halloween they dared me to go to the back.

Then, when I came back out, the boys had gotten scared out there waiting for me and left. I thought they were out there hiding and were going to scare me, but I called to them and got no answer, and finally I got mad and just went on home. They told me the next day that they had heard something and got scared. But life was like that for me.

I was born in the southern part of New Mexico in Ruidoso. The town was up in the pines in the mountains and was mostly just a main street that followed the river. There was a meadow on one side of the river with a lot of Indian arrowheads and shards and the biggest grasshoppers in the world. I used to go catch grasshoppers and find arrowheads, and my cousin Bob and I would wander around by ourselves.

I was an only child until about seven and a half and then had a sister. My father was a carpenter and my mother had planned to be a nurse until she stopped and got married. I think my father must have really wanted a son because I was quite a tomboy and grew up as his only son. I helped him dig and move rocks instead of learning how to cook and sew. We had a large family, uncles and aunts and a grandmother and great aunt, with houses right next to each other and big, traditional holiday dinners with everybody there.

My cousin Bob was two years younger than I was and we were inseparable. He was an illegitimate child and apparently not taken care of much, and he sort of thought of my dad and mom as his as much as any. It had been really strange because the family didn't know his mother was pregnant. One day, when she was seventeen or eighteen, she disappeared early in the morning, and later my dad was sent out to look for her. He finally found her passed out in an outside toilet that was near one of the summer cabins that wasn't used often. The baby was also there. Nobody ever bothered to tell the girl much and maybe she didn't know herself. Mostly her family just ignored her.

My parents took care of the baby until he was well enough to get along. He was a rough, tough little kid. He ran around without coats in the winter and hardly ever got sick, and he and I grew up together. It was almost like two boys because we used to go to the river and fish with our hands and churn the fish over a little fire and try to eat it. We just grew up like little wild things. My parents expected me to be on the premises by nightfall, but that was about it. We played cowboys and Indians with the other kids in the neighborhood, and we never played with girls at all; they were really something to be scorned. But he was allowed to cuss and have good tantrums that I wasn't allowed to have.

I read a lot. My mother always provided books and she would tell stories about Huckleberry Finn. The river in our town was much too small for a raft; it was rocky and was just a stream, but we'd pretend rafts and imagine running away. One time I got tied up on an Indian raid and left there, and I was too stubborn to call for help, so I was there past suppertime and my mother found me and brought me in.

I was always tearing up my clothes, and my mother was always tearing me up about that. I think she would have liked to have a daughter. It wasn't until my sister Barbara was born that she had a daughter. Barbara had long curls and was pretty feminine. That way mother had the daughter to play with and daddy had the son and everything was all right.

As I became a teenager a real struggle for me began. I was really having a hard time switching from a tomboy to a girl. I had been such a sorry-going boy that it was really hard. I thought girls were all dumb and pretended they were afraid of bugs. I looked upon females as being fake and phoney, and it was kind of hard to learn to be one when you feel that way about it. None of the boys I grew up with took me seriously as a girl and would ask me for dates because I had whipped them all sometime in our lives. We just had that other relationship and it was stronger.

In my secret fantasies, I was feeling very romantic. I wrote poetry and I dreamed about the old knight in shining armor, but I would have never admitted that to anybody I knew. I was just incredibly awkward. I could wear girls' clothes and look all right, but I would feel awkward and there were times when I'd be very hurt and embarrassed and humiliated because I would meet somebody that I would really like to impress and I didn't know how.

There was a lot of loneliness when the boys were first getting into dating. Then they got to where they were asking for my advice, and I became sort of an in-between, not a boy or a girl, kind of a neuter. I guess I had to go through that stage before I could move into being a girl. I often think that it was real good to be a tomboy and learn to be independent and that my potentials were as good as males, but trying to make that transition seemed like it was entirely different and twice as hard as for other people who just had to learn the rules for one sex role while going through puberty.

Many times I'd be so frustrated because I'd try to do something feminine, and I'd feel foolish while I was doing it, but I'd still be stubborn enough to try to do it, and then I'd get laughed at and I would get furious. When I did date, I dated outsiders that were in town for the summer or soldiers that were there for the weekend, because they didn't know me as a tomboy so much.

I had got a horse when I was eleven. I set pins in the bowling alley for money and paid seventy-five dollars for the horse. I used to ride it bareback all the time. I didn't have a saddle and didn't want one, and I roared around the mountains and the hills on that horse, full-tailed running and bareback. I would get sunburned and my dark hair would get matted, and my pants legs would be covered with hair from the horse sweating and shedding on me.

At that time I did have this girlfriend Marilyn, and there was a guy we did things with named Dale, who the other guys considered a sissy because he wouldn't play football. Dale's dad owned a place where they had square dances, and he would take Marilyn and me to the dance. We were sort of the Three Musketeers more than anything else. I would get home Saturday night in the evening from riding all day and I would be all sunburned, and I'd jump in the bathtub and get dressed and wear my black dress with a gore skirt and some jewelry. My hair would still be wet from the shampoo but it was naturally curly, so by the time I would get to the dance it would be nearly dry. Then sometimes we would meet people that had seen me during the day riding horseback, and they would ask, "Who's that crazy woman, that crazy girl that I saw who rode like an Indian?" Then we'd tell them all sorts of stories about that strange girl, that she was wild and lived alone out in a shack, a bunch of crazy stories. And Dale used to get a big kick out of those stories we would tell.

Marilyn danced but I didn't know how and felt so silly about it, but Dale was an exhibition dancer and he was determined to make me learn to dance and finally told me he wouldn't take me anymore unless I started dancing, so I had to learn. Then he'd get me in some of those wild polkas where we'd be going around and around. People would clear the floor and watch us and then clap afterwards, and I wished the floor would open up and swallow me.

I was still stubborn during that time, and sometimes it would get me in some hard places. I used to be afraid of the dark when I was a kid, but I bluffed that for so many years that now I enjoy the dark really. Back in those years I walked my girlfriend home in the canyon in Ruidoso. She lived quite a way out and it was late at night. Also, I was pretending to be tough as usual. Walking back I heard footsteps behind me. They may have been echoes; I was never sure. I'd walk faster and I'd walk slower and I'd stop walking, trying to decide. It was a long ways; it must have been a mile and a half up through the pines. Finally, I gave way to fear and ran all the way through town; I didn't turn off to my house at all. I was panicked and just kept running.

That taught me something and now when I hear noises outside that are frightening, I'll get up and go check them rather than stay awake all night and let them build up in my mind. Something funny happened in Taos that way. There was a noise outside the bedroom window, and I went out the door on the other side and crept around the house and just ran face to face into a cow that loomed up out of the black. But now I always check out noises if they have any capability of making me uneasy.

I worked as a cashier in a movie theater back when I was a girl, and once when I was fifteen or sixteen, a soldier offered to walk me home. It was a full moon and beautiful, and it must have been a romantic movie because I was out of my head. I suggested we walk down by the river in the moonlight, which he took to be two or three other things.

We sat down in the grass by the river, and suddenly I was flat on my back in the grass and couldn't move. I had never thought of our walk that way, and I was so astonished that I didn't have any power. I was helpless and that threw me for a minute. His shoulder was across my face, and I told him, "Let me go or I'll bite you." He either ignored me or didn't hear me, and I bit clear through to the bone. I'm surprised he didn't beat me to a pulp. I guess the shock of it protected me. Even then I was ridiculously stubborn. I wouldn't run. I got up and straightened my clothes and I marched straight home. I wasn't about to run.

The next night at the theater this soldier was walking around the box office looking at me from all angles; you know how those glassed-in cages are. He kept hanging around and watching me until he finally made me nervous. I asked him, "What's wrong with you? Do you want to go to the show or not?"

He said, "Is your name Lee?"

"Yes, it is."

"You're the one that wounded one of my boys."

"What are you talking about?"

He said, "You bit Private so-and-so." I was so embarrassed I could have died. This man was the medic and had treated the guy I bit.

I said, "Well, I warned him that I was going to bite him, and he didn't let me go so I bit him." I got very defensive about that.

Then the guy that I bit came in two or three nights later. It was after the box office had closed, and I was in the lobby just standing by the curtains watching the show. He was mad and said, "Come here."

"Why?"

"I want to show you something." And he unfastened his shirt and pulled it back, and it nearly made me throw up. The bite was just black and blue and green and yellow and just horrible with all these teeth marks. It was really bad.

I told him, "I'm really sorry, but I told you I was going to if you didn't let me go," and he just walked off. I really felt sick, pale and weak because it was hideous. But it was just done in panic because I had never been helpless before and that was the only way out.

I had worked with my dad and learned to drive my dad's truck with a two-speed axle, and I hauled lumber to the jobs sometimes. And I would dig those little ditches to put pipes in. I earned money working for him instead of getting an allowance for doing the housework and I liked it a lot better. I never really formally learned from mother. She tried periodically to teach me to sew and to cook, but lots of the time there was so much pain between us. But in later years, I'd shut my eyes and remember what bowls she used to mix meat loaf and remember her cracking eggs in it. If I could think back carefully and quietly I could usually put it together and do the things she'd done.

For all the freedom I had, there were times when my parents were hard on me. My father's hands were calloused from his work as a carpenter and he spanked me, and when he spanked me hard it felt like a two-by-four, but I don't think I was really physically abused. But now I realize that mother did verbally abuse me throughout my childhood and that hurt so deeply. She was an energetic, feisty woman and I was different from her, and she always said I was inept, I was lazy, I would never be able to do anything, and, on some level, I always believed her. When a child learns that from the beginning she just thinks it is part of her life, like, "The grass is green, the sky is blue, and I'm no good, and that's the way life is." It hurt and stayed with me all my life.

There were problems between my parents. I believe my mother was very frozen. She couldn't show affection as much as she would have liked to. I know she was a warm, passionate woman, but she was uncomfortable showing affection to her kids, even to my dad. She was always pleased when he'd give her a hug, but she'd say, "Oh, come on now, I've got to get dinner." But she wouldn't say that she was pleased. She just wasn't able to express those things.

My father and mother got divorced when I was about thirteen.

My dad had gone into the service, and when he came back, Mother had fallen in love with someone else, so my parents divorced. And at that time I felt like I was divorced from both of my parents and both sets of relatives and that I didn't have anyone.

Mother sued for custody of both of us, but I refused to go with her and there was a custody hearing. It was a mess and I wound up staying with my dad because I insisted that if she took me, I would just keep running away until she got tired of coming after me. It was probably hard on her because she was already cast in the role of the bad ugly anyway because my dad was in the service and she had not waited for him.

My dad and I lived alone together for a year or two before he married again. He had started contracting; he had talked it over with me and said that he was going to put all his money from the house and everything into a shop to do woodworking. It was going to be a big gamble and we might lose, or he said, "You might become the daughter of a contractor."

I said, "Let's try it." Mother had always kind of slowed him down because she was cautious with money and very fearful of taking chances. So he built a shop that had a little bedroom for me and a little kitchen and living room; he slept in the living room.

Then he met another woman and talked that marriage over with me too. He said, "I know you don't care much for Jane, but I'm thinking of marrying her; we love each other." I didn't like her but I was always making noble gestures and kicking myself later. So I told him that soon I would be out of school, and I would be going about my life, and he needed somebody for his life, and it had nothing to do with me, really. If that was who he loved and who he wanted to be with, then he should go ahead and marry her. I didn't realize how much longer I was going to have to be there and put up with her. It turned out pretty bad; she was very insecure. She had been married three or four times and had two children and was determined to make a lady out of me.

When I was in high school, I had a real hard time with my father once. I stayed out real late one night because I was afraid of seeing some people my stepmother had brought to our house. My father went out looking for me, and when I found out he was looking that scared me even more. So I hid out at my girlfriend's, and when he knocked at her place, she told him I wasn't there. About seven-thirty in the morning, he came back and said, "This is the only place she can be. Will you tell her to come out?"

And I gave up then. He used a belt on me and it wasn't like him. It was a terrible beating; I've never had a beating like that before, and it was partly because of my stepmother being on him all night and his worry and everything. But he really belted me and cut up my back quite a bit. I went to my room and I wouldn't let anybody in except my stepsister that lived in the room upstairs with me. She went down and got Vicks to put on my back.

My dad was very stubborn, but a day or so later, he finally came up and tried to apologize. I was so grateful to him for doing that, but he said, "I'm sorry I had to do it." Then it just dawned on me that he wasn't apologizing, he was just sharing his guilt in a way, and it sounded like words from Jane.

I said, "I wanted to hear what you had to say, but I don't want to hear what Jane put you up to saying." That shamed him and embarrassed him again and he went away. I stayed up there three or four days without ever coming down at all. The whole thing was unfair. Always before I'd accepted punishment from him because I thought it was fair, but that one wasn't fair and it made me angry.

Their whole divorce really was a mess. I was so sure that Mother was 100 percent wrong and Dad was totally right and I really missed my sister. Then my mother and sister and the man my mother was with moved to Pecos, a little village in northern New Mexico. I had chosen my dad, and, in a sense, I kind of lost him, and in the meantime I had alienated my mother. I really was nasty to my mother. When I sent her a gift or anything I'd send it to Helen instead of calling her Mother. And I just did things like that to hurt her on purpose.

The divorce was when I was thirteen, and suddenly, when I was seventeen, I don't know why, I've never been able to figure out what triggered it, but suddenly I understood that it was not all her fault. Just out of nowhere, the idea hit me that Mother hadn't been totally to blame, that it takes two people. I thought a lot of it out and realized that Daddy had been pretty headstrong about going into the service. He wouldn't have ever been drafted, but he was married at nineteen and had never done anything much, and that was his last fling at some adventure. He knew that with the allotment he could support us even though he was in the service and he took off. But he left Mother with a pregnant cow she was scared to death of, and when it gave birth the calf died and then the cow died. Mother had to have help from the neighbor man to bury them, and then the neighbor was the one that moved in on things. But Dad was really to blame for running off and playing soldier when he didn't have to. It wasn't excessive patriotism as much as it was a last chance to be adventurous.

So I wrote Mother a letter and told her how wrong I'd been,

and she invited me for Christmas and I went. It must have been just a total astonishing thing for her because I had bent over backwards for a couple of years being really rotten to her. When I came up to Pecos for Christmas, things were bad. My mother was going blind and later on I found out her new husband had left her. She was selling furniture just to keep them in food. I was having so much trouble living with Jane that I got dramatic and decided I was going to give up school and go take care of my poor blind mother. Mother insisted that I wasn't going to give up school, so then I went to school there and graduated from Pecos.

Mother's sight improved some and she was such a strong person in spite of her problems with her vision. After I graduated from Pecos, she got a job with a public service company in Santa Fe and was eventually married and divorced several times. But one of the men she was with sexually assaulted me when I was still young, and she found out and still stayed with him. I could never understand it. But with all her problems, she was still such a lively, feisty, sassy, energetic person.

Before I even moved to Pecos, I started a somewhat sexually promiscuous period. It was connected with always having to do things a little bit worse or a little bit scarier just to prove my worth and getting mixed up with the whole business of trying to become a girl or a woman. Also, like I mentioned before, when my parents were divorced I felt like I was divorced from the whole family, and I think an awful lot of the sex was trying to find somebody, some love, somewhere. But it started out with the whole little black book idea and the way guys score, and I decided I'd do the same thing.

At first, I convinced myself I felt good about all the sex. Also, I was close to a real good guy who was a person I could talk to, like about the belting from my father, but he was killed in a car wreck, which was a real blow. The sex got to be sort of a hopeless thing. It was sad and I came away from encounters feeling more down and more miserable.

When I was twenty, I became pregnant. Of course, I wasn't married. I always considered it a real lucky thing instead of a disaster whether the baby was illegitimate or not because I'd gotten to the point with the promiscuity that I felt like a gutter rat with absolutely no self-respect. I felt like I was worthless and having the baby and keeping him would be somebody to love and somebody who would love me. And it worked out that way. When I had him I was much more careful about things I did. I didn't drive fast; I wasn't out drinking and raising hell.

The baby's father was not any help, and I moved to Denver

with a friend and went to welfare. But I thought they were going to put the baby up for adoption, so I got afraid and didn't have any medical care until the sixth or seventh month. Then I finally got panicky and went to Colorado General Hospital, but I hadn't lived there long enough to be eligible. Then I just got desperate and started crying, and the doctor decided to waive the rules. I did get fine treatment and it was a really good hospital. John was born in October and it wasn't till New Year's that his father got in touch with me. I started to not even talk to him on the phone, and then it dawned on me that I could really rub it in because I had this perfect, marvelous baby. And I wound up back in the same relationship that it was with him before. And I got pregnant again, with Jill. And the father never showed up again.

I met Ed during that time. He and I had gone out a lot of times with John to picnics and he was really neat. He was married before and didn't have any children; he thought he was sterile. He said he wanted to marry me, but he was really wanting to marry John as much as me. I told him I didn't want to get married and then told him I was also pregnant again. After that he went away for about a month, and I figured that was par for the course. It was probably logical because it had really shocked him. Then he came back and said he had thought it all over and decided it was OK; he still wanted to marry me. I still didn't want to get married, but I remember every time he talked about it I'd wind up crying; it just panicked me really.

Then he took me to Albuquerque on a trip. By that time Mother had been transferred to Albuquerque, and while we were there he said, "We'd better go get the license."

I said, "What are you talking about?"

"I thought we were going to get married down here where your mother could be with us. I even brought my suit."

I said, "Oh, my God, did I say anything that made it sound like that?" So out of sheer being worn down, I went ahead and got married to be polite, to keep from hurting his feelings.

We lived in Denver when my baby girl Jill was born. I had nightmares about Ed. I dreamed that he killed us all, the kids and I and everything. I couldn't shake the dreams. Then we moved to Texas and had very little money.

Because Ed was worried that he was sterile, I figured that just as soon as I could, I would have another child for him if it was possible. He didn't want me to but I thought it was because he didn't want to know for sure that he was sterile. There in Texas I promptly got pregnant as fast as I could, this time with Paul. I found out afterwards that Ed had thought all the time I was carrying Paul that I had stepped out on him. Paul was just an absolute carbon copy of Ed when he was born, though, so there was really no doubt whose it was, but there was almost a year there that Ed had decided that I wasn't to be trusted.

Ed really wasn't a talker at all, and he was eleven years older than I, and he was very insecure about that. He didn't trust me so much that in Texas he used to water down the dust in front of the house so if there were any car tracks, if anybody came, he would know. It just drove me crazy because even if someone like a meter reader would drive up and read the meter and go away and I'd never even know, Ed would find the tracks and say, "Who has been here?"

I'd say, "Nobody," and that would just prove to him that I was lying.

Then I had another baby girl after a couple of years. Ed was never very fond of Paul. I don't know if it was disbelief or what. Paul was a lazy, fat, soft, cute little baby and Ed was pretty good with babies, but as Paul got a little older, he was a little slower to walk than John, and he didn't scream with delight when you threw him up in the air, and he was a little more cautious than John. As the years went by, Ed was more and more embarrassed by Paul because he wasn't the he-man that John was. It was really pathetic. I have pictures of Ed holding Paul on the arm of a chair, and Jill and John would be leaning against him, and he'd have this terrible look, looking at Paul. He just looked at him like he hated him. I have more pictures like that. Ed really treated his own biological children worse than John and Jill.

I often think how strange it was that I grew up so independent as a tomboy, and, immediately, when I got married I tried so hard to fit into the traditional woman's role. I didn't argue for my rights very much, and I tried to do all the housework things, and I never told Ed that I could hammer and saw better than he could when he was building something. I always encouraged him to do it and would say, "Gee, that was a great job."

It may have been a holdover from trying to switch from being a tomboy to a woman and thinking that was the woman's thing. I wasn't aware of anybody who had other kinds of marriages at all, equal type marriages. The only ones I ever knew about were the dominant male kind. I know I worked hard at that because I thought that is how you made marriages work, and if you were going to be committed to a marriage, you try to make them work.

I started having bad postnatal depressions. I had been gaining weight and the doctor prescribed amphetamines for the weight before they knew how dangerous they were. I wound up taking them two at a time at noon instead of three times a day like the doctor prescribed because I couldn't sleep if I took one in the evening. I'd take two at noon and clean the house and just have this marvelous energy. Then I started getting buggy and itchy; I couldn't go to bed at night because it felt like things were crawling on me all the time. There were scorpions there and I'd have nightmares about scorpions. I slept huddled up in an overstuffed chair pulled out into the middle of the room. And I was so strung out that I'd tell Ed to keep the kids away from me because I was afraid I'd hurt them. I kept feeling like the only thing that would release the tension would be to run through a wall. I was really messed up. Then, finally, one day while the kids were playing, I was so itchy that I decided to put some rubbing alcohol on a washcloth and just scrub myself. Something about the smell of the alcohol reminded me of ether, and I thought maybe I could get some sleep if I put the washcloth soaked with alcohol over my face like an ether mask. So I did and laid down and my heart started beating really slow, just once in a while, and I couldn't move. I couldn't even wiggle my fingers. I was just laying there completely dead but I was very conscious of everything.

I heard Ed come home and I thought, "Oh, God, he is going to come in here and won't get any response, so he'll probably slap me over the face like they do in the movies and then come back with a hot cup of coffee and burn me with it trying to get me to drink it." That's exactly what he did. He was real scared and panicky, but he never did call the doctor. I came to, but that scared me enough; I connected it somehow with the amphetamines and quit taking them. It was years later that I read in a *Reader's Digest* about speed freaks and symptoms and realized what had happened. At times I just had to hold myself; I was feeling like I was going to spin off into space.

Through those years I hated Texas so much. Any possibility I had I went to visit Mother in Taos in northern New Mexico where she lived. I just loved it. Ed talked to a dealer there and was offered a job. He took a cut in pay but we moved up there, and I was really happy to be back in northern New Mexico.

Most of the houses in Taos are out of adobe, and it was status to have indoor plumbing there. At almost any place there's a small farm, and you have a little garden and a little pigpen or a chicken pen. I lived on the edge of an old orchard, just outside of Taos. It was lovely and a neat place for the kids. I wanted them to have a place to roam without getting into trouble.

At one point Ed lost his job and wouldn't look for another. Finally, we didn't have anything to eat and we had to get commodities. That killed me because my family believed that welfare was really a bad thing. I had been brought up "poor but proud." You didn't tell people that you didn't have food and other problems like that. When I went to get the food everybody was so tense about it that they hardly spoke to each other. Like, they don't acknowledge you because it might be embarrassing to you. So you are down there with everybody pretending to be strangers.

Ed still wasn't looking for work so I went out and got two jobs. When I had six kids I worked in a bakery during the day and worked in the laundry at a motel at night. I hung on to the jobs as long as I could, and he finally did find a good job with the mine.

After we had the four kids I desperately didn't want more. Ed talked about getting a vasectomy but he wouldn't do it. So I went to a doctor and tried to talk her into an operation for me because contraceptives didn't work, the types that were available then. It was a woman doctor and she said, "If you have another child, that's not a disaster."

I said, "It's a terrible disaster. I cannot have any more children. I cannot deal with the ones I have now. I don't stretch far enough and if I had another one, it would be impossible. I think I'd kill myself or something."

And she said, "You're really indulging yourself in a lot of drama. There are women who have twelve and fourteen kids." And I just gave up then. She wasn't going to help me.

When I got up to leave it suddenly hit me, and I said, "If they have twelve or fourteen kids, they have one kid who is twelve and one who is fourteen. They could help." Mine were all so small, it didn't seem like any of them would ever get old enough to help. And with that parting shot, I went out the door. She probably believed I was being a dramatic, neurotic person.

I asked for a divorce when I found out I was pregnant with Lynn but Ed wouldn't agree to it. Ed wouldn't let me out of the house without sulking, and he was just more and more paranoid about the differences in our ages. He didn't like the time I spent with Mother and I was just totally miserable. I was penned up with a bunch of kids and no other interests or outlets. In Texas I had tried to join a group of women that bowled, but I only went once because Ed acted so badly about it that I just gave it up.

There was just nobody to understand the pain, even my mother. I guess I was a little more animated when I was around her, but she never seemed to be concerned or aware of what I was experiencing. I know when I told her I wanted a divorce, she said, "But why? Ed seems to be a good provider, and he doesn't chase other women. He doesn't go out and get drunk."

Even though I was miserable all the time she said, "Do you think that it is fair to Ed for you to just change your mind and not want to be married anymore?" So I didn't discuss it with her again. She made it seem almost like a frivolous decision, like here I have four children and I'm tired of being married so I want a divorce.

After I had Lynn, my fifth child, I got rheumatic fever and was in bed for three months. Also, I was so terribly depressed. The doctor I went to this time understood a lot of my depression, and I told her that I'd asked my husband for a divorce and he acted so crazy that I just pulled back and didn't talk about it anymore.

She said, "The only solution I can see is either learn to live with it or do something about it." That sounds so simplistic but it really helped a lot. I realized that with anything in your life, you could attempt to adapt to it or you could blow it up and start over.

I was still trying to figure out how to get out of the marriage when I was pregnant with Peter. I didn't even go to the doctor with that one; that was the bitter end. They had no contraceptives that would work. I had a tilted uterus and the diaphram wouldn't work, and I wasn't regular enough for rhythm and they hadn't invented the Pill. It was really a bad time and I just felt awful.

I didn't go to a doctor until I went into labor. Then I went and told the doctor I was having labor pains and that I hadn't had any checkups and I was overdue too. He was pretty upset about it. He said, "I don't like overdue, overweight mothers, but go put yourself in the hospital and I'll be there in a few minutes." I had Peter and after that I had the worst postnatal depression. This time I was sure that Ed was going to leave me, and we'd have no money and I was going to have all these kids to take care of. I was just so sure of it I didn't even feel panic. I sat and held Peter for hours in my reclining chair. All I did all day long was just sit and hold him, and sometimes I'd lose track of time. He would cry and I would check his diaper and change it, and if he still cried that must have meant that he was hungry, and I'd send Jill or one of the kids to get a bottle and feed him. Some people came by to see the baby and brought presents and I don't even remember them. I just sat in the room in the chair with that baby and that was all.

There were times when Ed and I would fight. The kids would be so quiet sitting around. I'd feel bad then and I would usually give in. I loved the children so much, but they just felt like bars on prison. I could never do anything that I wanted to do without considering first what effect it would have on the kids and whether they needed me for the next hour.

I couldn't do for all of them. I don't hardly ever remember reading to them. I did encourage them to read to each other. And I know a lot of times, when the kids needed a hug or affection, I was too wiped out to give it, even a small gesture. And I think back on all the things, the deprivation. When people say, "I'd like another child but we can't afford one," I'd say, "Forget that. It isn't the money. You just can't stretch yourself."

I was pregnant two other times and I did abortions on myself. I knew a lot of ways people aborted themselves and they were also damn dangerous. I had a friend that used a catheter tube that some woman that was an abortionist in Taos gave her and told her how to use. It was a metal hooded point on the tube, and she was supposed to insert that into her vagina, into the cervix, and push it in so far and just leave it until it accidently punctured while she was moving around. I took one look at it and it was filthy. The metal part that went into the tube had dried blood and junk around it. I just couldn't believe that somebody would use that thing. And then women attempted it with coat hangers and ruptured their uteruses.

I just read everything I could get my hands on. Also, once when I was pregnant, I had asked one of the doctors, "Why is it you don't take a tub bath the last few weeks before you deliver?"

And he said, "Sometimes the mucus plug gets disturbed in the cervix and water can seep in and cause infection." That told me that there is a mucus plug, and I finally just reasoned that if you could insert something that was blunt that wouldn't puncture anything but would disturb that mucus, there was a strong possibility of aborting. That's what I did. I used a glass swizzle stick that you stir drinks with. It had kind of a round ball on the end, and I disinfected it and tried to clean myself very good and then inserted it.

I know there were the days of anguish, and you would have to build up to it if you know you are going to do it yourself. You are so desperate because it needs to be done. I'd lay awake nights thinking how to do it, and I know a lot of times there were false starts. I'd get up in the middle of the night and decide to do it while Ed was asleep, and I'd go in the bathroom and get everything ready and I couldn't. So I'd put everything away and work on it the next day or the day later.

It's almost like I had to make a separation in myself, being so objective that I became like a doctor doing it instead of the person being done to. But I was just so desperate. I had a bad marriage and I wanted out and couldn't get out of that and I just kept having babies. Each month, two weeks after a period, I would start worrying about whether I would have the next one or not. I used to think it was damn ironic that you had to be so thankful for something as miserable as cramps each month. I had all of my six kids within a ten-year period and with the abortions also.

And the postnatal depressions were getting worse, and that was another thing I feared. It doesn't have much to do with having too many kids to support or feed. You'll manage that and I don't think it is particularly scarring to kids, but when you have too many kids to love and to talk to and to read to, I think that's the criminal part of it, really. There were so many things that I wanted to do with the kids, and I'd see that this kid would be suffering from some neglect, and I'd pat him on the head in passing or when they were hurt and that was about the only time. I always kissed them goodnight. That would be just about the affection that they got for years. And if they didn't get hurt, well, I was busy patching other kids and giving them a hug and a squeeze.

There was a sharp pain with the abortions. Apparently the mucus part has sort of this membrane because I know that I'd have to use pressure. I'd push the glass stick as far as it would go without resistance, and then I would just kind of position it and give it a push. It was kind of a sharp pain; that's all. Then usually within six or eight hours there would be cramping and the abortion would go through. I don't remember any guilt or any sadness for the fetus at all. I just felt like it was better off not being born because I couldn't take care of it, that's all. But I often wondered if they would have been a boy or girl. That is about the only actual personness that the fetuses had. Because you just can't allow yourself to dwell on what if it would have been another Mozart or such. That is a sentimental, romantic idea you can't afford to fool around with.

With the one I did after Lynn and after my rheumatic fever, I got so sick. I had a wild temperature, was delirious, when I went to the doctor, and when I told her what I had done she just looked pale. I knew it was illegal but I didn't think anybody was going to be prosecuting when you did it to yourself.

I had to be on the examining table, and the nurse that the

doctor had with her was determined to strap my hands down, and the doctor knew how I didn't want that. But I was having chills really bad with a fever and I couldn't control the shaking. I told them if they'd just examine me or clean me out and stop when I told them I was going to have a chill, I would be all right with my hands not strapped. The nurse was wanting to punish me and was determined to tie me down and was arguing with the doctor even, but the doctor was terrific and consented to do what I said because she knew that I was not a hysterical person and I would let them know when I had to move and they could stop for a second or two. But they were really upset and it must have been one hell of an infection because I was in the hospital two or three days that I don't even remember.

I think it was probably entered into the records that it was a self-induced abortion. I know the doctor asked how I had done it, and I told her that I had tried to use that particular glass swizzle stick so I could sterilize it. She kind of shuddered and made an awful face and let it go at that. I remember pressuring that glass a lot beforehand to be sure there wasn't a crack or anything because that would have been a mess for sure.

I guess I tend to think of things in relation, comparing them. This is pretty rough but it would have been rougher if I had done the other. I think that is how I always think about things when I have to make decisions between two rotten choices. I just try to figure out which would be the worse, and after I made up my mind about those things I don't remember any more really emotional stress about it. My big fear was that I was going to cause some damage and not be able to abort the child and I would have a deformed child. That was one of my big fears, and I felt like I probably deserved it.

I don't think Ed knew I was doing them. I didn't discuss them with him. I just learned that this was between me and me, and I'm the only one that is going to help me so I better do it. Even simple things like when a cat got mauled half to death by a dog and had to be put out of its misery, Ed couldn't do it. I wound up having to do all of that, and, for days afterwards, he'd look at me like I was some kind of murderess. But I always loved animals so it was hard to do it.

It was such a strange time. Agony or misery or terror or anything else can only be sharp for a short period of time, and when you're in a long drawn out period of misery, it gets to where it is just sort of a blur. I mean even from day to day, not in retrospect, but even just from day to day. The edges are not sharp and you just know you go to bed miserable, you wake up miserable, and it's just another damn miserable day and you get through it. It seems to take the edge off of everything that happens; even the good things that happen don't pick you up very much, and the bad things that happen don't get you down very much.

There were little things that were positive during that long bad time. Like I was determined to help the boys with football. I helped them practice to punt, pass, and kick when I was horribly pregnant. I'm trying to kick a football when I couldn't even see it. They won trophies too, whether I was pregnant or not. I found out later that it kind of confused them and made things a little difficult for them at school. Also, I would whittle them a wooden gun or something like that, and I'd warn them that when they took it to school, they should not tell the kids their mother did it.

Ed finally made them some stilts, and none of the rest of the family could walk on them and I did. I stepped right on those darn things and walked off. It was so funny and I felt so good about it. It was a silly triumph in the middle of a crazy marriage and all of those kids and all of the money problems, but the fact that I was able to get on those stilts and walk off and see the amazement in their eyes made it a triumph. I guess that's a pretty good measure of how little positive experience there was in my life.

Nutty things like that gave me more confidence. My German shepherd dog killed a pig in the orchard. There was a whole herd of pigs living in there, and the kids came running and said that he killed a pig. I knew that the owner of the pig would make me pay for it and I couldn't afford to, so I asked if it was a big pig or a little pig and they said, "Not too big."

I said, "Take the wheelbarrow out there and put it in it and bring it back real fast," and they did. I told the other kids to kick dirt over the blood if there was any. They did it and brought the pig back. It was a small one and I skinned it and put the entrails and the skin in an old well that had rocks and trash and put the big cement cover over it. Then I cut up the pig and put it in the freezer. I was forever having these damn little adventures that must have made everyone think I was crazy, but they were like a gift of a lifetime.

I stayed with Ed as long as I did because I was so determined to make a go of that marriage that I just refused to believe it wasn't possible. I just didn't want to go through marriages and divorces like my parents did. I know I was extremely stubborn about it, and I managed to put in something like fourteen years, which is amazing considering the fact that after the first year I wasn't happy and was continually more unhappy all along. It is kind of incredible how stubborn people can be. I inherited that from both my mother and father; they both were the most bullheaded people in the world. I also would have been so embarrassed if I'd have had a nervous breakdown; that wasn't allowed in our family and would have been a really weakling thing to do.

There were qualities of Ed that frightened me, but I couldn't understand my fears. I know there were a lot of times when I was first married to him that I worried about the kids, but I decided it was just my wild imagination and that I had to get over it. I didn't understand it, and it was just incredible that I couldn't put my finger on it, and I didn't know what it was. He didn't drink much, he didn't gamble, he didn't beat anybody; he seemed to be an all right person for a father for the kids even if I wasn't all that excited about him. I know I had nightmares. Like I said, around the time Jill was born, I dreamed that he killed us all, the kids and I and everything. I was having a lot of crazy nightmares like that, but I didn't know why.

One Sunday, when Terri, my second daughter, was about eight, Terri wanted to talk to me, and she was laying on my bed and we were talking. I was telling her I didn't think she should hang around the old barn with the boys so much. I said that the boys get ideas, and you could get yourself in trouble, and you shouldn't let boys see you or touch you until you get older. And she just said, "Then what Daddy is doing is wrong."

It was like somebody had hit me with an ax. I was just totally stunned when it dawned on me what I was hearing. I remember I was very quiet, and I wanted her to explain, so I didn't want my tone of voice to change. So I took a deep breath and asked her, "What do you mean? What has Daddy been doing?"

Apparently I kept calm enough that she went ahead and explained it all, saying that both she and Jill, my older daughter, had been being sexually assaulted and raped by Ed for some time. Of course, she didn't use those words. After a while I told her I didn't want her to talk about it anymore that day and we'd talk about it tomorrow. And I went in the other room and got the kids to bed and spent the evening with Ed and acted very normal.

The next morning, after Ed went to work and the kids went to school, I went to see my doctor, and he suggested that I talk to Jill before doing anything. The doctor was a really brusk, insulting, noisy kind of man, rough, but he was so sweet to me and put an arm around me and called me honey that he scared me so bad I didn't know if I had lost my mind. So I went and got Jill out of school and asked her what had been happening, and she said, yes,

Ed had been sexually using them. I later learned that it must have gone on for at least over a year. When Ed got home from work that day I told him to pack up and get out. I told him why and he didn't argue about it at all. He didn't deny it; he just packed up and got out. Of course, the sudden change was a shock to the kids, and we had to really struggle for a while to keep going.

I felt immensely torn up by the whole thing. I kept thinking that if I was any mother at all, I should have known. I should have been able to spot it. Now I realize that I was just so emotionally out of balance by the depression and despair I had been experiencing, that I just couldn't see anything. I was just so miserable that I didn't see.

I talked to an attorney and found out I could put Ed in a penitentiary, but the attorney advised me not to because there wouldn't be any financial support for the children if I did put him in prison. I think the attorney was just blown away that there were six kids and they were going to wind up just afloat. And I talked to a psychiatrist and Ed went to one, and the psychiatrist seemed to think that Ed did it to spite me mostly and that he wasn't really a threat to other children. I had told Ed about the experience with my mother's boyfriend when I was a child, and it kind of fascinated Ed at the time. I don't know what kind of threat he is. He never was put in prison or treated.

I thought back over the time when we'd been together and about Ed's relationship with the girls. It had been going on a long time. The one thing I had noticed was that when I went to the hospital to have a baby and came back, Jill and Terri were always so subdued and acted like I was a total stranger. I never quite figured that out; I don't know if it had anything to do with the assaults. Ed was really grumpy and grouchy but he never disciplined the kids unless they interfered with what he was doing. It was all such a nightmare that it still doesn't seem to be exactly real. It has that funny quality of something that I dreamed or read instead of really being what happened.

I was so obsessed with it all that for the next three months I got into this crazy sleep pattern. I'd always been a night person, and I was going to sleep immediately after supper, and anytime I slowed down during the day I'd go to sleep. I guess it was to keep from thinking. And for the next three months I was just obsessed with the idea that I wanted him dead.

Sometimes he would ask, "Could I do anything to help?"

And I'd say, "Sure, go drive off the gorge or something and let us collect insurance. That's the only thing you could ever do to help me." And for a long time, I wanted to kill him so much. It used to be so spooky. I'd get the shakes and cry for three days because of the intensity of wanting to murder him. And through it all he kept coming around, trying to effect a reconciliation, but I despised him.

I got to the point where I was thinking I'd give anything if I was a child again when there wasn't any strife, and I could sit on my dad's lap and he would say, "That's all right. I'll take care of you and nothing bad can happen to you." Just once in a while to be able to be a totally dependent little kid again.

When I was there alone with the kids and was so depressed about it all, I'd think I would probably commit suicide if I could, and then I would kind of laugh and think, that solution isn't even open to me because the kids need me and if I die Ed will have them. And I think it's so funny because the one time that I probably ever would have been interested in suicide was at a time when I couldn't see it as a solution at all. Women do and they have kids, but I guess my dedication to that responsibility is too much. I didn't even have the luxury of a suicide attempt.

I couldn't sleep late like depressed people want to because the kids had to be gotten off to school. And I didn't have any money to buy liquor and have never enjoyed drinking by myself. So I suppose the overeating was the only outlet I had, and now I have sclerosis of the liver from eating. You pay for any excess yet you need the excesses. I don't know when you come right down to it if overeating isn't probably the least harmful to everybody else. You can have a fat mother, but it's not that bad as compared to an alcoholic mother, which must be hell.

After Ed and I separated, I sent the two older boys to Boys' Town in Nebraska because I thought they needed male guidance and because it would cut down on the work load of trying to raise the kids. It would go from six to four and I could handle that more. Of course, Peter was too young to leave his mother and then there were the three girls. I was trying very hard to help the older two girls recover some from what they went through.

I always had support money from Ed because I wouldn't let him get around it at all, or I didn't let him see the kids if he didn't pay the support money that we agreed upon every month. I had locked him into that because I had really gotten hard and cold and cruel. I felt totally justified; I felt like I was being quite generous not to put him in prison, that was enough.

After Ed had moved out the old man that brought us wood propositioned me and it absolutely floored me. He was about eighty-five and hunched over and a funny little gnome of a man that I always talked to because he was interesting. And I had a lot of trouble with people that I had considered friends of ours who suddenly propositioned me because we were separated. One or two of them made me furious because they were good friends, and after they came on to me sexually, they weren't friends anymore. And I resented losing a friend more than anything else but didn't know how to express that. It just made me angry. I needed friends.

My mother had lived in Taos and we had seen her a lot. Then, after my divorce from Ed, she developed breast cancer, and even though she had the breast removed, it had already spread. I tried to take care of her, but I was working too, and she kept feeling so guilty because she was taking me away from the kids. She hadn't seen her sister Ruth in a long time, so finally I sent her back to Ruth's on a plane. Then I went to Ruth's in Indiana to be with Mother the last eight days before she died.

It's really strange because I had been at odds with Mother all our lives; even when it was peaceful we had the unspoken subjects that we just didn't dig into. But the end of her life was the first time that I really felt able to do something for her that nobody else could do. She didn't have control of her bowels, and Aunt Ruth said she was going to have to put her in a nursing home. I told Ruth to wait until I got there and to see if I could handle it. And I was able to clean her and turn her and bathe her and do all these things. But her dignity was so involved that when I was doing those things for her, she'd pretend that I was a nurse that had come in. She'd ask my name and I'd tell her, and she'd say, "That's interesting. My oldest daughter's name is Lee too," and she'd do that all the way through any of the personal things, and as soon as that was all over with, I'd go in and wash my hands and come back in and I'd be me again. It was the only way she could deal with me taking that kind of care of her. I think that was so funny. I also think part of it was the contentious relationship she had with me, and the feeling that she had to depend on me for those really basic things was more than she could handle.

I always would stay with her all night, and Aunt Ruth would get up about six-thirty or seven and come down and say hello to her and go fix breakfast for Uncle Bill. I'd usually have coffee with Uncle Bill and go to bed. My sister had come, so then Aunt Ruth and my sister would take care of Mother during the day. I'd get up and maybe go shopping and then come back. That's the way we worked it. Mother would talk day and night; she didn't sleep at all.

She didn't eat anything at all. She liked to have her lips wet but she couldn't swallow water.

Mother had some painkillers there on the nightstand, but they had discontinued them because the cancer had involved her spine in such a way that she wasn't getting the nerve messages of pain, no real pain. I remember that I asked the doctor, "If she suddenly complains of pain, how many should I give her and how should I give them to her?"

He said, "She won't. The nerves have been destroyed." But he didn't take the pain medicine away. He said, "If you give her more than so much it will cause her heart to race, to overreact, and it will kill her."

Mother had always said that if she was ever terminally ill or lingering on, she hoped that somebody would be humane enough to give her an overdose because she had worked with a friend for years before her friend died. Philosophically, I agreed with her. It just never occurred to me that she would ever be an invalid because she was such a lively, feisty, sassy, energetic person. You just can't even picture someone like that laying down.

I guess it was the last evening that I was with her when I decided if she wasn't dead by the next evening, I would go ahead and overdose her. I knew I couldn't talk to Aunt Ruth or my sister about it because it would bother them too much, and it just wasn't the kind of guilt that you can share. You just don't dare do that to other people. And I had made up my mind.

I saw her all through the night and she continued talking without stopping. I kissed her good-bye when Aunt Ruth came down in the morning, and I said, "I'm going to go to bed now, and Aunt Ruth will be here to take care of you." Then I went in and had a cup of coffee with Uncle Bill and went to bed. I had settled in the bed and snuggled down and shut my eyes, and I realized it was totally silent. Mother had talked twenty-four hours a day, and I knew that silence would be the sign that she was gone. I listened for a minute and she was totally quiet. There was just no sound coming from that other room. So I got up and went in there and she was dead. Just that quietly. And Aunt Ruth swore she was alive when she'd come down and kissed her good morning, but sometime during that half hour or forty-five minutes she had died, just quit talking. It was really strange, more the lack of sound than the lack of breathing.

We buried her in a red dress with a gray coffin, which was pretty. It was on St. Patrick's Day and she was a green-eyed, dark-haired woman, and it was snowing a little bit. I thought that was special because she liked the snow. It took a while to recover from her death, to have that feisty, energetic person gone.

When I was back home, caring for the kids and continuing to worry about them took so much energy. Paul, who was in Boys' Town, had problems getting along there. Jill, my oldest daughter, was trying so damn hard to be an adult and help me and not cause any trouble. Now she talks about her feelings of never having a childhood, and they have a good basis, really. She'd always tried to make up for the fact that Ed didn't act like a father and that I needed help and was always so worn down. Also, I'm sure Jill felt a lot of guilt for the incest and the divorce, and the guilt made it worse for her. Jill never wanted to talk about the incest, but Terri wanted to talk about it at the drop of a hat, when I least expected it, and sometimes I just didn't think I could handle talking about it one more time.

With kids so close together, the squeaky wheel gets the grease. The kids with the problems seem to get the attention, and Jill just always took care of the others and little Lynn was very quiet. Fortunately, Peter, my last child, has been a real delight. He's always been easygoing, open, friendly, and helpful.

Sometime back then, I finally forgave myself for being a bad mother. I realized I had been going through so many things when the kids were young, that I was as good of a mother as I could be at the time. I looked back and saw Lee struggling with all those things, how she was. She was pretty pathetic but was really trying and I could forgive. I felt a lot of guilt about Paul, because he was acting wild, and Terri had so many problems, and I took some of that guilt and also guilt that I didn't know what was happening to the girls until I was told. I always felt terribly bad about that. But I just came to grips with all that guilt and could feel sympathy for the woman I had been.

After the divorce I stayed at home until the kids were in school, and then I got a job working with retarded kids for the schools. I did it for three years and became quite interested in that line of work, but they paid very little. The people I worked with pushed me to go to college because I was really good at my work, and they said I should get qualified to get paid enough to live on it.

Finally, people talked me into applying to a small state university in another town in northern New Mexico. Then all summer long I sat out in our orchard, scared to death I'd be accepted. I was terrified at the idea of going to college, and it would mean moving to a town where I didn't know anybody. But the kids supported me so finally we moved.

We moved into the projects, where poor people had subsidized housing. Almost all of the people on that side of town are Spanish, but that's the way it was in Taos so we didn't feel uncomfortable. I tried to make it financially on my own but began to realize I would need some help to make it. I remember when I first starting getting food stamps and AFDC, welfare. I felt it was all right because eventually my kids and I would become taxpayers, and we would be putting money back into the system again. But when the welfare workers first looked down on me, I felt it deeply.

When I would talk with other people who lived in the projects, I taught them as much about their rights as possible because they need to know how to protect themselves. It's hard when you live in this twilight world of not owning anything and knowing that your whole existence is so transient. It depends on whether there is funding; it depends on whether the procedures have changed. The government is such an anonymous, huge thing that you feel like they're breathing down your neck all the time. The people on welfare and in the projects feel like if they don't say hello delightedly to an authority figure when they see one, they are going to get stepped on. The people don't band together for petitions or anything because they are afraid that if they put their name on a petition and it doesn't work out right, then they'll really be in bad trouble.

And if people can get just a little above welfare income, it scares them to death. Like my neighbor, who has six children. When she got a job at minimum wages, she said, "I'm so scared. I don't have the medicaid card for the children's injuries, and I don't make enough to pay any hospital bills." There is a no-man's-land between poverty and the middle class. She knew she really had to pray that nothing went wrong, and she has a job running an old people's nutrition program that could be dropped at any time.

The kids grew through those years, and I kept going to school. I changed my major from special ed to psychology and worked in the Crisis Center. I learned how to help people in all sorts of situations, both people with emergencies and people needing long-term help. The area was pretty poor, without many services, so we did all kinds of work. I dealt with suicide, rape, people having problems with their families, people without money, all sorts of problems. I ended my years there helping outpatients from the state mental hospital. I made close friends during those years and had several long-term lovers that are still important in my life.

The two middle kids were my main problems. One time Terri was having a hard time. I had tried to get help for her for a long time, and she finally agreed to counseling and I got it all lined up. But she got angry with me one day over housework and said she wanted to go live with her dad and took off. Ed had been writing and offering her money to come and stay and do housework for him. I was so angry with Ed for interfering the one time I'd had the opportunity to get help for Terri, and that triggered another episode of wanting to kill Ed, which I thought was dead long ago. After our separation, I'd had that obsession with wanting him dead. It had been so frightening and after it went away, I thought it was done. But when Ed interfered with Terri's treatment, I went through about two days and nights of just plotting his murder, down to the last detail, and laying there crying and being so angry I was just out of my mind.

Later, Terri married and then, in 1976, Terri's husband drowned, trying to save my youngest son's life. Terri and her husband Jim had invited Peter to go with them to Colorado, and I keep remembering that the last thing I told him was, "Take good care of Peter." And he died taking care of Peter. Leaving a baby girl and Terri, who was pregnant. Peter got caught in an undertow in a river and Jim went in after him, pushed him out of it, and was pulled into it himself and never came up again. He was found about a half mile down the river, drowned. Of course, it did terrible things to Terri, and Peter was also devastated. Peter had loved Jim and felt he was responsible for Terri's babies not having a father. For six months or so Peter seemed dazed and bewildered.

For a while, Terri and her little girl and baby boy moved in with Ed. All of Ed's interference is with Terri. She's the only one vulnerable to it. I tried so hard to get her out of there. Then Ed started telling her that she couldn't function alone, that she was more or less crazy, that she was unstable. Terri has to take heavy medication for epilepsy and who knows what happened while she was asleep. I kept saying, "Terri, you can't live there. You don't know what might happen and you'd hate yourself forever." But Ed's undermined her confidence in her own sanity to such an extent that she doesn't trust herself. Ed won't allow her to have boyfriends. If she starts losing weight, he brings her fattening things, just like he did to me.

Finally, I talked her into talking to a doctor about some of the things that were going on, and the doctor said, "You've got to get away from there." I referred her to a female psychologist who said, "You've got to get away from there." So, in a weird way, I seem to have been able to help build her a support system and she has moved out. Ed still has control over her, however. Part of the time she seems to be too paralyzed to do anything about it or to help herself. It is a tragedy that her husband died. He was a loving person, and strong, too.

I just keep thinking, I want to help Terri all I can, but I can't let it upset me so much that it puts me in the hospital. Yet, she needs to talk with me because she obviously is not going to go to someone else. And I've been able to spend hours on the phone with her sometimes when she needs me and not feel deeply depressed afterward. I feel physically tired, but I'm not emotionally ploughed under. I feel good because I can help to some degree and not become unfunctionable myself. And she has moved out.

The more kids you get, the more complicated it gets. But some of my kids remember some really pleasant times, and that is very gratifying for me when they get together. They said, "Do you know that I met this person who never had a birthday party?" And I remember that I never could afford birthday parties, but I tried to give each one at least one party as they grew up. Sometimes the kids didn't realize the happiness they experienced until later when the same situation presented itself. They said to someone else, "Well, people say it's foolish for an adult to roll up their pant legs and go wading or run under a waterfall. Adults are supposed to be dignified people, but I remember that my mother did that. I guess if my mother did it, it's OK, and I remember a lot of fun."

After I finished with school I moved to another small city in New Mexico and got involved with a group there that's primarily for parents who abuse their children. I was really open with the pain I experienced when raising my children and that broke down barriers between the women in the group and me. Then the leader of the group had to leave, and I took over the paid leadership role and am doing it as my occupation. The programs have continued to do well, but we've had some real, real struggles with funding.

I realize that the people in the group learned to think they were no good when they were little, and ideas like that are so insidious. You are battling them always. I think my mother's verbal abuse, telling me I was lazy and no good, hurt me more than my father's really hard spankings. I think my self-esteem now is at the best it's ever been and it's pretty strong, yet I keep finding myself believing those old messages. I'm still trying to defend myself against the idea that I am no good.

There are some people in the group who have money, and there are others who are on a welfare level. Living on a poverty level is very hard for the people in the group because it's so difficult for them to get any distance from their kids. Some of the girls probably wouldn't have gotten a job except that the first leader plugged them into day care. Now working gives them the break they need. No matter how much you love your kids, and the women in this program love their kids as much as anybody else, it's just the day after day after day grind with no end in sight that becomes too much. I know. I had six of them and I never got away from them except to go to the hospital to have another one. That was the only time.

I get very stubborn about not losing the funding for the program and trying to keep the program alive. My stubbornness helped me through a lot of crises in my life. I switch over to stubborn and I can get through practically anything. Sometimes I do myself more harm than good, but it's in more control now than it used to be, and with fund-raising, it is helpful.

I still have these crazy things I want to do. I want to learn to fly; I also think I'd like to try driving a truck. I've gotten a lot more reasonable and conventional over the years, but those were really strong desires that I've carried a long time and I probably will do them. I used to race cars and loved that. I'll probably die from a massive heart attack in the middle of one of these insane things that I keep trying to do. But, now, I really need to get the weight down and take care of my health because I've got this next period of my life for me, and it would be a damn shame to be cheated out of it by being sick or dying early.

All in all, I think I've had a damned interesting life. And a satisfactory life. I don't think I'd trade with anybody. A lot of it seemed pretty rugged, and it takes pretty rugged living to get through my head. Being born naturally stubborn, you have to get hit by a pretty good sized two-by-four to have it seep in.

A lot of what I've talked about is very sad and a lot of it is terrible, but I've always had people, like the kids when I grew up and the different men I've known and women friends. There have been so many good, unselfish people that were understanding and helpful. Otherwise I would have never made it. I think that is what is really important, and I think that is what I understood about working at the Crisis Center and with the child abuse program and why it mattered so much to be there to help when I could. Through callousness and lack of foresight, I got myself into some terrible messes, but there was always somebody there when I couldn't swim anymore and that person took ahold of me. That's the good part.

Mary and Mildred

Countless individual and group efforts by southern textile workers, often ill and poorly paid, took place in the eighteen-year struggle to unionize the powerful textile industry. With sales that are 30 to 50 percent higher than southern agricultural sales, and accounting for one quarter of all the jobs in five southern states, the textile industry is the bedrock of the southern economy. But the industry's history of fervent antiunionism made it the only major industry in the United States that was not unionized, with barely 10 to 12 percent of its workers represented by unions. Textile workers were the lowest paid industrial workers in the nation, with wages at the powerful J. P. Stevens textile plants averaging 31 percent below the national average factory wage.

Textile work originated in the South during the Reconstruction, when mills moved south due to tax incentives, potential control over the local governments by setting up "company towns," and the South's promise of "one hundred-percent Anglo-Saxon cheap, contented labor."* Towns were created around and controlled by the mills. The mills drew impoverished white workers who had lost their land during the Civil War, and their descendants toiled in the mills for generations. Over time, more and more mills moved south due to the southern tradition against unionization and the easier exploitation of non-unionized workers.

---

*Mimi Conway, "Gonna Make Some Changes," *Journal of Current Social Issues,* Fall/Winter 1979, p. 29.

J. P. Stevens, the second largest textile firm in the nation, flagrantly violated collective bargaining laws as workers throughout its plants fought to be represented by the Amalgamated Clothing and Textile Union, ACTWU, which is pronounced "act two." Between 1963 and 1979, Stevens was involved in over 1,200 law violations that were consolidated into over 130 individual cases. As a result, labor boards spoke of Stevens's "corporate-wide proclivity to violate the [National Labor Relations Act]." Stevens was cited in federal courts for racial discrimination and also for violation of the Occupational Safety and Health Act, not only for its use of unsafe equipment, but also for its factories' high cotton dust levels, causing brown lung (the often fatal disease byssinosis), and noise levels, resulting in loss of hearing to workers.

As a result of these practices and Stevens's continued resistance to unionization, a nationwide consumer boycott of J. P. Stevens's products began in 1976, thirteen years after the beginning of the struggle for unionization. Another drive was organized to oust company directors and officers serving on other corporate boards. These actions were backed by many religious and service groups, including the National Council of Churches. Many of these groups began independent investigations of Stevens's illegal practices and resistance to unionization, and gradually Stevens was forced to respond. Much publicity was generated, including the popular film *Norma Rae*, which documents the story of Crystal Lee Sutton in her fight to unionize her mill.

I've thought about what if the kids would have to go to work in the textile mills. The main thing that has made me fight against Stevens is that I don't want my kids to have to work under the same conditions that I had to. Or anybody else. Because I know it can be better.

—Mary Robinson

I had heard of these workers and traveled to Montgomery, Alabama, to interview women mill workers. I spent a number of days with Mary Robinson. Mary was a petite, delicately shaped black woman of thirty-six with golden brown skin, a long graceful neck, wide-set intelligent eyes, and finely arched eyebrows. Her face lit up when she smiled and was animated while she told of her past and her deep union involvement. Mary was an intensely intelligent, warm, and loving person, who was open and friendly with me from our first conversation.

She slept sporadically during the day, waking to frequent phone calls concerning the union campaign, and then drank large quantities of coffee in the evening, in preparation for facing the night shift at the mill. During the time we spent together in her efficiency apartment and at the union organizing office, I was impressed by her constant alertness, regardless of how little sleep she had. During the four years of her union activities, she got by with three or four hours of sleep a day, working full time in the mill and organizing on a nearly full-time basis. She even managed to talk with me while working on the files and placing phone calls in the ACTWU organizing office. While there, Mary showed me photos taken secretly at the mills, showing the deadly textile dust that had accumulated and hung from pipes above great spools of thread.

Mary cooked several elaborate meals which we ate with her close friend, Mildred, whose story is told here also. Mildred is a thin white woman who works with Mary on the night shift at Stevens and is also active in the union movement. Mary and Mildred laughed and groaned together, talking in their deep southern accents and telling of their common backgrounds of poverty, early marriage, the mills, and their struggles for unionization. Both Mary and Mildred chose to use their real names.

Mary   My father was a tenant farmer, and there were eight of us, eight kids. At the time when I was growing, I thought it was so hard for us. I kept saying, "How much poorer can you be in this world?" Because we only got shoes, clothes, once a year, and that was after the crops were in and my father had settled his debts with the white man he was sharecropping for. Then we'd go to town and get a pair of shoes and that was for the whole year. We never got in school until around the last of October, the first of November, so then we was always behind the other kids and we had to try to catch up. Then around April, we'd have to come out again to start working again in the fields.

We'd work out in the fields sometimes when it was so hot. I had a sister just a little older than me, and we'd just pray for it to rain so we wouldn't have to work. We had all those old tales 'bout what you could do to make it rain. One of them was to take a cricket and put his head down in the soil and leave his legs hanging out and then it would start to rain. Another was if you killed a snake and left him hang in a tree somewhere, that would make it rain. So we did all this kind of stuff trying to make it rain so we wouldn't have to work.

One day we started fixing for home for dinner about eleven-thirty in the morning, and me and her was way ahead of everybody else. At that time of year there's a lot of wild plums out, and they're real tasty when they're ripe and yellow. We used to go home early to stop and get us a whole lot of plums to eat at dinnertime. The sky was just clear, a good spring day. But while me and her were getting the plums, we run on this snake. We decided to make it rain so we killed the snake. There was this sweet gum tree down by our barn, and we hanged the snake in the tree and went on to the house.

Everybody came and ate and we was finishing up when, all of a sudden, we heard something, and Daddy said, "What was that? Was that thunder?" He just stopped with his fork in midair.

Mama said, "No, the sky's clear as it could be."

Then in a minute we heard it again, and Daddy said, "That is thunder too." Listen, in ten minutes, it was just a terrible storm, a tornado almost. The little house we were staying in was stuck up on pillars, and there wasn't anything underneath it, and the wind was blowing so hard it was like the wind was trying to raise the house up off the pillars. Me and my sister, we just stopped eating, and we dove into our little bedroom, there was nothing but two bedrooms in the house, and I started crying. I said to my sister, "I told you not to hang that snake up in that tree! Now we fixing to get blowed away!"

So she said, "Let's see if we can go outside and go down to the barn and take him down." But, oh God, it was thundering so bad, I said, "I ain't gonna do that!" So we went in to Daddy and cried, "Daddy, we killed a snake and hung him up in the tree and that's why it's storming so."

But he just laughed and said, "No snake caused it to rain," and laughed some more. Finally the rain stopped, but after that, even if we had to work every day and killed more snakes, we never hung another one up in a tree.

My parents were good to us. They were up in the morning time by daybreak and worked from sunup to sundown to provide for us. It was hard, hard work for them. My mom had a sad time. She had birthed thirteen kids and only eight of them lived. She especially felt bad about losing her set of twins.

Also, she was illegitimate and her mama had died giving birth to her, and she never really knew her father. I know she felt real alone when she was growing because of having no sisters or brothers, mom or dad, or aunts or uncles on her mother's side. Her father had brothers but they was all married, and they didn't have time to fool with her, so she more or less just raised her own self.

Back then black people were always taught that sex was something you weren't supposed to talk about to nobody. They told kids all kinds of ideas about where a baby comes from, anything except the truth. And when my mother was fourteen she got pregnant, but she didn't know anything about how she got pregnant. She knew she fooled around with a boy, but she didn't know what took place, how it happened. But, anyway, she was so happy she would've had that baby if she had to go out in the woods to have it. She just wanted somebody.

Wherever she was staying at, they told her she couldn't stay, so she went and started living with another somebody. And then they found out she was pregnant, so they run her away. So she went off to Bessemer where she didn't know anybody. When she got up there she stayed with an old lady and took care of her until my sister was born. And then she came back to her people to work. Nobody ever wanted her till it was time to harvest the crops, and then somebody would come and get her.

I guess the closest somebody that she had, my great, great aunt, took the baby away from her and started to raise the baby. My mother felt bad about that, but before long she found out she was going to have another one. She wouldn't let her aunt take that one; she took him and run off. So my great, great aunt raised my oldest sister. But when my sister got old enough to where she understood, she left her aunt and went where my mother was. By that time my mother was married to my father, so they took her and finished raising us up. My oldest brother and sister, they always considered my dad to be their father.

Bless her heart, my mother wanted people so. She just took my father's sisters as her own sisters, and they worshiped the ground that she walked on too. She'd go up to visit my auntie who was a good cook and who had a gas stove, and my mama would bake a pound cake which she'd bring home. She'd say, "I sure wish I could afford me a gas stove like the one Jessie has got." But we couldn't afford it. The only thing we had the whole time she was living was a wood stove.

It always makes me really sad to think about the kind of life that she lived because she was my ideal person. She could take just about anything and make a meal out of it, and everything was always clean. She washed all our clothes by hand, and she made all our linens for the bed. She was just what you'd call an expert housekeeper. Plus, she worked in the fields.

They had little houses in the cotton fields where they put the cotton, and I remember so many times when I was real little, before I could work in the cotton fields, Mama used to put me in the cotton house and let me sleep on the cotton. At that time I couldn't wait to be able to pick cotton. Mama always got flour sacks, and when we get to be 'bout three years old, she would make us a little cotton sack out of those bags. She'd carry us along, or sometimes we'd ride on the back of her's or Daddy's sack. Then we'd crawl down to the field and pick us up some cotton, and we thought that was really doing something. We thought we was big. Dad would always go on about how much cotton we'd picked, paying us a compliment. He'd say, "Oh, my baby picked a lot of cotton!" when we had only two or three bolls in the sack. But then we got old enough to where we was really picking, and, boy, we wished we had a flour sack then 'cause we didn't want to pick no more. We didn't play around in the fields because we wanted to get out of there as fast as we possibly could. We used to race with my uncle's kids to see which one could get out the most bales of cotton or hoe the fastest.

I used to get so black out in the sun working there. You talk about getting a tan. We'd wear the strawhats, long pants, and long-sleeved shirts, and it didn't help any. Nothing helped, and, boy, there were bugs. Everything was bad. The fields were so hot in the summer that my dad would come home sometimes and his eyes would be real big and sick looking, and he would be as white as a sheet. He would be like that for three or four days and would be so weak. I remember one time he passed out in the field. A guy was traveling up the road, and he seen the mule just standing up there under the tree. The man went over there and my dad had passed out in the rows. Daddy stayed sick a long time after that.

Oh, it was hot, I'll tell you. We never had no mattresses like there is now; we had the mattresses that you stuff with cotton, and in the morning you stir it all up till you get it good and level. Well, that made it doubly hot 'cause you just sink down into that kind of mattress. In the hot weather Mama used to weigh the milk down in the bucket in the well so it would be cool enough for us to drink at dinnertime. And then at dinnertime she would let another jugful down in there. Also, an iceman came along and sold blocks of ice. We'd buy maybe fifty pounds and by night, it'd be melted down.

Then in the winters it was real cold. The ceiling in our house was up high and the walls weren't sealed, and it was up on stilts so you couldn't heat it. We would be trying to keep warm, but our legs would be freezing cold. I never had a coat until after I was married. I'm telling you, I don't know how we survived. I really don't. I used to try to forget about the times like that; they're some good memories in there, but there's more bad than good.

Also, there wasn't no such thing as going to the movies or going on vacation. We just worked. We used to cut our wood, and I learned how to swing an ax as good as any man and pull a plow as good, matter of fact. And I remember the blackberries. We used to stay out in the fields till sundown, then we'd go pick us some blackberries so Mama could make some blackberry pie. Those were the best parts, I guess, out of life.

I thought times were so hard back then, but now I think about it and I think about the problems I have now, and the ones I got now look like mountains compared to those. We had a lot of love, and there was always plenty to eat, and not one of us says we ever went to bed hungry. I'd go back there any day now. I don't know if I could do it as well, but I'd do it again.

I was real close to my sister who was a little older than me, and she was always getting herself and me in all kinds of trouble. We used to have this old cow named Pet that we milked. Pet had a little bull and one day my sister says, "I bet you can't milk that bull." So she gets by his head and feeds him some corn shucks, and I get on back behind him and I mashes his balls. My sister laughed her head off, and I have a scar on my lip where he kicked me. Mama come running 'cause I started hollering at the top of my voice, and Mama grabbed my sister and tore her up, saying, "I'll teach you to do these things," but it didn't change her.

Another time, we had a radio. The volume would go down on it so you'd have to hit up the battery and it would come on again. Every song that would come on the radio my sister would try to memorize so when she'd get out in the field she could sing. She'd be singing away out there, standing in one spot, hoeing over and over. So Daddy would show her how to hoe right, and pretty soon she'd be back there singing again. Then she'd get whupped, but whupping didn't last no longer than five minutes with her. She'd be right back out there singing and chopping those little spaces. Sometimes we'd be to the end of the row, and she'd have gone just a little ways. Daddy'd whup her the whole season and it didn't do a bit of good. When she comes home now, she'll tell you some stuff and just die laughing, 'cause she knew she was doing wrong and just didn't care.

But the best time of my childhood was every Fourth of July. My daddy's cousin lived down the road, and the third of July we'd all start making ice cream, and we'd make it all day the Fourth. Every year we did that, and that was the best part of the whole year. The only things we usually got for Christmas were apples and oranges and candy. We had this one closet, and Mama and Daddy would put what we were going to get in the closet and we could smell the apples. One time my two brothers got a bicycle; one for the two of them. But some big kid sat on it and pshh!, it broke. You talk about crying!

I remember having only one doll my whole life. It was a little, old bitty doll, little bitty. I was about six or seven, and I beat that doll to death. I did it 'cause my older sister got a white doll and I got a black doll, and I didn't want no black doll. Mama and Daddy told us that there was only two left 'cause Santa Claus didn't have but two. He had a black one and a white one so he gave me the black one.

It was a hard rubber doll with no hair, just lines on it. And I took that doll out there behind the smokehouse. We had a big stick, and I started beating it and beating it and beating it till I beat off all the legs, the arms off, the head off. And all the time I was beating it, I was just crying, "I don't want you, you old black doll, you!" I just cried and cried. It was hard and it took quite a bit of beating to beat it apart. Then I went and got me a hoe and I chopped it into pieces, and I buried every one of those pieces in a different hole.

For a long time, didn't nobody know what happened. My sister who got the other doll made hers all kinds of clothes, and I thought her doll was much prettier than mine had been. Finally, one day she was playing with it and Mama asked me, "Mary James?"

"Ma'm?"

"Where is your doll at?"

I told her and she said, "Well, I bet you one thing, young lady. I bet you ain't never gonna get you another one!" And she whupped me up good, and I never did get another one. My sister kept her doll up until about three years ago, and then she sent it to my daughter Tracy. I beat that doll of mine 'cause I just could not stand the idea that my sister had a white doll and I had a colored doll.

Thinking back, I was scared of being black. Oh, God, I was scared plumb out of my wits by the Klan. I can remember vaguely when I was just little. It was in Eclectic and the tree is still up there. I remember my mama crying, and I could not understand what she was crying about. Later on she told us about it. This black man had left his wife and a bunch of kids to go north. He got him a job up there and saved some money, and when he came back to get his family, the Klan got him. And they took him to this tree and they hung him and then they burned him. The tree is dead and there's no bark on it at all, but it's still there.

I worked sometimes for the son of one of the men who did it. Late one night, the son came to get me to stay at his house 'cause he and his wife had to go somewhere. When I got over there, the woman was crying. His father, who had been in the Klan, had killed hisself that night. Before he did it, though, he revealed every bit of burning that black guy. Then he fixed a sawed-off shotgun on his bed and blowed his head clean off. Eclectic was a bad town. The only thing that changed since slavery time was that they built a bank.

My first encounter with the Klan when I was little was about a family that lived a good ways from us. There were five boys and one girl, and they didn't have much morals. Also, they owed a white man, Jim Tom, some money and hadn't paid it. One day somebody came to our house and told my daddy, "You know, the Ku Klux went to their house last night and nearly did every one of them to death."

"What for?"

"They just didn't like 'em and they beat them, bad."

For a long time they thought the man wasn't going to live. Finally, one of the men admitted he did it and told the names of every one that beat those people up, but, of course, no charges was ever brought. It wasn't no law and order in that day. They had sheriffs and all, but they didn't help the blacks. The sheriff at that time was Lester Harley. He had this big farm and huge rocks all over it, and he'd take the black prisoners up there and make them carry those rocks and pile them in ditches. And he used to beat the prisoners; people used to come up dead in that jail, but nobody stopped him.

Of course, kids hear other things too. There was one family where the woman was black, but she looked like she was white. They had got run out of Lowndes County by the Ku Klux Klan because of how she looked and that she was married to a black man. So they came up near us. One day I was up at the store and so was this black woman who looked white and so was Miss Walker, the white woman whose place we stayed on.

Miss Walker went up to the other woman and said, "Hum, I don't believe I know you, do I?"

When the black woman who looked white talked, she didn't have a black accent, and she said, "I don't think so," and told Miss Walker her name and where she lived.

So Miss Walker said, "Well, my name is Miss Walker, and when you're down my way, come see me." So the black woman thanked Miss Walker and left and walked down the little dirt road to where she lived.

Then the owner of the store said, "I heard you telling that woman that you'd like for her to come and see you. When did you get where you're entertaining niggers?"

I was standing there listening. And Miss Walker just went all to pieces 'cause she couldn't think about that she'd invited no nigger. So she said, "Why, she ain't no nigger!"

"Yes, she is. They just moved in from Lowndes County."

Well, she got all upset, but I got all tickled. Oh, it was funny. I thought to myself, "That'll teach her." But, still living there was hard for all of us.

Another thing happened that later inspired some of my civil rights work and especially my union organizing. The farm that we lived on and worked was owned by a white man, and his wife's brother and sister-in-law worked at the same textile mill that I later worked at and am trying to unionize. We kids used to go up on Saturdays and work for them, and we'd hear them talking. They were making a fairly decent living, enough that you could tell they was accomplishing something. And the subject came up one time that there were no blacks working in their cotton mill except for a few working as janitors on the outside. That's when it really dawned on me how much injustice there was in the world. Because we was out there; we was the ones that was making the cotton for them to send through these plants. And we had the hardest part, and we weren't getting anything for it. I didn't really become totally aware of the injustice at that particular time because I was young, but I started thinking, and as I grew older I found out more and more how much injustice there was, like our not going to school full time and trying to travel somewhere and not being able to use the facilities.

But there were good times growing too. I loved to go fishing and my mother loved to go too. Me and her have got lost so many times in the woods 'cause we always fished on these little creeks that run off some river somewhere. We'd get lost and I would say, "Mama, how we gonna get out of here?"

And I could tell lots of times that she was scared her own self, but she didn't want to admit she was scared 'cause she thought it would start me to crying. So she said, "All we have to do is get in the water; just follow the creek and we'll come out somewhere."

I'd say, "Oh, Mama! You know we don't know where we going."

"Now, shet up," she'd say. "We got in here, and we can get out." That was always her explanation, and we would walk and every now and then she'd take her pole and if she found a little bitty hole she thought a fish was in, she'd throw it in there. And we'd find our way out of there. When we'd get home, we'd be so wet, but we'd have our little syrup buckets with maybe eight little bitty fishes in them. [Laughing.]

One time we come on two huge snakes, teasing and fixing to kill a rabbit and skunk. Mama said, "Oh, my goodness, we better go get out of here!" so me and her started running. But then she stopped and said, "Come on, let's go back and see what's happening."

I said, "Uh, uh, Mama. Let's go back to the house."

But she said, "No, they ain't gonna hurt us." So we climbed up on a dead tree and watched them tease those animals before killing them, and then we left them there and went home. She was always curious like that.

When we got home Mama told Dad about it, and he got all upset and said, "I want you-all to stay out of them woods 'cause you-all ain't got a bit of sense. If those snakes had ever turned around and even had the slightest idea that you were there, you-all would have been the ones they tied up." But, we still went back fishing.

There was plenty of snakes out there, and when I was growing up, it was nothing to go out and see one getting a sunbath. We'd kill rattlers with a stick or hoe, but we got to the point where we didn't pay most snakes much attention. We kids used to chase some of them like crazy, 'specially black runners. That was the runninest snake; you got in behind them, and you had to be Jesse Owens to keep behind them. And, boy, if one ever turned around like he was going to come after us, you talk about running, we would run so fast to get away.

There were other special people too. My grandfather and step-grandmother used to live near us. All the furniture in her house was old and beautiful. I wish she was alive; I never seen a woman like her in all my life. Her house was like ours, not sealed, but she took something like clay and whitewashed all of her house with it. It was so thick it looked just like plaster. 'Course the house wasn't but one bedroom and one kitchen, but still it was beautiful. And she took newspaper and cut little designs out of it and put it on the shelves in a beautiful china cabinet. It would be so pretty; she was just a fantastic lady with the wildest imagination of anyone I ever seen. She could do anything.

I can see her just as plain as day even now. Her skin was ash color and she had no teeth, but she was the most kindliest person I have ever known. My dad thought of her like his mama, and I loved her to death. She could make the best syrup bread. They stayed so close to us that when she would be making it, we could smell it, and we'd go and she'd give us as much as we wanted.

And my mama was really a good person. She would always help anybody who come along. I remember one time five women prisoners broke out from a women's prison about thirty miles from where we were living. We knew they were out. The sun was almost down that night, but you could still discern things. I looked outside and the women prisoners were coming up the road, walking. Mama was out in the yard, sweeping it with a broom and she seen them. They walked on up there to the yard and she spoke to them. We kids were standing in the doorway; our house had no door on it. You could tell they was out of prison 'cause they had on their uniforms. They said they were hungry and that they had traveled a long way.

Mama said, "Well, the only thing that I got is some peas. Let me finish sweeping this spot then you-all come in." So she swept it and put the broom up on the house and led them inside and said, "You-all sit down now and I'll have it warm in just a minute." Then she fed them, just as good.

All at once my daddy walked in the door, and he knew exactly who they was. They were sitting there, eating away. My mama's name was Sarah and he said, "Sarah!"

"What?"

"What are you doing?"

"What does it look like I'm doing?"

"Do you know who they is?"

"Yeah, I know who they is; they're them prisoners that broke loose." Just like it was an everyday thing.

My dad was short and bald-headed and just stood there looking at them like he didn't know what to do.

Then one of the women spoke up and said, "We're not gonna hurt you-all. We're not gonna do anything; we just want something to eat."

So Daddy said, "Ain't they looking for you-all?"

"Yeah."

So they went ahead and ate, and when they were through they said, "We sure thank you," and they left. Then about an hour later the sheriff came by looking for them, and Mama told him, "Sure, I fed them." The sheriff caught them, though. But that was the type of person my mama was.

There used to be a railroad along where we were living. It had been there long, long years before I was ever born. They called it the Old Georgia Road. It was a freight train line, and people used to ride along in the cars. That was the way that everybody knew how to travel. All kinds of people would come walking along, and Mama used to get what we called hoboers asking for food. She used to feed them and feed them, and my dad would say, "You don't have to go around giving food to everybody that wants something to eat." But she never paid him no mind.

Of course, things were hard. I hadn't ever seen a doctor until after I got married; none of us had, and we certainly never went to a dentist. And school was always a problem too 'cause we could never stay in it long since we were needed in the fields. We had a little rural school to start with, and nobody came from different backgrounds, but when I went to junior high in town, everything was different.

I was just an outcast; that's what you was. The kids that lived around town would talk about the clothes we were wearing. They could go to the beautician and get their hair done; all of those things. I just was never accepted, not only me but the other poor rural kids too. Also, once we got home, there wasn't no way we could get back into town for the prom or football games. There wasn't that much to look forward to with school except getting out. It was the most difficult part of my life, and I never did adjust.

I always wanted to be a nurse, but you can't live on dreams. Many of the kids in town went off to college 'cause their parents worked at the hospital or the glass plant. It was just much better for them, but not for us. We'd be late going to school and the first ones to get out.

I was young when I finished high school, only sixteen, and all I could see was having to keep going into the cotton fields because I knew I couldn't afford to go off to college. So when the first and the only boy that I ever dated in my whole life asked me to marry him, I went and talked with my dad. I was always close to him, and I said, "I want you to sign for me to get married."

He said, "I'm not going to do it. I know ain't nothing wrong with you, like being pregnant."

I said, "No."

"Why do you want to get married?"

"Because I just cannot see myself going back in those cotton fields in September."

"That's a good reason to get married, but I'm still not going to sign for you because I don't think you should."

So then I told him, "Well, if you don't, I'll run away from home." I was going through a stage at that time, and, of course, I hurt him real bad. I don't know if he then signed for me out of anger or because he didn't want me going out in the fields again, but he gave me every blessing, and I went ahead and married at sixteen. But it was a really big mistake. I wished so many times that I could just turn back the clock.

Right off the bat I got pregnant with Jamie. I had too many strange feelings then. I had never been to a doctor before, and I remember the first time I ever had to be put up on a table. I was so tensed up, in complete knots. They're saying, "Relax. Relax."

And I'm laying there saying to myself, "I'm so embarrassed this ain't even funny." How are you going to relax when someone's looking at everything you ever had and ever are going to have?

My husband James was in the service, and we stayed in Arkansas until after Jamie was born, and then we came back to Wetumpka and moved right next door to James's parents. Maybe the marriage could have worked out better if we'd just stayed gone. Whenever we'd have an argument, his parents would treat me like the big bad wolf. So it's just not been what you'd expect out of life, not at all.

I had three sons and a daughter right close together. I got mumps when I was pregnant with my youngest boy, and it like to have killed me. And while I was sick I got into a fight with my husband and decided I couldn't stand it and was going to walk to my daddy's. But James's sister came out and said, "You know you ain't got no business out here with the mumps and being pregnant. Now you go back where you belong." So she finally convinced me to go back home.

Of course, I worked while I was raising the kids. With a man, he works eight hours a day, and the first thing he does when he gets home is flop out on the couch with a newspaper and his day is over with. But for a woman, the day is never over. I'd work nights and then I'd come home in the morning and have to cook and pick up after the kids. Then I'd sleep some and when they'd come back after school, I'd have to be back up, and I'd cook again and go off to work for the night.

My mother became very sick before all my kids were born. I never will forget one morning when we were in the kitchen of her little house. That was where we all got together in the morning time to talk. She was standing at the wood-burning stove and had the frying pan in her hand. All at once, she just dropped the frying pan and that startled everybody in the kitchen. We looked at her. She was looking down and we looked down too, and then everybody just kind of went crazy for a while. Mama was standing in a puddle of blood. We grabbed her because she was fixing to pass out, and my daddy run up to the man whose land we were living on, and he told the man he had to come down there and take my mama to the doctor. When she had been in the hospital about a week, they called and told us to come down. When we got there, the doctor came out and told us that she had cancer, and he didn't hold out no hope for her.

She weighed about 165 pounds when it started, and she had so much vitality and so much energy, and I watched her go from that down to where I could run my hands underneath her and pick her up and do anything I wanted to with her. Also, she always had long hair, down to her waist, and it started coming out from the treatments. She was bedridden for about three years, and, I tell you, it was many, many days that I seen her in such pain that I actually went out, and I prayed for her to die, 'cause I knew that if she died she would never hurt no more. I went to work in the textile mills about two weeks before my mother died, and that made her happy even though she was laying there on her bed and almost at the point of death. She thought it would be a chance for me to get more, and blacks hadn't been allowed in there in the past.

But when she finally died it was like my whole world fell apart. I felt like it was so unfair; I just couldn't imagine why it would happen to her when I could see other people that just did such cruel things. But at the funeral the minister said, "Have you ever went out into a flower bed and picked a bouquet of flowers? Did you ever go out there and pick a bouquet of dead flowers? No. You went out and picked the prettiest ones that was in there. That's the way it is with God. God likes pretty things, good things, too. And sometimes he comes and he picks the best that he can find." Then after that I got to where I could deal with deaths of somebody real close to me better.

But before Mama died, my dad got involved with some old woman that wasn't no good. And after she died he gave the other woman everything they had. So then I kind of lost respect for my father even though I had always been really close to him. And I think about my mother. She never did have an electric stove. During all of her days of dying, we had to go out and get wood in order to keep her warm.

Through those years the civil rights movement had begun. I was on the march from Selma to Montgomery, the one where Viola Liuzzo was killed. After she was shot, everybody was sad and remorseful looking and feeling. You could hear murmurs among the marchers saying, "Is it worth it? Every time we try to do anything, somebody loses their life." There were hecklers on the side, but nobody really paid much attention to them; everybody's mind was bent on what had happened.

Dr. King gave us so much. He inspired us with his speeches, and he gave the black people courage to stand up and say, "Look, man, I know you're not doing the thing that is right." From the time he started being in and out of jail, it made the man realize that if it takes going to jail to get my civil rights, then I'm willing to go. But, then in that process, with all the beatings and the burnings and the killings that happened, sometimes I got bewildered.

When Dr. King was killed, everybody's dream really died. I feel sometimes, "Why did that have to happen right when we were making some progress?" I never have been one to hate but that morning when those kids were blown up in that church, I felt so lost. I didn't want to hate no one, but that particular morning, I wondered, "Where is God now?" It was the most awfullest thing. I thought, "To let this happen in a church? God must just not care anything about the black people." At that particular time, everything was happening. Bull Connors was up there in Birmingham, and I'd watch him out with water hoses on the people and big dogs on the kids. I didn't see any hope for blacks at all. And it's really not a great river of hope left in me now as far as the blacks are concerned.

And I read about black history and the way the women were

used, how they breeded them. I know I would have just killed myself; I wouldn't have been able to take it. And during all that time, all the black women and men had was their hopes and they had a dream, but that dream has not been fulfilled yet.

I work with whites and I associate with them, but I know there's still going to be a prejudice in there. There's no way that you can completely get rid of it. And I think about the life of my family, and, in a sense, my father was just a slave. And we were slaves to him and to the man he was working for because we had no say so about when we could go to school. And we'd have to just sit there and wait for the man to give us what he thought we needed. So slavery was never completely gone.

And even with all the trouble we went through in order to get the civil rights enacted, I feel it came a hundred years too late. Now, sure, we got all the privileges of buying in any neighborhood, but who has got the money. I mean, what's the use of giving a dog a bone when he hasn't got any teeth to chew with any longer? The civil rights deal was fine, but blacks are no better off because they do not have enough money.

But my kids are learning to fight for their rights. They forced the schools to integrate but that doesn't mean they've stopped discriminating against the black kids, and the black kids are smart enough to know exactly what they're doing. An example was with my son's football team. The team was made up mostly of blacks, so they had these black guys out there running their hearts out, but the cheerleaders were chosen by the teachers and were all white. The black parents met with the superintendent about it, and when that didn't work, the boys walked off the field and refused to play. And they had been the champs of the state of Alabama for the last three years.

At that time I was really into the union campaign, so the school people said I was the one that was instigating it, but I had just talked to my kids and told them, "You can be pushed so far, then all of a sudden you got to take a stand and say, 'Look, I've got rights too!' Now if you-all feel what you're doing is right, do it and if you don't, then don't do it." So they walked off and newspapers and television came.

There was a big meeting and the next afternoon, the kids came home from school just grinning like crazy and said, "Mama, we're going back out on the football field. They decided to let the student body vote on who they wanted on the cheerleader squad, and we voted and got four whites and two blacks. We're satisfied now."

And the next year they voted three and three. I'm proud of them for standing up like that.

I first went to work in the textile mills in '67, right after the civil rights movement forced them to let blacks in. I'd drive into the mills in Montgomery and work nights and then go home again. I'm still working in them now. Then about three years ago, things got bad with James. I think the hardest blow was what happened on our anniversary. I had worked that night and I came in at one and went to bed, and the next morning I heard somebody ringing the doorbell. I went to the door and it was the sheriff. He asked me if I was Mary Robinson, and I said, "Yes."

He said, "Well, I have some papers here for you."

I said, "What kind of papers?"

He just handed them to me and I looked at them, and they were divorce papers! I said, "I don't believe it!" At that particular time James worked at night too, so I went back in the house to where he was, and I said, "You just don't do things like this; serve me papers and not even tell me." I was devastated. James didn't move out right then, but he got involved in a couple of bad things and decided he could use me as a punching bag, hitting me, so I went and got me a lawyer, and he moved right next door with his parents.

I had heard rumors about James and another woman, but mens are going to be mens, so I actually didn't pay that much attention. But the woman was a teacher in Tracy's school, and that was hard on Tracy. Then there was the divorce and they got married and had a child. The state of Alabama stinks as far as women getting any kind of consideration from the judges. James hired a lawyer who was the son of the judge, and so I only got $150 a month child support for all four kids. The kids would go over to visit James every weekend, and they'd take them bowling, take them out to eat, spend all sorts of money on them. Then the kids would come home and I wouldn't have anything.

I saw it all mess my kids' lives up. Their grades went down in school, and I saw my second son go from a happy little boy and then withdraw into himself. Before, every day he had wanted to go hunting or fishing with his daddy, but afterward it was just like he died or something. You know, that part of it hurt me worse than anything. And I had so many money problems. We'd bought a little house but I couldn't keep it, and for a while there, I thought I was fixing to crack up. It can be almost devastating when you see things not going right, and there's not anything you can do about it except sit there and watch it go wrong. So it took a bad toll on me when I got divorced.

I was having to drive back and forth to Montgomery to work which was about forty-five minutes each way, but the kids didn't want to move down here. I just couldn't keep everything together, and I said, "What're we going to do?"

Their aunt on their daddy's side said, "Well, the two oldest boys are big kids and aren't home that much 'cause they both work in the afternoon, so they can stay with us." And James took Tracy and Ronnie and I stayed in Montgomery during the week. But Tracy and Ronnie are unhappy staying with him, and that part hurts me more than anything. You can talk to Ronnie and he'll tell you so much, and then he'll just hush his mouth and he won't say anything. And I still can't get it in my mind that I'm not married anymore. If I go out, I feel like I'm being disloyal even though James is married and has got his own life. But mostly, I'd feel I'd be being disloyal to my kids because I've seen so many kids with problems with stepparents. It's like I've been left alone, like being an orphan or something. My kids are really the only ones I've got, and after they're a little older, they'll be gone.

But I do care about something else; I care about bringing a union to Stevens, the mills I work for here in Montgomery. I'm thirty-six years old and I say, "Well, I've did the best part of my years here anyway, so I'll take what remains and try to do something constructive with my life." And trying to bring a union to Stevens is constructive.

J. P. Stevens used to run their mills up North, but they left the North 'cause they knew that they were going to have to have unions there. So every now and then they'd bring a plant south because the South has so few unions. Many ended up in North Carolina and South Carolina, which is two of the worse states there is. Not Mississippi; I guess they figures, "Ain't no use going down there 'cause 90 percent of the population is black." Stevens more or less owns North and South Carolina, and they still have their own little company towns surrounding the plants. They rent out houses to the workers, like they showed in the movie *Norma Rae*. It's almost like living in slavery without having a master. Textiles is the main industry down South, and they get together and put a monopoly on wages.

It's really bad working in any textile, but it's been overly bad at Stevens. When I first started working in this plant it was not J. P. Stevens but United Elastic. Then Stevens bought it and made altogether different changes from when it was United Elastic. We lost holidays, and they picked supervisors who were outsiders and didn't care about us. We have no benefits, no insurance, no sick leave.

And there are mostly vulnerable people working there, so it's easy for Stevens to take advantage of them. We got some workers in the plant that cannot even read and write, and there's nobody out there that has not had a bad life of it. We've got about 60 percent women out there now and 40 percent men. And so many of the women are divorced and having to take care of themselves and usually their kids. Many haven't even graduated from high school, so Stevens thinks they can pretty much make them do what they want. And they've never did anything for the workers no matter how long they've worked there. Louise Baley went to work in that plant when she was thirteen years old and raised her three kids on it, and now she's fifty-five years old. And they take someone with six weeks training and give that person the same pay as Louise is making even though she spent her whole life in there. People work there for their entire life, and they end up with a pension of forty dollars a month.

Also, they definitely discriminate against women. The highest paid workers in there is the fixers, and they don't do nothing. Because she's a woman, they wouldn't consider my friend Mildred to be a fixer, even though she had seniority. I said to her, "File you one of those discrimination suits so the company will think twice before they give it to a man next time." You see, they want to keep a woman down to where she cannot be independent and cannot have any power. There's no women in supervision, in management, no way. And it's no reason at all that a woman can't do it. Who can't drink coffee, and that's basically what the supervisors do.

And a lot of times, when men think they've got the advantage over women, they start making wisecracks. In an offhand manner, they'll come up and tell you a joke or something. If they think they can use it in order to make a play for you, they're going to use it. And when the supervisors come at them sexually, a lot of women, rather than say anything about it, just keep quiet and take it. And that just burns me up; when you got somebody pawing you and they got like octopus arms. Makes you want to just slap the taste out of their mouth. I just really don't feel a man has any business being over a whole bunch of women like that.

And they are really hard on the black women. I see women out there right now doing jobs that women never did before. What they're doing is jobs that men held down because they was heavylike jobs, but the women they put there don't feel they have a choice. And I've noticed that they're all black women, doing those heavy jobs back behind the carding department where raw materials start and come forward. Once we were having a committee meeting, and I asked, "When have you seen a white on those jobs?" and nobody could remember ever seeing a white person back there.

There are a lot of health problems from working in the mills. Of course, there's the brown lung, when people get cotton dust from the air in the mills into their chest, and it just hurts their breathing and hurts it till they die. I went to a stockholders' meeting of Stevens a couple of years ago, and, I'm telling you the truth, I sat there and I cried. 'Cause there was this lady, her name was Muriel, and she was one of the members of the brown lung association. She had brown lung and she was coughing and struggling to breathe, and she just looked so sick and tired. Louis Harrell, another old worker with brown lung who started in the mills at thirteen, testified with her, but since that time he's died.

Muriel came up to the mike, mikes were set up all over the auditorium, and she tried to talk to James Finley, who at that time was board chair of Stevens. Finley had a fixed face that didn't show any compassion. Muriel told him how long she had worked in one of their plants and how she retired on seventeen dollars a month and had brown lung from working in the mills all those years.

This was during the question and answer period, and he looked down and said, "If you didn't have no better sense than to work in there until you got brown lung, I don't have any sympathy for you." And she had given up her life for that durn company, and then for him to stand there and tell her that! It even made the stockholders angry. I sat there and was crying and thought, "What kind of heart do you have?" Then I thought that he didn't have a heart; he got a pacemaker.

A lot of other workers came up and they'd ask him questions, and a lot of times Mr. Finley just refused to answer. He even shut the mikes off, so he wouldn't even hear them. That's the kind of man we work for.

Also, there's so much noise in the mills that people lose their hearing and so much vibration from the machines that your body is constantly being jarred. Then there's the overwork, the overstraining; it's your whole body being affected by stress. And the women get varicose veins. It's really just an unhealthy place to work. It does nothing for your life and your emotions and is a constant battle. You see a worker that has lost a finger; you see workers that have worked in there so many years until you can see the strain on their face and on their body. It's really a pathetic sight.

I went down to Tallassee with a couple of other women to do some organizing in a real old textile plant there. The plant is right at a river with a road that goes beside it. You can just stand there and watch the workers come out and look at the people's faces who come along in their cars, and you can tell who works in that plant and who's just traveling through. The mill workers' faces look so tired and strained, like life is being worked out of them.

I went to work one night two years ago, and I'll never forget it. One of the guys came up to me right away and said, "Mary, Richard just got his arm cut off. It's been forty-five minutes, and he is still just laying there."

I started out to where he was, and somebody caught me and said, "No, don't go out there."

"Why?"

"Because his arm is completely amputated, and he's just laying there in shock."

So I called our union organizer and told her that we'd had a bad accident, and by the time I got off the phone, the ambulance had got there and took him away. He got his arm cut off in a card machine. It just cut it clean, slam off. The machine did not have a safety switch on it like it was supposed to. Richard had put his arm in there because the machine was supposed to stop and instead it cut it off.

The doctors experimented with him, and they put his arm back on, but they said it'll be five years before they know whether it works or not. In the meantime, not a day goes by when he's not in pain, and he is only living off of $116 a week. And he has six kids! And the company has not given him one dime! I don't know how they're surviving 'cause his wife was working up until the accident, but she had to quit her job so she could take care of him.

But there's accidents like that and what really makes me mad is that OSHA [Occupational Safety and Health Administration] is supposed to be inspecting the machines. If OSHA thinks the managers are going to tell them that the machine doesn't have a safety latch or safety switch on it, that's crazy. Because that's going to cost the company money.

So this year when I went to the stockholders' convention, I found out that another worker in a Stevens plant had his arm cut off in the same machine. The plant had finally come in, after his arm was cut off, and put safety switches on the machine. So when they started the question and answer period at the stockholders' convention, I got up to the microphone, and I asked Wendel Stevens, the president of the company, "Mr. Stevens, in the plant I work in in Montgomery, you-all are constantly talking about safety. But almost two years ago, one of our fellow workers in our company had his arm completely amputated, and he's been living on $116 a week with six kids. Now you-all talk about safety, but still you do nothing about the dangerous machinery in the plant. I understand that in another one of your plants here, in the Carolinas, you have had another worker have his arm amputated in the same kind of machine.

"You say how concerned you are, but I consider that the only time you are really concerned about health and safety is when you-all make a tour of your plants. That's the only time that our plant management considers it. When they know that you-all, the big mens, are coming into town, they have everything cleaned up. They sweep the floor; they get up all the oil; they cut the machines down so it's not so dusty in there. But by the time you walk out of that plant, they speed the machine up; they don't care if the oil is all over the floor; the guards are not kept up on the machines. I think that's bad."

Of course, the stockholders were surprised to hear somebody say those things and they all made an aahhh sound.

Then Mr. Stevens said, "Are you telling me that when we are coming into the plant, the supervisors get the plant all cleaned up for us?"

I says, "That's exactly what I'm telling you. And once you leave, they don't give a damn what kind of conditions that we have to work in. They sweep up, clean up, mop up, when you-all are coming in just to walk around for thirty minutes, but we have to work in that stuff forty hours a week."

Of course, by the time I got back to Montgomery, the company knew that I'd went up there and spilled the beans on them. The guys from New York have been down one time since then and surprised the company here and didn't tell them they were coming. So the managers were caught with their pants down. Now they started having safety classes with the workers involved in them, so the workers could tell them the conditions they considered to be unsafe. But, still, if it's going to cost them money, they just ignore it. They don't pay any attention.

The day-to-day working in the mills is so hard, and you get really tired. My friend Mildred runs a winder, and she has from seventy to one hundred spindles to take care of. And right now, I'm being what they call a yarn person, but I'm still in the spinning room and classified as a spinner. I spin in my dreams all the time that I sleep. And your whole body aches from the strain and the bending. I think that if you took a survey of people who work at the plant, most drink a lot or take nerve pills or smoke dope in order to go to sleep. You get so tensed up working there, and most people can't then just relax. Also, you don't know what the temperature will be in the plant. Sometimes it's so hot that it just drains your energy away completely. Then, a few years ago, they bricked up all the windows so we couldn't look out anymore. You just get to the point where, whatever work you do, you do it without even being aware of what you're doing. The noise is so bad and you can't get the noise out, so you try not to think. And, of course, the dust continues. In the spinning room at about eleven at night, I can look at the wall and see it completely covered with dust. You can brush and blow dust off your skin or clothes, but you can't blow it off your insides.

But what disgusts me is that those machines seem to have got more knowledge than I have. That's what makes me mad. What I'm thinking when I look at them is that I'm looking at a human being; I'm looking at somebody that was very, very smart in order to make a big old monster of a machine like that. So every time I run a spinning job, it is a challenge to me. I know I got to work 'cause if I don't it's going to beat me. I've got to beat the machine.

As I said, I became aware of oppression little by little as I grew, and then, during the civil rights movement, I saw that people could fight to change things, and I started being involved. After that I got the opportunity to go into the textile mills to work, and that's when I really wanted to see conditions change because there was so much injustice in there. Finally, one day I heard a union organizer was coming to town, and I said, "Yeah, and I want to see him." That was in '76 and when the organizer, Henry Mann, hit the gate, I hit it with him. And it all started from that.

In 1976 we really worked to get people to sign their union cards, and we got over a majority at the plant so Stevens got a bargaining order in '77. After that they weren't supposed to make any changes in the working conditions, but they started making all kinds of changes. Also, they were using every little thing they could come up with to get people fired. They did so much I bet that there are approximately 275 to 300 workers out there now; whereabout, when we starting organizing, we had about 450 to 500. They both fired people and harassed them so much that many couldn't stand the pressure of it and quit.

And the company appealed the bargaining order so they

wouldn't have to deal with the union. Then in 1979 a judge found the company guilty of massive unfair labor practices in our plant and refusal to bargain, but Stevens wouldn't comply. All over the South, they did the same thing. Courts would rule against them and they'd pay the fines or appeal, and they'd go on refusing to recognize the union. They'll do anything to keep out the union.

It's easier to organize the plants with a lot of blacks in them. The whites have usually been there so long that they feel like they got a lot to lose. But the blacks usually think, "What have I got to lose if I sign a union card? I ain't got nothing no way. If they want to get my job, they're going to get it anyway." They just sign the union card right off the bat. Many of the young white workers will also join right away, but lots of the older ones, no way. They'll walk by and look at you like you're some kind of murderer. And Stevens has tried to turn white workers scared of blacks; they put up pictures of whites who had been killed by some blacks in San Francisco. Like I said, they'll do anything to stop the union.

You never know what's going to happen when you try to start organizing a plant. There is a plant in a little place called Tallassee, Alabama. It is a bad place to work. I worked down there for two weeks one time, and one day I just walked out and said, "No way. I'll starve before I work in here." The dust levels were so high that when you saw the workers coming out you said, "My God, what have they did to them in there?" They looked like someone sucked all the blood out of them.

So Alice, another organizer, and I went down there to tell about the union, and we split up and were passing out leaflets when the company men came out like a big swarm of bees to complain about where I was standing. You could sure feel the hostility. Then a patrol car came, and I said, 'Uh, oh, I'm fixing to go to jail." But he helped direct the traffic where Alice was working. Finally, I saw two guys go by and park and then come back. I thought, "Oh, no, somebody done hired someone to come out here and get me."

But the men came up and said, "Would you give us a whole stack of those leaflets?"

"You're not going to throw them in the trash can are you?"

They said, "We've been looking for somebody to come down here and help us for a long time. It's awful in there." And so they started trying to organize.

Stevens is hard on me, and friends of mine sometimes say, "Why don't you go look for another job?"

I say, "Well, I could do that." But I think of all the years that I've already put out there, from '67 on. If I go somewhere else, I've got to start from scratch. Plus, there's the fact that I feel that if you've got to work somewhere, never be satisfied with just working in that place and letting it stay the same. That place is like a house, if you don't constantly try to keep fixing that house up, that house goes down, and that's the way it is with a job. If you're not constantly trying to improve that job, the conditions on it, it's going to stay the same or it's going to get worser. And I know that place can be a better place to work at. I know that we can have the same working conditions and the same wages that other plants have. If it was a little bitty company, I could understand it staying bad, but when you're dealing with a company that's as big as Stevens, with eighty-five plants, you're not dealing with a little empire. You're dealing with a huge empire that has got the money to pay the workers and make conditions better for them. And a union would help. A union is not an organization out there that's bent on destroying a company; it's the workers banding together to better their own selves.

I'm living here in Montgomery now with Alice, one of the women organizers, because money is such a problem. You just cannot hardly make it now with the price of everything. If the kids were small, it would be easier because things are a little bit cheaper when they're small. But when they're teenagers, their clothes and everything cost as much as an adult. Sometimes I think to myself, "Now, what am I going to do?"

I don't sleep much, work all night at the plant and spend most of the day organizing, so I just get patches of sleep, and then sometimes I get sad and think, "Nothing really good ever came out of my life but my kids." And I think, "Why don't I just give it up and do nothing and just lay down for awhile?"

Yes, I've thought, "Why do you keep hanging in there?" but if the kids don't need you for other things, they need you for moral support. They have always looked to me as being a pillar of strength, and I need to be there for them. And I've never wanted my kids to have to live the kind of life that I had to live. I've thought about what if the kids would have to go to work in the textile mills. The main thing that has made me fight against Stevens is that I don't want my kids to have to work under the same conditions that I had to. Or anybody else. Because I know it can be better.

And I'll keep on fighting for the union. I think about the union in terms of my mother. She would have been proud of me for doing it. She would have supported me all the way. Because her life had been devastating too, and she'd been oppressed all of her life, and she'd want a change for us all. There were just too many kids and never enough to go around, and she was depressed when we couldn't be in school. She would have been very proud of me for trying to change that. And I think somewhere along the line, she knows about it now.

We didn't have much then, just
outdoor toilets, no TV, nothing. Also, we
worked so hard that by the time we ate
supper, we were tired and went to bed.
And we were very, very poor. Sometimes
we had chicken or meat to eat, but mostly
we had cornbread, peas, potatoes, and
corn. But I was loved. Even though we
were poor, it was the best time of my life.

—Mildred McEwen

Mildred McEwen and I drove together past an impoverished black ghetto in Montgomery, and through an area in which poor whites gathered outside trying to escape the heat, to the West Boylston J. P. Stevens plant where Mildred and Mary worked. The plant loomed up like a prison, surrounded by high chain-link fences topped with barbed wire. It consisted of a sprawling, three-story brick building with clearly outlined windows that had been bricked in so the employees could no longer look out. In the past, the workers were able to sit outside and smoke on the fire escape during their night shift breaks; now however, once inside the building, an employee was not allowed to leave until two gates were unlocked at shift change time. There was a small entrance gate between the fence and barbed wire, but it opened only out and no one could enter. Guards watched the entrance from a white house across the street, and any requests to enter the plant went through them.

I planned to take Mildred's photo with the plant in the background and pulled the car up close to the gate. She was very nervous about the process, and we worked quickly, aware of being observed from across the street; the heat seemed even more oppressive because of the speed with which we had to move.

When we arrived back at Mildred's efficiency apartment, we spoke of the constant tension under which Mildred worked. Mildred's feelings of tension had increased within the past few days due to the beating death of a man in a nearby apartment, which reminded her all too clearly of a time when she was nearly killed in a similar way. While I was there, she started carrying a pistol and was in the process of buying one for her nineteen-year-old daughter.

I interviewed Mildred several times in the early morning, after she returned home from working the night shift at Stevens. She was forty years old and looked fatigued, with a narrow face, large, thick, round glasses, reddish gold shoulder-length hair, and freckled shoulders and arms. She was very thin, with a slightly concave body, and usually wore a blouse and blue jeans and was barefoot while we talked. She chain-smoked throughout our interviews. The first day we sat in the kitchen eating biscuits and gravy. Mildred drank several beers, trying to relax after a difficult night at work, hoping she would then be able to sleep more peacefully.

Her apartment was carefully furnished and had a color TV running soundlessly in the background. Several photographs of her daughter, Lisa, were on the wall. In one, Lisa appeared at her high school graduation, and in another she was smiling with her young husband. A large brightly-colored poster hung over her kitchen table instructing her "How to be happy in spite of yourself," and included such ideas as "Smell swell smells" and "Astonishing cheap thrills."

Mildred My father was killed when I was real young, and my mother went back home to my grandmother and granddad. Then, when she remarried, I just stayed there because I loved my grandparents. In the beginning, my granddaddy had a dairy and sold milk. That was before I started school, and that's where my half-sister was born. Later on, my grandmother and granddaddy and I moved farther out in the country where he planted cotton and corn. It was really flat land, no hills whatsoever. I used to go out in the cornfields and make dolls out of corncobs, the cob for the doll and the silk for the hair. And I'd put clothes on them and sit out under a tree and watch the older people work. My granddaddy had a couple of men that would come in and help, and then my aunt and her husband would work.

The first thing I remember was when I was four and my stepsister was being born. We lived on the farm, and I remember that my grandmother was holding the baby and the baby was blue. It looked like she was dead, but there was a pan of water, and my grandmother just took Brenda and dunked her in that hot water. That somehow revived her and she started screaming. We were out on the front porch, they always had those front porches that went all the way 'round the house, and I was crying because I was afraid. Then I heard the baby and they came out and told me I had a new sister.

The next thing I remember distinctly was the first day of school. I had to go on the bus, and, oh, I didn't want to go and I was crying. My grandfather was standing on the porch, and he said to my grandma, "Jula Mae, put her on that bus. I don't care if she cries, she has to go." They had to put me bodily on the bus and I hated school. I wanted to be with my granddaddy. I had never been around anybody except them, and I was scared to death.

School never got much better, partly because I didn't have nice clothes like the other girls. And I was embarrassed when I had to fill out those forms that said, "What does your father do?" I had to put, "I don't have a father. My grandfather is a farmer," and it hurt. I was always different and kids can be cruel. There weren't any other kids around there. I didn't have any friends; the houses were few and far between. There was a little store, right beside us, just a little country store.

My granddaddy made me a little cotton-picking bag out of a flour sack, and after school I'd go out with him to pick. He wouldn't make me pick much. It was fun, and the times that I remember were happy times. My granddaddy was a fabulous man, a Christian man and a compassionate man. I really loved him; he was my favorite person in the whole world. My grandmother loved me, but she yelled at me. But my granddaddy never did. He was a big, tall man who weighed about 200 pounds, but he would always ask me to do things in a soft, kind way, and I'd do anything for him. Every Sunday, me and him walked the mile to church. We never failed.

I was the ugliest little kid you have ever saw. I swear I was ugly. I look better now that I ever have. I wore pigtails and was skinny, skinny as a bean pole. I wore long-ago dresses and was just pathetic looking. I have one picture before I had braids, but I had bangs, just like a bowl had been set over my head. And I was looking like, oh, I lost my best friend. I always wore dresses, never overalls, and went barefoot in the summertime. But my granddaddy loved me no matter how I looked.

I have some special memories of when I was real little. My big treat was that every afternoon I got a Coke from the store next to us. Also, we used to take the bus to town every Saturday, and one time when we were in a store, I saw the prettiest big doll I had ever seen. I wanted it so much that when they started to leave, I just laid down in the store and was crying and screaming and kicking. They had to whip me to get me out of that store, but they saved the money for it, and they got me that doll for Christmas. I remember it was so beautiful, about three feet tall with dark hair. And I remember the heat in the summer, and my grandmother laying in bed and fanning me. She was a tiny little lady who always kept her hair real short with a permanent in it.

We didn't have much then, just outdoor toilets, no TV, nothing. Also, we worked so hard that by the time we ate supper, we were tired and went to bed. And we were very, very poor. Sometimes we had chicken or meat to eat, but mostly we had cornbread, peas, potatoes, and corn. But I was loved. Even though we were poor, it was the best time of my life.

When I was about twelve, my granddaddy started in with skin cancer on his hands. They removed two of his fingers, and then it just spread over his body. They wouldn't let me in the hospital because I was too young, and, oh, I was just devastated that I couldn't see him. I knew he was fixing to die, so my aunt snuck me in there real late at night, but he didn't even recognize me and I was just crying. Then, a little later my aunt told me that he had died. I just couldn't accept it; I couldn't believe it. It hurt me really bad. I felt so close to him, more so than anybody else in my life, other than my daughter now.

Then my grandmother sold the farm, and we moved with my mother and stepfather and sister to Cylacauga. Cylacauga is just a small red-necked town, where the only industry at that time was the textile industry. I felt so strange, so different. Because I had never been around anybody except the kids at my earlier school, and I was real shy. I went to high school in Cylacauga, and if you didn't belong to a certain group, you were just alone. I never belonged to it; I was always an outsider. That is just the way I felt all my life, alone. My parents were not poor, but they did not have a lot.

Also, in a small town like that, there's nothing to do, but a bunch of us girls would go driving around when we could get a car. One night when I was sixteen we were sitting in the drive-in, and a guy parked next to us and slammed his car door into ours. He came over and said, "Hi, my name's Harold. I'm sorry I bumped you."

And I said, "Oh, well, I'm Mildred," and that's how we met. We dated for about five or six months and then decided to get married, which was ridiculous. I think a lot of the reason I decided to get married was just because I was so unhappy. We were both seventeen and ran away to a little town in Mississippi, which I thought was exciting. Harold had to go and get an old man to be a witness for us. It seemed thrilling, but it wasn't. It was stupid, very stupid, but I thought it was all going to be so great. I was sorry just two days later when Harold slapped me around. I don't even know why, but I didn't have the good sense just to walk out and leave. I thought, "It'll get better; it won't be like this." But it got worse and worse.

Then, when I had been married for about a year and a half, my daughter was born. I had to grow up real quick after that. Lisa was born and then Harold and Walter came soon. I had all three of them before I was twenty-one, and I was working too. I had had dreams of being a doctor. Who knows, I might have too, had I not gotten married. But I was so young I didn't know what I was doing. You do wild, crazy things when you're young. I regretted the marriage, but then I had the kids.

It was hard. We had no running water and I had to get up at

five in the morning to build a fire. It was so cold in the house that when Harold took his coveralls off, they froze to the floor. I had to work and there weren't any choices for jobs, so I went to work in the mills. I remember the people who worked in the mills back then. They always have the look, so you can tell. They look old and they look tired and worn out.

I had so much trouble trying to find somebody to keep the children. My husband was not dependable enough to keep them, so he did not care for them even though we worked different shifts. I would have to pay somebody to keep them, and he would just go out and have his fun.

It was hard to do everything when the kids were so young. We lived next door to my mother-in-law, and she used to come to the house all the time and put me down because I wasn't clean enough. She didn't realize I had to go to work every day, from two to ten at night. One time I had just had a baby, and my sister Brenda was over and was in the kitchen trying to cook. I'll never forget it. My mother-in-law had a split personality like my husband; she could turn on you any minute. We had a fireplace and my mother-in-law had a fire poker and was stirring the fire with it and nagging Brenda. Brenda had a smart mouth on her and said, "If you don't like the way I cook, you do something." When she heard that, my mother-in-law got so mad she came at Brenda and almost hit her with the poker!

Later Brenda said, "I'll never try to cook something and have her up here again." I think there was a history of mental instability in that family; my mother-in-law's father went insane. And my mother-in-law was just cruel. I've seen her take an unwanted puppy and just sling it against a tree. I could never do that.

Life was so hard because of my husband's violence. He was beating me all the time, practically from the very beginning, and it got so I felt no love for him. I was ashamed, but I didn't know what to do. I really had no money. I had my parents, but they still had two children at home, and I felt like I had nowhere to go. I had no money, no car, three little kids, and I felt just trapped. Everybody knew he beat me, and nobody helped. Still, his mother would come up there and she would see that I was beat up. Sometimes I couldn't go to work and I'd just be in a terrible condition. I'd have my arms all bruised and my eyes black and my glasses broken and all sorts of hurts. My mother-in-law even said, "Don't live with him; leave him. I wouldn't live with him." She never really helped me, but she always told me that. But, then, when I did leave him, she turned completely against me.

Harold never hurt the kids. He threatened one time to whip one of the boys with an electric cord, and we got in a terrible fight about that, but I told him I'd leave, so he never hurt them. But they witnessed it, though. They saw what he did to me, so they were afraid of him. All he had to do was look at them to scare them.

But I was close to the children, and I somehow believe that the love you have when you're very young sticks by you. As babies, they were the only things I lived for. They were beautiful children, all three of them. They were my life. It was like me and them, against him. The kids knew I'd always be there. The boys were five and seven when it happened.

Harold used to have a little pistol that he'd always pull on me, and that really got to me. One night he came in the house and put the pistol up in the cabinet. When he left I said, "I can't take this anymore; I've got to get away from him." Lisa was at her grandmother's and I just had the two little boys with me. So I got the pistol to get it away from him, I put it in my purse, and I took the two boys and I just walked out; I left. I took the car and went to a friend and her husband's house and asked them if I could stay. They let me; they let me stay.

I had been gone three weeks when it happened. That day we had been to a funeral. Harold's uncle had died and I had agreed to ride in the car with Harold. I had left the kids with my friends where we were staying. We had a house trailer and I asked Harold to stop back by there so I could get the kids more clothes. I had no idea what Harold had planned. I walked in that door and I just immediately walked back to my closet to get the clothes. And Harold just threw me down on the bed and started beating me up with a Coke bottle, all over my head.

He weighed about 200 pounds and was sitting astride me, just beating me to a pulp and choking me, hitting me with a Coke bottle and cutting big gashes in my head. I blacked out a couple of times even. I don't know how or what revived me; I just don't know. He told me when he was beating me up that he was going to kill me and him; that was his plan. But I didn't see a gun or anything, and I figured he couldn't beat me to death surely. But he might could have. I was just panicked. I could feel myself going, and I thought, "You're fixing to die. Do something! Do something!" So I just kept fighting to get away from him. I was bleeding and had lost my glasses and couldn't see, but somehow I rolled over on the floor. I was over there between the bed and the floor. And I saw him. He was sitting right on the edge of the bed, and I saw him raise up.

He got a gun from under the mattress and when I saw that, something happened. I revived up and I just walked out. I just walked right past him. I was barely walking, though. I had on high heels and a dress, both of my shoes were gone, my dress was torn off, and I didn't have my glasses on. I had lost them and I can't see without my glasses. I was barely moving. But he didn't try to stop me or anything; he just let me go.

I was bleeding real bad and we didn't have a phone there. So I was walking up to the next-door neighbor's to use the phone, when I heard the gun shot. I heard it, but I didn't go back. I just went on to the next house, and I called his sister to come immediately. And when they got up there, Harold was dead.

I guess he had planned to knock me out and then kill me and kill himself. It was just not my time to go, because all he had to do was reach right there and shoot me. I walked right past him. Then I walked out that back door, and he still could have stood up and shot me in the back when I was walking away. I don't know why he didn't.

My head was just pouring blood and I was just barely seeing. The people who came thought I was dying, and they took me over to the hospital, and I was in there three weeks. I must have been in shock. When they let me out of the hospital to go to the funeral, I still couldn't comprehend it. It never really got to me until I saw Lisa and she was crying, and then it hit me what had happened.

And they started suspecting me. My mother-in-law said, "There is no way that Mildred could have gotten away from him; she is so tiny." So she thought that I had killed him, and she sent the sheriff up there to the hospital to question me. I told him, "I don't know anything. I just know that he beat me up and that I walked out the door."

The sheriff said, "Woman, if you had a killed him, I wouldn't do a thing to you." But I think everybody thought that I really had killed him. And gossip, gossip, gossip.

After I got out of the hospital, I stayed with my friend, and finally it just got too much. I called my sister who lived in Nevada, and I said, "Brenda, I feel that I have just got to get away from here for a while or I am just going to go crazy."

She said, "Well, why don't you just come out and stay a few weeks with me."

I said, "OK, I'll talk to Mrs. McEwen and ask her to watch the kids." So I told my mother-in-law exactly what I planned to do. I said, "I'm just going to go and stay for a few weeks." I left the trailer, I left the car, I left everything sitting there. All I took was my suitcase. And I said, "I'll be back in three to five weeks."

While I was gone my in-laws got a lawyer and had papers drawn up. My mother-in-law's cousin was the lawyer, and the judge was their friend that they had worked for. I got home one afternoon and the next morning the sheriff came with papers saying that I had deserted the children, that I didn't intend to come back. My in-laws had set it up and were trying to take the kids from me.

I don't even think it would have been allowed to happen here in Montgomery, but in Cylacauga those few people had all the power. There was no way they could prove I was unfit because of the children. They were healthy, they were fine-looking, beautiful children, and they always had care when I was at work. And, so, they didn't try to say that I was unfit; they said desertion.

I borrowed $250 from my sister and got a lawyer, and my sister came back from Nevada. But it didn't do any good. And my in-laws knew I had just intended to stay for a visit, just to get away. They knew that. But it was all fixed with the judge. It was all fixed up. So there was nothing I could do.

And then I almost really did crack up. It almost destroyed me, all that. I never remarried and those are the only three children I have. And my in-laws offered me money. Harold's sister was involved in the whole thing, and she said, "Mildred, we know you don't have anywhere to go; we know you don't have anybody to go to, but we'll give you money if you sign the adoption papers. We want to adopt them."

I said, "No, Sue. I'll find somewhere to go. I don't want the money and the only way you'll ever adopt is when I'm dead." But they never did; they could not do that legally.

My sister-in-law kept the two boys and I'm sure they loved them. I have no complaint about that. And they're fairly well-off. And Lisa stayed with my mother-in-law and father-in-law. They only let me see them at my mother-in-law's house. I would go there whenever I could take it, but it got so I didn't see them much.

The kids knew, though. Lisa saw through it. The older she got the more she understood, and she had every bit of it figured out. And my son that is eighteen and the other one that is sixteen figured it out too. Because the kids have been around my in-laws, and they see how they are and what they've said about me. And the kids see me and they know; they put it together. But I don't know why my in-laws did it to me. Revenge, I guess, is the reason. I never will know why they did it. They never told me; they've never talked to me about it.

I moved to Montgomery and started to drink some because of all that had happened. For a while I was so depressed, I couldn't even lift my hand to eat. Then Lisa got real sick with lupus, and for about five weeks she was really, really bad in the hospital in Birmingham. That was devastating because I was afraid she was going to die, and I had not really gotten to see her to amount to anything in two or three years. That's when I really started the drinking. If I went to visit the kids, there was so much tension I could not relax and enjoy being with her or my boys.

But after Lisa got home from the hospital, I called her, and she said, "Momma, please come."

I said, "I'll be there." I went to see her regardless of what my in-laws said or did. And I've seen them regularly since then.

After losing them the drinking was the only thing I thought would ease the pain. I drank for about four years almost constantly, day after day, when Lisa got sick. But it didn't help. It just made me more depressed and more depressed. I was in the hospital twice. The last time I stayed almost four weeks, and it really helped because I got psychiatric care. Somehow, somebody got through to me and made me see that I was a worthwhile human being.

I believe in God. I'm not saying I'm a Christian, but I believe that God has helped me definitely; otherwise, I don't think I would have made it. During that depression, a psychologist, a young girl, got through to me. She said, "So what." She kept repeating over and over and over again to me, "So what if it didn't work out; forget about it." She kept telling me that over and over, but in a kind way; she was always smiling. I had been always thinking that nothing was going to work out, and I was supposed to be devastated, but she said, "So what if it didn't work out." Those two little words; I keep thinking them. I know it sounds strange but now when something happens I think that. "So what. There is always something else there. There's something else." That's the attitude I've taken towards my job. That's the attitude I've taken toward my in-laws. I say, "So what if they don't like me. I don't care. So what. It's not gonna devastate me anymore like it used to."

I've been thinking lately about dying. I say, "Well, I'm not going to be forever, so why should I worry about that little thing out there." And that's how I stopped my drinking.

When I first moved to Montgomery, I needed a job immediately. I had known the man who is now my supervisor from back in Cylacauga. We had been friends our whole lives, and I went out to the mill where he was working, and they hired me the same day. I had worked in the mills in Cylacauga, and when I first went to work, it was not that bad, not nearly as bad as it is right now with J. P. Stevens. It was all dreary and boring, but it was not a really hard, hard job in the beginning. But it sure is bad now. Most of the people that work out there have got no education whatsoever; a lot of them can't even read or write. The majority of the people that work there now are blacks, and the white people in the mills are uneducated and just followed their families into the mills. It makes it easy for Stevens to exploit them.

There's another aspect to it too. If you're a fairly good-looking woman in a place like that, and you flirt around with the supervisors, talk to them, go along with them, it's much easier. And if you don't or if you have and stop, it's bad; it's terrible. That should be brought out somehow because it's definitely true. Nobody's just had enough guts to say it. I have a friend who got involved with a supervisor, seriously involved. He was getting a divorce from his wife, but it didn't work out. It ended, and this girl has been harassed for a year by him. That should definitely be stopped. It makes you feel so small.

I told her that I would not put up with it. I would say, "OK, if you don't like what I'm doing, you fire me because I'm not going to do something that I don't want to do or something that I feel is wrong. If you want to fire, then fire." But she's not like me; she's really a shy, sensitive person. And she's got two children that she's responsible for, and she knows that he'll get her fired. The whole place is sad.

When they started trying to get a union, I got involved with the campaign through Mary. We were friends and she started talking to me about it and I got a union card. I believe if you don't stand up for yourself, nobody else is going to. But they'll do anything to keep a union out. And they do too; there are just very few of the original people left out there. They've either fired them or harassed them so bad they quit.

After I signed up for the union, life changed for me with the main supervisor of the mill, the one I knew all my life. When I was drinking a lot, he used to come over here and sit and we'd go out. I was involved with him, not seriously, but we'd go out and he was fun to be with. But when we started to organize and I signed a union card, it stopped; everything stopped. And he always comes at me before anyone else. Mary can tell you that. If I leave my job five minutes early, or if I stay in the break room five minutes over time, I get written up. And he gets Mary too because she is my friend. Now I regret being with him before, but I'm only human. Yes, he's got the power, and he uses it too. One time he told me, "I can fire you and laugh at you while you're walking out the door." I'm looking forward to the day when I can just walk out, yes I am.

And the job keeps getting harder and harder as part of their desire to make me quit. They keep pushing me around from here to there and laying me off. Finally, it's got so bad I can hardly handle it. I have to fight through the job almost the entire eight hours in order to keep them off of my back. It's physically killing me and it is nerve-wracking. I'm only supposed to have one seventy-five-foot machine, and I almost have another one to operate now too. It's a constant moving your hands around. I work on production rate and since we started organizing, it gets worse and worse every day. They stay on me constantly. They've raised the production; they've speeded up all the machinery; they've just done everything to get the people for the union to quit.

Just working there is so hard on you. My neck and my back and my feet ache; everything on me aches right now. And for the last month or so I haven't been sleeping, even with drinking beer before I go to sleep. And when I sleep, I dream about those machines. Also, it's a problem to work nights because there isn't anything to do during the day. But you can't change to days unless you've been there for twenty-five years. And we've been working six days for about eight months now, with no sick pay and only two weeks vacation after you've worked there five years.

It all makes me feel just like a slave or robot or something. I am so depressed every morning by the time I come home, I sit here and I say, "Why am I still doing it? Why?"

But I'll try to keep working there because of a promise I made to Henry Mann. Henry Mann was our organizer and he was a fantastic person. He was in Montgomery two and a half years, and we got to know him so well. Mary and I were two of the strongest people in the plant, and we promised him faithfully that we would stay, just for the sake of helping. We promised him because we believe in it. I said I'd stand up to them, and that's why I stay in so much trouble all the time. But I feel like the union needs some strong people to be in that plant, if and when we ever get a contract.

Because of how Stevens has harassed us since we started trying to get a union, the National Labor Relations Board has laid all kinds of penalties on them, but they ignore it. They've ruled against Stevens every time, and in each case almost nothing has been done. They have been ordered to bargain with us, and every time they have appealed it to another court. They're just buying more time because they know eventually they are going to lose, but it makes me so mad.

I try to forget about my job sometimes and think about my family. When Lisa turned eighteen, she immediately got married and moved away from my in-laws. And we have a really fantastic relationship now. Her illness is not too bad, and I just believe she'll be all right. I guess it's faith. In the last year and a half, we have gotten really close and we can talk about anything. Emotionally, I feel almost no different than I did when I was twenty years old, so I can understand things she's going through.

My father-in-law has cancer and after his surgery, I was the first person that he wanted to see. He wanted me to forgive him for all that they had done. He has been saved lately and he realizes what he did. But my mother-in-law still hasn't come around after all these years. But I forgave my father-in-law. That made Lisa especially happy because she's really tender hearted and sensitive. But my in-laws had almost destroyed me completely. They don't know how close they came.

I'm better off now than I ever have been in my entire life, but sometimes it seems like there is nothing in my life; it's just empty. That's especially because I work nights and I sleep all day. That way you really can't have any kind of social life. I can't really say I've ever been happy. I love music and I always liked cars, but my grandfather gave me more happiness than anything since, except my daughter.

Often I wish I'd of been a man. It seems like they have it so much easier. They don't have the responsibility of the kids, and they know if they lose a job they can go out and find one just doing anything. I think back to what had happened, and all I felt was that I had to survive; for what, I don't know, but that I was going to make it. Maybe I'm a fool, but I've always had a dream that someday, everything would work out fine. I guess that's kept me hanging on. I haven't really given up hope.

I remember during the drinking time, I prayed, anything to save me because I felt like I was drowning, like I was just blowing away. And something did help me. Now I enjoy watching the 700 Club with Pat Robertson, a preacher on TV. He's just a true, down-to-earth man. With us, you have a personal relationship with Christ; that's the only way you can be saved.

For a while I wondered about the religious aspect of working for the union because someone talked to me about how unions were wrong for people who were Christians. But I can't believe that people wanting their dignity and their rights can be wrong. I can't believe it; you're supposed to love your neighbor.

There was a reporter who came down from New York, and he asked me, "What do you think Jesus would do in a position like you're in?"

I said, "Jesus never got involved with any kind of politics, but he picked up a politician for one of his disciples, so he must not really be against what we are doing."

I think working with the union is a real Christian act because you're working for other people, not just yourself. I could do something else; I don't have to be there. But for people in later years who might have to work there, my kids and Mary's kids and others, I want to see it through.

Epilogue

On Sunday afternoon, October 18, 1980, a settlement agreement between the Amalgamated Clothing and Textile Workers Union and J. P. Stevens was announced. Seventeen years after Stevens said it would never sign a collective bargaining agreement, it bowed to the continuing organizing efforts of its employees, a nationwide consumer boycott of its products, and an intensive corporate campaign to publicize and protest its business and financial ties. The agreement affected some 3,500 of Stevens's 44,000 workers and opened the way for organizing drives among the nonaffected workers.

Workers in Roanoke Rapids, North Carolina, who had first voted for a union in 1974, filled their high school auditorium and cheered after the final vote. Crystal Lee Sutton, the real *Norma Rae*, held a contract above her head, re-creating the movie scene in which she is shown holding up a cardboard "UNION" sign, and said, "Today makes it all worthwhile . . . I sort of feel like running out in the street and shouting."

Mary Robinson received a phone call that she described later. "I wish everyone could have been down here. We had waited for so long. I knew they were about to sign it a couple of weeks ahead, but they had told me not to say anything because they was tying up the loose ends. Then they finally called me up and told me I could just go ahead and holler it from the mountaintops if I wanted to. So I drove out to the plant when the shift changes at two o'clock in the afternoon. The workers were coming and going into the plant, and I'd stop them and tell them, 'We have got a contract.' Some of them, their eyes would bug, and some of them would say, 'Really?' like they didn't believe it.

"But I think the full impact really hit us when we went to work on Sunday night. The company had posted a notice on the board about the fact that they had agreed to a settlement with ACTWU. Then everybody went absolutely wild, and they wanted to know all the glorious details. I spent half the night talking with them about what was in the contract. It was just fantastic."

Mildred described how she first heard the news. "I first found out on TV, would you believe. Everybody was calling me and saying, 'Turn the news on. J. P. Stevens has finally agreed!' And everybody was watching TV that night and was ecstatic. I was just laughing and laughing. It's been worth waiting for; it's been worth waiting for.

"It makes me feel good to just be able to say to them, 'Now, look, this is in the contract; you can't do this to me.' I carry my contract booklet with me all the time and I get it out. And, now, if we have bad yarn or we're out of yarn so we can't get our normal amount done, they have to pay us our average earnings for the previous three weeks. And if they move us to another job, they have to pay us like we were on our own jobs."

Mary spoke again. "One of our agreements was that the workers who were fired because of union activities were to be reinstated and paid back wages. They got up to $38,000 in back pay! Enough to change their lives! I had the job of trying to locate all these people who had been fired; about sixty-four of them. And half of them had moved away up North, and half had moved to new locations without leaving an address. I had to get out and be Kojak or somebody, running them down.

"It felt wonderful to tell them. I had this one little, old girl. She's very religious, and when I told her, I had to put the phone down 'cause I could go into the kitchen and hear her shouting through the phone. She was just having a fit of happiness. I thought, 'Lord, that girl is going to have a heart attack.' She was just actually overjoyed by it."

Mildred added, "Yes, we are overjoyed, and it's not going to be something you just put away in a drawer. We fought for four years so we could live by a contract, and we're going to make sure the company lives by it too."

"It took a lot of hard work; I lost a lot of sleep," Mary concluded. "But I told one of the men this morning, 'When you work and you achieve something, you don't mind working. But if you just work and nothing ever comes out of it, it gets you down.' But I feel so good because I know that out of all the hard work that I did, all the sleep that

I lost, a lot of people has got a second chance on life. And, when we sit there and talk to the plant manager or personnel manager, we can do it as a person with some kind of dignity and self-respect. So, it's really a joy; it really is."

But as time passed and the economy became worse, that goodness faded. Plants and factories closed and more people were out of work than at any time since the Depression. At the end of March in 1982, I received a letter from Mary Robinson in which she talked about our friendship, our families and also said:

. . . Things are very bad here right now. The plant closed down to two floors and now they are talking about shutting the whole plant. I have been working three days every other week for many months, so had to give up my apartment. Luckily for me I had some very dear friends that let me move in with them. . . . Mildred is no longer staying in Montgomery. She was one of those that lost her job because of the top floor shutting down, so she went to where her daughter lives. I never see her now but I still miss her very much.

Then I received another letter in early May:

. . . I am doing okay, but am out of work. ACTWU would like to have me on staff, but right now they have got a lot of people laid off too. . . . The layoff is completed at the plant, there are ninety-five workers still there. That is a long way from what we started with. But I guess we are lucky, so many plants closed down. . . . I sit sometimes and think about all the wonderful people I met during our struggle, and I think I wish that part of it was not over. Life is so short and the good things always go by so fast. . . . But, as long as I can stay close to the labor movement in any way, I will be happy.

I tell Pablo, "Hey listen, Pablo. Maybe
what God wants us to be is very simple,
to be a symbol to the people that we're
suffering but can endure. Maybe that's
why we don't have a very nice place with
all the commodities. Maybe if we didn't
have a thing to worry about, we wouldn't
have this feeling, this kind of belief that's
so powerful that we want to make social
change and fight for justice for the rest.
Maybe that will keep us going."

—Maria Elena Ortega

The tattered and sloping front porch of Maria Elena's house held cacti, old furniture, and large boxes of homegrown tomatoes and peppers. When I arrived there early one cloudy summer afternoon, Maria Elena was out assisting a woman who had a new baby, so her friendly fifteen-year-old son Oscar greeted me. It began to thunder as he showed me their two large gardens and the hollyhocks, petunias, and iris growing around the house. He told me that his mother had *las manos* (the hands) when it came to gardening.

The storm developed suddenly as we waited on the porch, and I looked through sheets of rain toward the small, conservative, and predominantly white Illinois town in which Maria Elena and her family lived. I saw an old cannon rusting in a small park, and a grain elevator whose high rectangular grayness dominated over the town's old, low, store buildings.

As Oscar and I sat together, I thought of my visit the previous summer to Delano, California, a small agricultural community located in the hot and dusty, but irrigated farmland of the San Joaquin Valley. It seemed far away from the humidity and lush greenness of the Midwest, but Delano had been the headquarters of the United Farm Workers, the UFW, with which Maria Elena and her husband now worked.

The United Farm Workers established a major service center for migrants in Delano, giving the workers medical, legal, and other kinds of aid. In the late sixties the UFW, led by Cesar Chavez, had organized the greatest agricultural labor strike in the history of the United States, a strike that included a nationwide boycott of wine and table grapes and that brought the plight of the migrant farm worker to the attention of the American public. When I talked earlier with Maria Elena, she had explained that it was the dream of having such a service center in the Midwest and her knowledge of the labor organizing process that gave her current work its direction and strength.

Maria Elena returned home shortly, running in the rain with a young woman carrying a baby. Maria Elena held the hands of two small, dark-haired children, hurrying them through the rain. She was a short, dark, graceful forty-year-old woman with a beautiful smile, even, white teeth, and a sculptured face with fine cheeks below deep-set brown eyes. She wore her thick black hair with red-brown highlights pulled back from her face in one braid that fell partway down her back.

We entered the first room of the house she shared with Oscar and Pablo, her sixty-three-year-old second husband. Serving as a kind of office, the room displayed a large black-on-white United Farm Workers banner and was crowded with other UFW materials, as well as religious objects, papers, and a television to entertain children as their parents talked.

Maria Elena seated the children in front of the TV, reached for the baby, and talked in Spanish with the young woman. She and Pablo were in the process of buying the house in which they lived and worked, but had no money to make the house safe and sanitary. They had gone through several winters without central heating, one burner to cook on in the kitchen, no hot water, plumbing that barely worked, no bathing facilities, and extremely old and worn wiring that forced them to live with the constant threat of fire. Still, a multitude of people came to the house seeking help, which Maria Elena and Pablo gave as fully as they were able. While dealing with such endless practical problems, Maria Elena, using her real name, told me her story.

Maria Elena

My mom was an orphan and about thirteen years when my daddy found her at a *charreada*, a Mexican celebration, in Texas. They have a parade and carnival. From what I've heard, my mom didn't have much hair because she had had sores in her hair on her head, and they had cut her hair off and she was wearing a scarf. But she was pretty.

She was with an aunt and she suffered a lot. That's what she tells us. They'd get her up around three-thirty in the morning to start breakfast, tortillas, and they were used to having cupcakes and food like that besides breakfast. So she had to get up very early in the morning, and she didn't go to school, I guess maybe to the third grade.

So my daddy met her and asked her to marry him, and he took her to my grandma's house. Grandma didn't have any daughters so she was thrilled. So there was some love there then, for my mother. My grandma was like a mom to her.

Then I was born and I was my grandmother's favorite granddaughter because I was the first one, and I loved my grandma so much. I wanted to be with her all the time but I couldn't. She was an Indian woman, a Yaqui woman. She was very strong and very pretty; when she died at fifty-eight she had all her teeth and had long beautiful hair. But just before she died, they cut it all off. I was about ten when she died and I missed her. On my mom's side, my granddaddy was an Indian too, *Chichimecas*.

I guess my daddy had a terrible time when he was a child too 'cause I hear stories about him, that he just used to tramp the trains since he was a very small child. I think he was very young when he joined the Navy. He was more like on his own since he was a kid, a little kid. He went to school in the Navy and was very, very intelligent. He would talk about politics and religion and other countries and geographical areas when I was young, and I used to listen to him and admire him, how much he knew about everything from the sea to the sky to the land, the vegetation, everything. I'd say, "My God, he knows so much." He'd talk to just about any person.

I was born in Brownsville, Texas; that's way down South in Texas. When I was very little my daddy had to go to the service right about the start of World War II. I remember that my younger brother and I were alone with my mommy in a house, and then I remember Daddy coming home all dressed up in his Navy suit. And that was a very happy occasion, when I saw my daddy that time. Then he had to go again, and when he came back he was a different person. He had been changed in the war. I remember that our problems started real bad at that time. We didn't have enough food and the winters were bad, and in the winter we shared our house with lots of other folks, especially relatives.

I guess my dad went through some terrible things in the war. I know about one incident. They were in a big ship, and he was radio operator in communications. He said all of a sudden, the bombs hit the ship. By the time he got to the deck, Navy men were running all over. He saw many of the guys, including his best friend, burn alive. He tried to help his friend, but it was too late. He says that this young man was on fire, and he fell on his knees and put his hands out like praying and looked up to the sky and managed to say, "Go see my wife and my mother," but he was all in flames. My daddy couldn't do anything. He burnt himself through the process trying to help him but he couldn't. Also, he looked around in the water and it was full of flames. I don't know how he escaped, but he was one of the ones that was alive. It was in the bombing of Pearl Harbor, and he was also injured and had to go have surgery on his leg.

The first time he came to visit us he was very happy and was sad to leave us, but the last time he came out of the service he was a total stranger. I think it was real hard on my mother because they were so young, both of them, and my daddy became cruel. I can't say that he was like that all the time; I have to say that he was a great daddy because he never quit worrying about food and he was a provider. If was just unfortunate that he had to go through so much. I guess when people suffer a lot and go through horrible things it changes them. It can make you very bitter and a mean person, or it can make you understanding and so you try to help other people who have been in bad situations. Like I said, when he came back from the war, the bad times started.

We were a big family; my mother had seventeen babies and I was the oldest, so I began working right away. One of the first things I remember was the shrimp basin, standing up on a big wooden crate, competing with grown-ups on how to learn to do the job. About every day I would go with my daddy and mom to the water port, and the big boats that carry shrimp would come to the docks. I think it must have been before I even went to school, when I was under five. I was very little so they would have to put a big wooden box for me to stand on, and they taught me how to take the head off the shrimp. The head would go to the bucket; the body would go out to the stream of water. I would do this mostly during the night. This way I could help to provide food.

After that my daddy started taking us up North, to work the crops. We went mostly to Michigan, Wisconsin, Ohio, but we went also to Arkansas, to Indiana, and as far as Montana. Around Idaho, South Dakota, North Dakota, we were working in sugar beets and potatoes. I was such a strong girl; my God, I was very strong. I could pick up a basket and the baskets seemed so big, but I could put one on my shoulder, with one knee on the ground and the other one bent. I could also pick up a sack of cucumbers for pickles, the tiny ones, and a sack of potatoes.

And I say that my dad was cruel because I couldn't have no friends or nothing when we were working in the fields. I tried having one girlfriend once, and he really got upset over it. He said, "I don't want you to associate with nobody." I was very sad all the time, very depressed. He was just not loving. But he wasn't hateful, real hateful, with us but I said he was cruel because when he got upset he would spank us and he would really be real strict. So we couldn't have any friends. It was very hard and my mom, she was always pregnant.

I guess my daddy, he must have become bitter toward the whole situation. He was very cruel and hard on Mom. My mom worked a lot and he was a very hardworking man, but he was so strict. I can understand why he was like that because there was so many of us, and he was always forever taking care of us. But it just kept getting worse and worse. We'd go out and work and pick pickles, tomatoes, for God knows what. One time I was counting how many different jobs I'd done and got to fifty-two, and I says, "Ooo, that's it. Forget it. Forget it. I don't want to count any more."

But my daddy was very, very strict. When he was upset, we couldn't say one word. Sometimes we couldn't even look at his eyes. We'd have to look down and not give our faces. But Dad's changed a whole lot. He was very, very hard, but when we got older, he couldn't be. I've never been disrespectful but still I told him, "Hey, Daddy, it's not right." When there's nine brothers and eight sisters, what can he do? He had to get gentler. We wouldn't harm him, but we wouldn't allow him to be cruel.

My daddy was against my mom using birth control. He would say no. I would listen to him tell my mother, "You better not do it. I better not find out that you're taking stuff." So my mom was never taking care of herself. I remember she was always pregnant. One time she almost lost her life when she had the twins. She had a bad hemorrhage. After the twins, the last baby was born, and she finally had to have a hysterectomy because the doctor said, "No more."

We went back to Brownsville every year and we lived in little houses, little old shacks, very run-down places. Then they built the Point Sierra Project, a public housing project, and that was very nice. It was like, oh gosh, fancy. It was brick apartments with three bedrooms, a hall, and a restroom with your tub and everything, then your kitchen and your living room and your dining room. Oh gosh, it was very, very nice. It was built especially for low-income people so we were able to move in there.

I remember once we tried to buy two lots, and for fifteen lousy dollars, which my parents couldn't pay once, they lost the two properties. Fifteen dollars. Now that I think about it, I sometimes say, "Oh gosh, why didn't I go beg in the street so that they would have had the money." But then we just lamented, how do you say it, felt bad that nobody could do anything.

I still feel like my home is in Texas. If we ever accomplish our mission or our goals up here in Illinois, I really and honestly want to go back there because I don't want to be here. You suffer too much up here. It's not that I'm not trying to take responsibility. I know that when I leave, I want to think it is better for people here. But it still seems like Texas is my home.

I worked in the streets in Texas when I was little and we weren't following the crops. I was always dressed as a little boy, always. Most of the time I wore a straw hat and sometimes I put my hair up. Many people thought I was a boy and I hung around with boys, too. My daddy didn't allow us to do this but I was very sneaky, I guess. Sometimes he was gone to work. Whatever we had, whether it was shoes, clothes, vegetables, or fruits or cactuses, I would have to be in the street selling. You meet a lot of people in the streets, and you see and learn a lot of bad things, too. That's one reason I always tried to keep my kids from it, but it's hard. You also learn a lot of good things because you learn there's another way to survive, too, not just working in the fields, that you can work in the street selling. But there's a lot of stealing and a lot of bad things that go with it.

You don't see any girls in the streets, so this is one reason I kept my hair up and put my hat down far. And they couldn't tell the difference because I was too little. I learned a lot. That's where I learned to smoke. Well, the first time I smoked was with the Indian girls, when we were working the crops. That's when I really learned how to hold a cigarette. But I did it more in the streets. And I know that while some of the boys went to steal bread and food, I would sit there and wait and take care of the shoe-shine boxes or whatever they were selling so they could do it. I waited and took my share, too. Also, I learned how to say bad words, and I saw other things that were bad, like men who would rub against girls. Sometimes we would be on a bus and we would all be crowded, and I could see that older men would hurt and bother a girl who would pass by, and then they would just sit very innocent like they hadn't done nothing. They wouldn't even move, which was so bad. I learned how to take care of myself in these things, like how to bite.

I would go with the boys to the warehouses where they packed potatoes or tomatoes. The water would carry the little potatoes out to a big pond of water which flowed to somewhere else. It was dangerous but I didn't know it was dangerous, and we'd get under all that equipment which came out of the factory. We would just dig for the new potatoes and fill up our baskets and then go wash the potatoes and sell them or cook them for ourselves.

Another thing that I did too was to get on the freight trains and throw pineapples across to the other kids. I was a monkey really. I was very light at jumping, and I guess I could smell the pineapples. I start thinking about these things now and I start wondering. I want to remember how it is that I knew how to get the pineapples and that pineapples were there. It couldn't be anything else but the smell. It's so strong, the smell of pineapple. Also, in the water port there was another section where they brought bananas in. I knew how to ask the workers and persuade the people to give us some.

Maybe they just felt sorry for kids like myself. Also, I guess I was very curious, and my daddy would allow me to go around some of the time. So I would go to the banana boats and get bananas, too.

Like I said, I was not allowed to go out or talk to the girls when we were up North, but when I was in Brownsville, my daddy would work and in the evenings, after school, I could raid the garbage cans. Saturdays and Sundays I would go sell in the street, and this is where I got into all these things.

Sometimes we would sell bananas, sometimes fish, 'cause we caught fish. Different things. My mother would also trade, like clothes for food. I don't know where she got the clothes from, but I remember she could get clothes and trade it for food. Sometimes we would go oyster fishing or crab fishing. We would also trade for eggs. But every time we came up North to work, my daddy would be overly protective and very, very strict, especially hard, extra hard.

Life was hard because Mom kept having kids all the time. It was bad because I was the oldest so I had to take care of them. I would have to do the watching mostly, and the dishwashing, washing clothes, and cleaning house, and taking care of children, and going to school. Going to school wasn't easy because I had to walk about six miles from where we lived clear across town, and we had no shoes and no sweaters during the wintertime when it was getting cold. My brother was the same. All the older ones had to go through the same thing; they were also raised the same way. I remember that all the time we would hit the garbage cans, raid the garbage cans in the neighborhoods and just pick up anything we could.

Whenever we were up North working we would get rich eggs and milk and cheese and lots of vegetables and fruit, but once we were back in Texas, it was terrible. There was just very little. Sometimes, at the end of the summer, my daddy would have money from all the work we did, and he would fill a whole wall with food. I mean all kinds of vegetables and everything. My mom and dad would also can. So I remember that we would all stand back and look at the wall and it was such a beautiful sight. Then when all the food started going and going, oh, it was sad.

But Dad never wanted us to get government help. He's never allowed Mom to take food stamps, but my mom, she had done it behind his back. He never allowed us to go ask for a can of tomatoes or an onion or nothing, no matter if we didn't have enough. That's the way he was and he still is.

But it was difficult 'cause every time we went up North, it got harder. I guess you've been told before about the discrimination.

You weren't allowed to go into a place or to restrooms. It was awful. But when you're a kid, you don't really care so much about these bad things because you don't understand. I do remember that I couldn't understand why we wouldn't be allowed to go into a restroom. I didn't understand why I was told to go where the blacks were. I didn't understand why we had to sleep in a tent sometimes and cook outside. I didn't understand a lot of things, when I could see that a lot of other people had places to eat. It was especially hard to sleep outdoors with army blankets. My daddy would sleep inside the car, just sitting down to keep an eye on us. Sometimes he would just lay across the hood with a pillow while Mom and all of us kids would sleep on the side of the road, 'cause if we went to a public park we would get run out of there. We would stop in a little stream to wash our dishes and to wash up. And my dad was bitter, and especially hard on Mom.

But my dad did try to make sure that when my mom was pregnant, she ate very good. He tried for her to get very good nutrition even though we were very poor. Daddy would bring her liver and I could see that my mom would sit down and eat good. After the babies were born and my mom was working the fields, she would stop every so often and go to the truck and cool a little bit and then nurse a baby and then go back to the fields.

There was a lady who lived with us, her name was Anna, and she's still alive. This lady was such a wonderful person and helped to provide a lot. She lost her husband and two kids in Mexico and she was all alone. Anna was a prostitute. At that time I didn't know it, but she provided food for us with it. I guess she did it to have food, because as I grew older I realized that all she did was bring food to us. She would go with my brother next to me and myself to garbage cans, and we would pick up a whole bunch of stuff, sometimes vegetables, and fruit and about everything that we could get, especially clothes. Mom never worried about her. Anna was real good.

I went with her one time to a junkyard. There was an old man there, his name was Che. That's when I started to understand that what Anna was doing was selling her body for food. I stayed in a near room while she went someplace else with the man. I thought, what is she going to do out there with that man? And, all of a sudden, I realized.

One time it got real bad and we were really hungry. There was no food. Most of the time it was beans, tortillas, butter, and potatoes. But that time it was really bad. I was about twelve years old and Anna asked for permission to take me to the movies.

My mom, she trusted Anna real good and I had never been out to a movie, so she says, "Yah, go ahead and go to the movies."

So this boyfriend of Anna came up and instead of going to the movies, we went out in the country. They had another young man in the back seat. We went out far into the woods, and I told Anna, "Hey, listen, Anna. Why are we here? Why aren't we in the movies? You said we were going to the movies."

Well, anyway, she took off with her boyfriend in one direction, and I was left alone with this other guy. This young man said, "Do you know why you're here?"

And I said, "No. No, I don't."

And he said, "You know what, if your mom and your dad knew where you were, this lady would be in a lot of trouble. I know the reason she's doing it is to provide food for the rest of the family, but this is not the right thing to do." He said, "She came to sell you to me and I was supposed to pay her." That's when I really understood. But he was nice and he said, "I'm not going to hurt you. Don't be afraid." He didn't even touch me. He was so good.

I think Anna took about two hours, a long time, and it was raining too. So when she came back we were still sitting in the back seat talking. I was talking, but I was scared too. She was surprised to see me just sitting there. I guess maybe she expected to see me in another condition.

We went back home and I told Mom. I felt sorry for Anna, but I never did go out with her again. That was just a bad thing that happened. After that, when I was still twelve and working as a busgirl in a hotel, I got followed one time by about six guys. I was so scared, but I wasn't hurt either that time.

I had three bad experiences when I was a kid, one more. My mom would let me go to babysit because I would get paid fifty cents or whatever. This time I went to stay with a girl I went to school with. She was about two years older than I was, and I was just supposed to keep her company at her house. When I got there she started locking the doors and shutting the windows. I said, "Why are you locking all the doors and windows?"

The other girl said, "I just want to lock the house up so we can watch TV quietly."

"OK."

So all of a sudden she let her cousin in. My God, I had never gone through so much. It was terrible. He tried to rape me. He tore my clothes off and it was horrible. I remember that I didn't know what to do. It was so bad. But then her brother came and he kept knocking on the door, and she had no choice but to open the door.

When he opened the door, the other boy had me in the restroom. I was still about twelve years old, and that time I found out that you can get hurt.

I remember I went home and my mom was asleep with a whole bunch of kids all over. She was always with a whole bunch of kids. I remember that I was crying, and I went to wake her up, and I said, "Mommy, Mommy, do you know what happened, Mommy?" She was tired and so she just turned the other way. I guess she just didn't, couldn't, she was just too tired.

She would say, "Say nice things. Say the nice things. Don't talk about how bad it's been."

But there were good things back then. I loved music, especially a lady singer, who was beautiful. In her younger days this lady was very popular. At that time I was a little kid, and I learned all her tangos, just about every one of them. I guess she would come on the radio every day and through the radio I picked up all her songs, 'cause I don't remember having any records.

The people would say, "Maria Elena, Maria Elena, sing me a tango," and they would tell me which one and I would stand there and sing for them. I just knew them all. As I grew older I quit listening to the music and this way you forget. But that was my favorite, tangos, beautiful music. Her songs, they always say a story.

Yes, since I was a little girl I was always singing. Anna knew that I liked to sing a lot. One day when I was about nine years old, she said, "Maria Elena, why don't we go to the Amateur Hour in the theater and you sing, and maybe you'll win a loaf of bread." The first times I did that, my legs would tremble and I was so scared but I never gave up. I still sang. I guess I must have been funny or something that first time, 'cause I won a loaf of bread. The first prize was two bags of groceries and next place was one bag of groceries and then maybe a five-dollar award and then one loaf of bread.

Then after that I liked it and went every time we found out there was a place, like the Mexico Theater in Brownsville where they had an Amateur Hour every week. I had to sneak out because of Daddy but I managed it. And when I was working in the fields, unless I was sick, I was always singing. A lot of other girls would sing too, sing together. We'd start competing against each other just for the fun of it and start imitating people.

I learned a lot of things as a kid. I paid attention when I saw a person. One thing that I learned about men, I learned that I could look into men's eyes and know exactly what they were thinking. I could see when they were honest and good men, and I could see the evil too when they were bad. It was mostly in men that I could see this, not in little kids, not in boys my age. But when I saw it in big men, I'd get frightened. I would get out and away from them. I don't know how I learned it but I was always able to do that.

Sometimes we would have to cook out in the open. We had a tub and we'd burn wood in it and put like a grill on top of it and with tin all around. We would cook tortillas and a pot of beans and coffee and then meat with potatoes. It was never meat alone or chicken alone. We ate vegetable soup very often because my mom said it was good with all the juice of the vegetables and vitamins. So we ate that a lot, chicken soup, vegetable soup, when we had it or money to buy it. Then sometimes when we're back home it would only be like potatoes and beans and tortillas and butter. While we were up North it was good 'cause we ate very good.

It was exciting sometimes while we were traveling on our way to someplace new to work in the fields, but when we were working, my God, it was terrible. Some of the places were very, very bad. The water was bad and we'd drink water that was real bad, get sick in our stomach, and we wouldn't go see a doctor or nothing. We'd just get over it with the medicine my mom had. Then we'd have to buy from this store that they called the *comisarios*. I don't know why. We went to town anyway, but mostly we would go to the garbage. We picked a lot of lard left over from the meat, pork meat and beef, and a lot of fruits and vegetables. Then we came home and washed them and ate a lot of that.

We worked all the time when we were doing the crops. We would work the fields and get to the house and do the housework. We lived in cabins often about the size of a small room. Sometimes there was bunk beds and some of us slept in them and the rest on the floor, and sometimes there was a little table, a stove, and a bench. I remember that we used chicken coops, with three walls and then an open place. Then I remember also just being out in the open in Texas when we were working in straw you make brooms out of.

Also, when we were in the fields, we were told you had to stay working all the time. If it was wet, Mom would say, "Well, the sun will be shining soon." You get wet with the dew, but she'd say, "We'll get dry." Then, when it was so hot that I think if you put a thermometer between your hat and your head it would really register a high temperature, she would say, "Well, we'll put water on our heads to cool off." We would wet our hats and put them back on. It felt like your eyes would get real red and irritated, and the dust, it was uncomfortable.

My neck would hurt a lot and I was just a little girl. I can imagine how Mommy felt, being so many years older and pregnant so much and doing stoop labor. We would hoe with hoes with that short handle, so we were bent over all the time. The reason they used a short handle was to make sure that we were doing the job. If they looked out across the field and saw that we were standing straight up, they thought that meant we weren't working. How terrible! Isn't that terrible? They made us do stoop labor and suffer that way when we didn't need to. I remember, oh God, it used to be so hard all day long with a short-handle hoe. Then my back would ache and ache at night.

Sometimes we would go to bed in straw mattresses; other times it was just boards or the floor. I wouldn't really feel rested the next morning; I'd feel terrible. My muscles all ached. And I was just a girl. Not an older woman!

You couldn't really keep the kids clean. My daddy, wherever we were at, him and some other guys would make a big hole and that was specially to burn garbage in to keep the place cleaner. And Daddy was very strict about being clean. He wanted no flies. We would have to be watching out if there was any flies because of the food and the baby bottles. He constantly kept us on the ball. Don't let any flies in and wash up to eat, and the food has to be very clean, our utensils, everything. So my mommy had to work very, very hard to keep us healthy. We all worked extra hard but it kept us from getting too sick.

When a woman had a baby while she was working the fields, she would stay in camp till she got on her feet again. Three days later she would be up doing housework, not heavy work, and nursing the baby or feeding him the bottle, whichever. Then probably by one month she would be in the fields. I know Mom, she didn't take too long. Mom wouldn't and later I didn't either. Mom would get up on the third day, and she'd start housework and to recuperate real fast. But, like I say, Dad always saw that she would take good food. There was other women that didn't look that good.

I could see the ladies, all pregnant, working in the fields, doing stoop labor or whatever. But they'd try to let up on the work a little. Like if it was tomatoes, most likely the husband, he would carry the basket across the rows to the road to be picked up. If it was pickles or potatoes she wouldn't drag too much. If it was the kind of work when you're planting, it was easier, but when it was with a hoe, that was hard. I know that there was this lady in Montana. Her name was Maria Elena, too, and gosh, she was about seven or eight months, and as soon as we got there, she was working. She was real big. She would press her hand against her back in pain. Then at nighttime her mother-in-law would massage her back. They were from Monterrey, Mexico. She said she was working because they had to but otherwise she wouldn't. I guess there must have been a great need.

Sometimes we traveled with my daddy's other relatives. We were a very large family. My daddy only had two more brothers and my mom had one brother and one sister, but the children were many. On my granddaddy's side there were a lot of brothers and sisters. Once we were all traveling together, my aunts and uncles and their kids, us, and my granddaddy and grandma, and we were in Kentucky. My granddaddy, he was an Anglo from Kentucky, from a big, poor, hillbilly family. He was my father's father, a very tall man with real blond hair. He had one blue eye and one green eye. In the blue eye his eye pupil was elongated, so he looked like he had one cat's eye.

My granddaddy hadn't seen his folks for forty years, so they didn't even know if he was alive. My aunt was going to have a baby, and when she got sick, started labor, my granddaddy went to find his brothers. I remember that when we got to Maysville, this big man came out of a building. I guess that building said Lucas, which was my granddaddy's name, and so my granddaddy talked to the man and asked him, "Do you know a family by the name of Lucas that lives in Willow?"

The man said, "Yah," he was kind of in a hurry. "You take route so-and-so and you'll get there."

Granddaddy says, "OK, thank you, sure." This big guy was really dressed up.

When we got to where the directions sent us, I remember that I got out of the car with my granddaddy. He knocked on the door and the man who was my Uncle Ed opened the door, and he says, "Hi, can I help you?"

So my granddaddy looked at him, and he says, "Yah," and just kept looking at him, staring at him, and then my granddaddy says, "Are you Ed?"

My uncle says, "Yah, I'm Ed." He just looked at him and then Ed says, "Oh, my God, Ray. You're my brother Ray." And, oh gosh, they started hugging and kissing.

My uncle was real, real poor. He lived in a little shack, and he had a wooden stove so you had to burn wood so you could cook. Later we learned that they had never had any tortillas or Spanish food at all, nothing.

My aunt was very, very sick with labor, so my granddaddy said, "My daughter-in-law's real sick and she's gonna deliver a baby." There was no beds or nothing in the cabin; there was only burlap, sacks of burlap. All they could do is throw a lot of burlap on the floor, and my mom threw a bedspread and more covers on it. We could barely get my aunt inside. My mom delivered the baby and that time I was coming in and out, watching it. So I saw when Emilia was born and I was very excited.

Then that night we slept in the cemetery. It was just next door. There was no place in the house, so we slept there on the ground, but I wasn't afraid at all. I was watching the stars and thinking how beautiful it was. So then I got to meet all my cousins and a whole bunch of family. We went back again, one more time, and then that was it. We never saw them again or heard from them again. My granddaddy died and that was the end of it. But we always teased my cousin who was born there and called her hillbilly. Emilia, the hillbilly.

Sometimes we worked in the fields, just our family, and sometimes we worked under the crew leader too in the fields. The crew leader wouldn't have to do any work, just see that the work was being done. He would take the people to the field and back to the camp, and he would be in the fields with all the people, checking your work and seeing that you didn't take too much time to go to the woods to the restroom and getting to the parents so the kids would do the work right and keep at the same pace with the rest of the people.

The crew leaders would get paid good. They would get paid a certain amount per person, then transportation, and then they would get some out of the work you did, part of your earnings. They were pretty good to you if you did the job good, kept up, but if you were slow or something, they would push and push and push. It was not likely that they would get on the kids directly, they would get on to the parents. They would say, "Well, you can't bring him anymore if he's not going to do the job or keep up at the same pace as the others." So the parents put a lot of pressure on the kids.

I remember that sometimes we wouldn't get paid. What happened was that the crew leader would give us some money every week to go buy what we needed, soap and whatever. Then at the end of the season he would give us all the money that we earned, but then we'd have to pay him for the transportation and have to pay him how much we owed for those necessities. That didn't leave too much money, and sometimes it was better and sometimes it was worse. Also, I remember that if you were traveling with a crew leader in a truck, at night you would have to just sleep in the truck all crowded. So one time my dad, he bought a car for ninety dollars so we could travel on our own. I think that back in those days it took about thirty-five dollars of gasoline, so he had very little left when we got home.

And, of course, there were just the dangers of traveling all the time, lots of time in cars and trucks that weren't in good condition. One time we were in the camp, and, all of a sudden, we heard a loud noise, like you hit something real hard. Everybody started coming out and saying, "What happened; what happened? What was that?" Then we started running towards the road.

Oh my God, when we went out there, what a horrible sight! I'll never forget that as long as I live. These people, they were migrants coming to camp, and it was raining and foggy and their car skidded or slid and it slammed into a tree. And the lady, oh my goodness, her breasts were cut almost off and her chest was torn open, and she's going like a little doggy when it's a baby and it goes, "Mmmhh, mmmhhh, mmmhhh!" Just a sound, oh horrible. The two children were thrown too and laying unconscious but they weren't torn apart. The car was completely smashed and one guy was laying on the ground and was awake and he was crying. The other man was cut and his eyes and expression were like his mind was gone, horrible.

I guess I must have been the first one to reach the scene 'cause I was always running. Anyway, the police came and my mom and my dad, and they said, "Hey, get Maria Elena out of here, and the other children." But I saw the lady. Her chest was torn open. Oh, just awful. Her eyes were closed but for a while she was making that sound, like trying to cry, then they covered her all up. I didn't understand then but now I know that when they cover a body like they did, it's dead. They put her in the ambulance and the children too and took them away. So, there were bad times for many people.

My daddy always tried to teach us skills to help us through hard times that we might have. He was always saying to learn how to work in the fields and learn everything we could because if we were going to survive, we would have to learn lots. He would take us into the woods, and he would say, "This is an apple tree. This is a pear tree. And this root is good to eat and this weed is good to eat." So we learned a lot of different weeds that were good to eat. He would say, "You have to know these things." He was very strict and would grab us and say, "Listen to me; pay close attention. One of these days you're going to need it." So it was always constantly a worry to find food and how to get a little money to get food. It was always the same thing.

But sometimes my daddy'd have to go out of the fields, and we stayed in them working and then we had a ball. We had a ball. My brothers and I and my sisters, we'd start playing and running in the fields. Boy, I guess we knew we were going to get into trouble, but that time, it was so good to play that we didn't stop.

I remember one time we were in a tomato field, and green tomatoes can hit you pretty hard when you throw them like a rock. And so we had a tomato fight. Of course, that was destroying tomatoes and a serious thing, because the grower gets after the crew leader real bad, and then the crew leader gets after the parents. But, when my daddy wasn't there, they couldn't keep us quiet, my brother and I and a couple of other kids. We were having a blast throwing tomatoes back and forth at each other. We would pick tomatoes regular but the first chance when we'd get a green tomato, we'd hit somebody with it, and then go back to work and play dumb. But, finally, they caught us and then when my dad got there, oh boy, we got a spanking for doing that, yah. We wasted a lot of tomatoes. Also, we'd do it with red tomatoes and maybe that was a little worse, because when the red tomatoes hit, they would splat.

I remember one farm we worked on. The farmer's wife was very Catholic. She managed to get Mommy and Daddy married through the Catholic church, against Daddy's wishes and will. Mom was very religious but Daddy was against religion. I also think that woman baptised a whole bunch of my brothers and sisters, and she was constantly there with Mom. She would help Mom a lot, give her clothes. I guess my mother somehow persuaded my daddy to get married in the church, maybe she begged him. I remember that Daddy said he was going to go through with it but that was it. I guess he did it just to get them off his neck. That's the only reason I could see, 'cause I've really never seen Daddy go into a church. I hope that before I die someday I can see my daddy go into a church or pray.

My mother started being a midwife while we were working in the fields. I think it started in Portage, Ohio, where there was this lady who was real heavyset, real, real big. She was in labor and there was nobody else; it was an emergency. My momma had to deliver that baby. She had a terrible time doing it too, because it was a very big baby, but the baby was born all right. They did go to get the doctor, but by the time they got back, the baby was already born and my mom had taken care of it.

After she delivered the first baby, it would happen again and again. I guess she gained self-confidence. Then every time we were away working or would be up there in the North, the pregnant women would just go and get her, talk to her, and have her check them and massage them. They would ask her to deliver the baby and she would. In some cases I helped my momma, by getting hot water and being around when she needed me. I could see the pain the ladies were going through, but I wasn't afraid because it was just something that was normal with my mom having so many kids, so I always knew about it.

My mother would pray during the deliveries and religion was very important to her, but my daddy wouldn't allow us to go to church. I remember when I was a little kid I tried to make my first communion and he was against it. He said no. But before that there was a period when he let me go to church. I remember in the month of May, when the little girls carry flowers to church. They call it "the distribution of the roses," and that was a very special occasion because I remember that I got to do it several times, taking a whole bunch of flowers and just giving them out. Then I remember there was the last time, and my father didn't let me go anymore.

To this day, I've always said, if I can ever convert my daddy, I'd be so happy. He's not like he used to be at all, but if I can ever get him to pray, it would be wonderful. I don't understand how he got that way, but he would say, "There's no God. That's a lie. There's no God for us." But through the years my mom kept praying all the time, to God and to Mother Mary, Our Lady of Guadalupe, Our Lady of San Juan, and Our Lady of Refugio. And even today I dream about Our Lady. Sometimes when I need her she comes to me in my dreams.

I remember one time we went to church to ask for help, though. It was very cold and I was wearing boy's clothes and my straw hat and my braids. It wasn't even inside the church. It was at the house where the priest lived and he scolded me. He said that I should know better than to walk into the house of God dressed like that.

I was real hurt because this was coming from a priest, and it wasn't even the house of God. That's what I kept saying to myself, "This is not the house of God." Anyway, I had to step outside and I was ready to answer back, but my mom said, "Maria Elena, go outside and wait." Oh, it was so cold. My mom was going to ask for five dollars. I don't even know if she got it.

On our way back home, I was arguing with Mom. I could

complain to Mom; to my dad I couldn't, not one word. Most of the time we wouldn't talk with Daddy, he would just say to do something or to correct something, but we wouldn't get into talking. Anyway, after we saw that priest and as we were walking home, I told Mom, "Oh Mommy, that's wrong. That's not the house of God. The house of God is next door in the church."

She said, "Oh, it's all right. Don't pay attention to the priest."

I said, "No, I don't like that. It's bad, Mother."

My mother was praying, up until today, but she couldn't come to church because my daddy wouldn't let her. So it was like that with Daddy.

When we were working up North we had cans of Carnation and Pet milk. We'd empty those out and make a slit in the can to save dimes in. Every week my daddy would give us the change in dimes. He'd say, "This is for when we get to Texas to buy you clothing and the supplies for school." So we would put our dimes in there. But when we got to Texas there was never enough. We could only get one pencil and one writing notebook and then a pair of shoes and two pairs of socks, and I don't remember getting any dresses, but maybe panties. Then my shoes wore out and I would go to school barefooted. My mom was always trying to get clothes, used clothes. Sometimes when I was barefoot, I wouldn't go to school.

I was very shy at school and only had one little friend at school that I talked to. She was from Mexico and she was very, very friendly, very nice, and her name was Frances. She couldn't speak English very good, and it was just a short time that she stayed there and then she left. She was very poor too because when she was going to school she had very old and patched clothes. You could tell it was sewed up. I felt sorry for her and she was so good. She looked sad; she looked like she was sad all the time and she was so pretty. She was light complected and her eyes were big, with curly lashes. She had a very beautiful mouth. I was a kid but I paid attention to everything. I was like that.

Also, school was hard 'cause I always would be taken out of school to work the fields three months before school was out, and I remember going back to school three months late all the time, so I didn't get much school and I was very, very dumb. I just never could learn and I only went to sixth grade.

I grew and then, when I was fourteen, I met my first husband. I met him overnight in the government housing project where we were living. He was living right next door. There was a big screen on the outside with movies, and I was sitting down on his porch with his sister and she went in and he came out. He just sat next to me, and, all of a sudden, told me, "Will you marry me?"

And I said, "Yes." That's how it was. Then he kissed me and said, "Are you sure you'll marry me?" and I said, "Yes," again. So I think it must have been about three days later that he went to Ohio. I had an aunt and I told her that he was going to write me, and she would go and get the mail so my daddy wouldn't get to it, because if he would get to it that was the end of me probably. In every letter my future husband would ask me, "Will you still marry me?" And I answered back and I said, "Yes." So when he got back, I guess about a month later, I married him. It was sad, because what I was trying to do was get away. That was what I was trying to do.

I don't think that I even loved him when I married him. I was only fourteen and it was just out of desperation. When I met my kids' daddy I thought, "Oh my whole world is going to be different." It wasn't. It turned into a nightmare very, very quick. Two weeks after I married I started having problems. Then it all came back to me, the same thing as with my daddy. I tried and tried; everything I did and everything I said was wrong. I really never did anything wrong, but still I wasn't meeting the expectations. It wasn't just my husband; I had to answer to the whole family and be what they expected. Each person has a different way for you to meet their expectations. It was very hard to please everybody, and he was just too attached to his mom for many years. And I couldn't get him to move away and start our own life, so we were never left alone. Then I felt guilty because she was his mother, and I didn't want to offend them.

I ran away once not long after I was married. I was barefooted and I was really in bad shape. I ended up in the *mercado* in Mexico in Matamoros, and I decided I should give up and come back to the United States, to this side of the border. But I only had one nickel with me, an American nickel, and it took two nickels to get across. Then I ran into my friend Frances from school, the girl I had liked so much who had moved away. She was working as a salesgirl in the Mexican market, and I don't think she was married yet. I told her of my trouble and she gave me a nickel so I could come back to this side. And we said goodbye and I never saw her again, which was sad. She was very good. I didn't have no papers or nothing to use to cross the border, but I could speak English. I took a bus and then crossed the border, and I guess I must have looked pretty bad. People usually wore shoes to cross. I don't think I've ever seen anybody cross barefooted. This was the last time I saw Frances. And I went back to my husband.

My first daughter was born in Post, Texas, when I was fifteen years old. I worked in the cotton fields all the time I was carrying her. But I didn't have a hard time having my child. I guess I never did with any of my kids, probably because of Mom. It was very natural and I guess I thought that since Mom did it so could I. I remember that I was just happy. I acted like a kid, really, not like a woman. I was just a kid.

Then, when Eva was a little baby, I was working in onions. We were taking the tops off the onions, and then we would make little hills of them. They would dry a couple of days, and then we would go back and put them in sacks. There were big weeds there. I had a little wooden tomato crate for Eva, and I fixed it with blankets and a pillow. I would take Eva and put her under the weeds in the shade and then I would nurse her. But I was very hot when I nursed her and she'd get sick. Finally, I was told that I wasn't supposed to breast feed her while I was very, very hot with the sun, to cool down a bit first. So I did and she stopped being sick.

So I began to have babies, and some of my little brothers and sisters came to stay with me too. They were really no trouble. They helped me very, very much. In a way, they kept me company. We loved each other a lot and we were very, very close. We still are, especially the oldest ones, because I had seven of my brothers and sisters stay with me, five boys and two girls. They didn't stay all together but they lived with me at several different times while they were growing up. It's just that my mom, she had so many. They were a lot of fun and I was very happy that they were there.

I had even more of my ex-husband's family with me than my brothers or my family. My mother-in-law lived with me. She'd come and go but she was mostly with me, so her sons, her daughter-in-laws, and the children were just about there everyday. Then on the weekends I never could go no place 'cause they would bring all their children, and since she was there, she would have to babysit and I couldn't go because of my family. So I was constantly cooking. It took a lot of my energies. I had no rest.

I had seven babies in all. It was three days before my son was a year old when I delivered twins. My little girl was just about two years old then. I was still very young, maybe seventeen or eighteen. The twins were very tiny, both of them.

When my girl, the first twin, was born, what happened was that I was laying down in bed, and, all of a sudden, I felt something like when you tie a knot and pull both ends to tighten it, something like that. I even heard it; it was a pop, really. It was my water bag that tore. I had a real bad time with the babies. The midwife, Dona

Elena, didn't know if we would make it or not, but, finally, the babies were born, a girl and a boy. The twins looked like little monkeys, newborn monkeys. Then the Department of Children and Family Services tried to take them to the hospital because they said that the babies were going to die on me.

But I cried and I said, "No you don't. If my babies die, well, I did my best, but I'm not going to let you take my babies."

I guess I thought I was not going to see them again and that they were taking them away forever. The department people couldn't reassure me that this was not so. They never convinced me so I never accepted. Then they said, "OK, if the children die, it's your fault."

I said, "No, they're not going to die."

The man said, "How do you know?" They couldn't even eat or open their eyes or open their mouths.

I said, "Well, I'll feed them anyway." I was very young and I didn't understand.

The twins would only take about a half an ounce of milk every three hours when they were very little. I would try cotton and a dropper too, open their mouths and just put milk in there, and you could hear the hard gulp as they swallowed. But I'd still stick it in there and I tried to nurse them. Well, about a month and a half later, they started to move more and to be bigger.

It was hard. My shoulders, they were killing me and it was very difficult. I couldn't keep up with anything. Every time I fed one the other one started crying, and I had everyone else to take care of too. Then, when they got older, I'd put a pillow across my stomach and I'd give one breast to one kid and the other breast to the other, and with one leg I would pat Tommy, my year old son's, butt, and rock him with my foot and give him his bottle and pat him on the shoulders. Then, as Tommy would sleep, I'd rest my leg and try to feed the babies as much as possible. As the twins got older, I'd set them on my lap and I'd just stick the breasts in. It didn't look too good but they were satisfied.

I think my oldest was a little over two years when the twins were born. So I had babies just about one after the other, seven babies. It was very hard. Now that I'm older, I say about young mothers, "Oh my God, how can she do it?" Well, I went through the same thing and it must have been real hard, but now it's past. And I'm glad that my children are grown up. I feel free and I feel I can do so many things and no problems with diapers and bottles.

It wasn't until after all the kids and I went to Arlington and I worked very hard there, in the factory where they made planes, that

I was able to save money and I was able to buy a washer and a dryer. It was a big celebration when I got them.

In an airplane factory I worked in a unit with 150 guys, but the guys tried to get me out of there. They would say jokes and have pictures to get me upset. They didn't like me around because they thought they couldn't have freedom of speech if I was there. So one day I got upset and I said, "Hey, listen. I don't care what you say. I've got a job to do and if you want to joke, if you want to say dirty stuff, if you want to put naked ladies in the gear and tool boxes, it's not going to do nothing to me. Because I've got my job and you're not going to make me quit my job if you keep on doing those things."

So I was accepted and I was one of the guys. It was fun. There were a lot of Spanish and white guys and Negro guys; we were all like brothers and sisters. But they didn't like it because after I learned the work, the company started to get me to train newcomers. I guess that was an insult to them. But I kept at it.

My marriage was so bad, and, finally, when my mom and my brothers and sisters were going to come up North to work the fields, I took my seven kids and left my husband and came with my mom. And I found out I could make it on my own, very good. I went back to my husband when we finished working that first summer, but it was so bad and when it came time to work the crops again, I told him, "I'm not coming back." So that's the way it happened. It was sad but I had already made up my mind that I wasn't going back. I found out I could make it on my own. I said, "My God, we're so happy and I'm so happy now." The pressure was gone and even though I was working very, very hard, still I felt good. I felt free.

I had a lot of problems because my daddy, he was very upset with me, very, very upset. He didn't want this to happen. He said that I got married and that I should stay in my marriage. And, in a way, I will never forgive myself. But the only reason I say that is because of my children. It hurt them very bad. But I know it was wrong to marry my husband in the first place, and I'm not sorry that him and I got separated and divorced. Because I know that was for the best.

Still, when you divorce or separate, it breaks the home and hurts some kids. I love Pablo, my present husband, a lot. He's been very good and we both believe in the same thing. We work together, but every time I talk to a mother who is thinking of divorce, I say to try to work it out rather than separate, because of the kids. But I think about my life and pray, "God, there's got to be a reason for all that we have gone through." And I think that reason is 'cause God's got a purpose for my life.

When the kids and I came North, we'd work the fields, and then we stayed more in one place and I worked in Libby's cannery in Ohio. The housing Libby's had was real small cabins with a bed and a wooden table and a little stove on the wooden table and a stick to hang your clothes on. Although, with my seven kids we had a bigger cabin and bunk beds that we put together to make two full beds and a cot, which was where I slept. So my kids all did sleep in beds. Then I had one wooden table and a stove and one door and one window. It was crowded and a hard way to live. The restrooms would all be outside. One thing I disliked very much was you couldn't have any privacy in the restrooms. Everything was open. So if your monthly time was happening, it was terrible. I disliked that so much.

I was a supervisor in the cannery for five years. I don't want to brag about it, but I think I was very good. I loved people and they loved me, and I never had any problems with people. My boss, he wouldn't butt in for nothing. There were complaints by other bosses about why they would see people outside during working hours. They'd see workers out because I'd give the ladies a chance to go eat with their husbands. But the women would make up their time. I'd say, "Let her go take lunch now so she can eat with her husband and then you take her lunch hour." So everybody was happy in my lines.

But when I was working in the cannery, there was nobody to take care of my kids, so even though I had a cabin, they were running free. And I usually worked sixteen hours a day. I tried to tell my kids, "Please stay home. Just play in the camp." But it's not easy to keep kids away from the street when you're working, and they don't have anybody to tell them. They were going to school while school was open, but then school was out so the kids were free. And I was working sixteen hours a day, and there was nobody to take care of my kids.

Then the kids started going to what people called a "joint." They had billiards and pool and playing machines in there. From what I gather, the owners were not supposed to allow any children under age in there, but they did and some of my kids would go to it. When I found out, I started getting after the kids. I said, "Don't go to town. If you do, I'm going to give you a spanking," but they wouldn't listen to me.

So one day a friend of mine came into where I was working in the cannery and said, "Maria Elena, your kids are at that joint and I came to tell you because that is not a good place. There's drugs and a whole bunch of things going on in there, and if you're not careful, your kids are going to end up very, very bad."

I got out of work and went up there just to see and sure enough, they were there. When they saw me they ran but I managed to get one of them, and I gave him a spanking on his butt. I didn't bruise him or anything, but somebody seemed to think it was terrible. I was alone with my kids in there and it was very hard. I was trying to work and to support them. But I didn't have anybody to babysit and with seven kids, it was bad.

Then somebody reported me to the authorities for giving my son that spanking, and the authorities came looking for me. They went to the office of the company and they called the company managers. They made me look like dirt in front of my boss and everybody else. But my supervisor, he didn't stay to hear what they said. He says, "I'm not going to listen because I know Maria Elena. I'm not going with you." He stayed away but the rest of the people that managed Libby's came, and I was terribly ashamed and humiliated.

Also, the discussion was right in front of the children. The authorities were really attacking me, saying, "You're doing wrong. You're not treating your kids like you should! You shouldn't have spanked them." This and that. That's what they were telling me in front of my kids. While they were doing that, all I could do was cry.

I asked the lady that was talking, "Have you ever been a migrant or a farm worker?"

She says, "Well, no."

Then I says, "You don't know what you're talking about, lady. Listen, if anything happens to my kids, I'm going to hold you responsible."

They just gave me such a funny look because they thought, "Well, we are the ones who care. We are the ones that are doing something about her problem. Look what this crazy woman is telling us." Something like that.

I thought, this is not right, right in front of the kids. They are going to feel like, well, Mom is wrong.

Sure enough. I went back to work and I sent my kids home, and, the next morning when I got off work, they were gone. The youngest two ran away. They were eight and nine. For one week I went looking for them all over the farms, and it had rained a lot and the water was about knee high. I've never been so scared in my life. I was crying, I was like crazy. I thought any minute I would find my kids drowned or killed.

Right away after the little kids left, I went back to the authorities, and I said, "This is your fault. I told you. You were wrong. If anything happens to my kids, I'm going to hold you responsible."

They were looking for my kids all over till finally I got a call from Texas that they were already back there. The two little kids had hitchhiked with another boy, and they were so excited because they had been in the arch in St. Louis, Missouri.

After that happened, I thought, "Never, we're never going to come back here again." And I didn't. So I never came back even though I kept getting letters from the company asking me to.

At that time, there was talk that farm workers were organizing, and I was listening to all this talk about the farm workers getting together. I guess it was just beginning. I thought, "This is going to help." But I wasn't coming back there anyway.

The second year that I took the kids north to work, I met Pablo. Pablo is quite a bit older than I am, in his sixties now, and was separated from his wife for many years. He came from Mexico, where his folks were not too poor, about medium. But when Pablo was young he insisted on coming here, and now he lives with a constant, how do you call it, sadness and conflict inside. He believes he should have never left Mexico. He says that if he were in Mexico he wouldn't be in these conditions, because we have such problems with money. I feel sad that he should always feel that way.

Pablo and I had a lot of money problems because every extra penny I earned went to pay money for transportation for my kids going back and forth to Texas. Also, we were working very hard in the fields and living in the camps. I used to dread laundry days. We worked such terribly long days, and on laundry days I had to take an extra two hours to do the laundry. Of course, that time came out of my sleep. There was nowhere else for it to come. And the camps were so terrible for us to live in. There were so many flies and they were so dirty and run down that we used to sleep in the back of our truck.

We began to stay more around this town here, this little town in Illinois. There were nurseries around here to work in, and we began being here most of the time. Most of the people in this town are white, and there has been a lot of prejudice. The grown-ups don't come right out and show it too much, but the younger kids do, and I remember hearing of kids saying, "My father hates Mexicans."

My kids were in high school here, and they started dropping out of school. I was very disappointed. I cried a lot because that meant that they had to go back to Texas, because I was afraid they would get hurt in the streets here just anytime. That's what happened constantly. They couldn't walk downtown to the park because they'd get beaten up, so I thought, "Well, what choice do I have?" Hector was about fourteen years old when he left high school, and I had no choice but to send him to Texas. Now he's not seventeen yet and he just got married. Gloria did the same thing, got married very young.

And Johnny, Johnny had such a terrible time in here that he enlisted in the Marines. Now that he's come back several times to visit, he's told me, "I would never come back to live here. I wouldn't put up with the things that you do." He says that he respects what I believe in and says that it's good that I have something to work for and to look forward to, but he says, "Mother, if I came back here it would be disastrous because I wouldn't put up with all this stuff we put up with before."

The big things hurt and sometimes the little things hurt too. There is a grocery clerk here and my friends would tell me that they would give her the money to pay for their groceries, and she would get the change from the register and throw it on the counter at them.

As I said, Pablo and I, we started staying pretty much around here and working, and we started trying to help out some of the migrant workers who were around here. At that time everybody was so separated; everybody was just going their own way and nobody was sociable. But I met a young girl, Alicia. She and her mom were Mexicans who had to leave eight children at home in Mexico with the grandparents so they could come here and work. Alicia and I got acquainted and pretty soon I found out that Alicia had a lot of experience in Mexican folklore dances, and I love music and dancing too. It was near the bicentennial and we thought, "Why don't we ask Alicia to teach the young people to dance, and we'll celebrate the bicentennial that way?" So we got a group of about twenty young Mexican girls and boys together, and before long they were performing all over. It gave them lots of confidence and was wonderful fun.

But in our town and around the farms, I could see all the trouble the people were having, and I tried to think of ways we could all be helped. I thought that we needed to get our help from

God, and then I thought, "Maybe a priest, maybe a priest could help us and lead us, could be with us and make life better for us." Also, we had to go to another town if we wanted a Catholic church, and then the service would be in English. And so we had many meetings and we organized. Of course, I didn't know the word, organized, at that time.

Once we had the church, everybody started working. We were washing floors and scrubbing, polishing and painting, and I sewed the curtains to Our Lady of Guadalupe. They're still hanging there in the Mexican colors, red, white, and green. There are these curtains and Our Lady of Guadalupe is in the center.

Also, with the Latin American Association we built a fund that anytime that a person was in real need of money, we'd give them automatically twenty-five dollars to provide transportation and immediate medical attention, whatever they needed. And the dance group practiced in the basement of the church.

Pablo and I got working for the Illinois Farm Worker Ministry because of the dancing group. Olgha Sierra Sandman, who is the director of the ministry, came to one of the dances and talked to me. She was born and raised in Mexico and married an Anglo minister who lives near Chicago, and she works with the Migrant Ministry. This lady, I've never seen any woman work like this beautiful lady. She is really a gift that God sent to the people. She's very active and goes out of her way and talks to all kinds of people.

She had a hard time, at first, trying to get us to work for the ministry. I was just like everybody else at first. I had doubts, even though she was Spanish. I thought, "Wow, they're interested in us; I wonder what they want?" I was full of curiosity and doubt, but after going through so much, you learn to distrust people so bad. Also, I didn't know too much about the farm worker's movement in California. But I knew I was trying to support the idea that we were going through misery and that I believed something should be done. So Pablo and I had been helping the people around here anyway, and then we started being backed by the ministry, and I went to California to study union organizing and started organizing for the United Farm Workers, Cesar Chavez's group.

So many of the people around here have such extra problems, besides all the problems of just being migrants. They have these extra problems because they are undocumented, illegal. They come from Mexico because they are so desperate and because they are so poor. Some people say undocumented workers take too much from our country, but I don't think that is true. They work and pay taxes and social security, but they don't get benefits like unemployment or food stamps.

When I was working in the farming businesses, it was sad to see the women workers being mistreated. I don't like to say the words, but our boss, she'd say, "You Mexican son of a bitch, come on and get to work. Move it!" Like that.

I had complained once to one of the owners, and he told me, "Hey, if you want to keep your job, keep your mouth shut and bear with it." So I needed the job and needed it bad, and I had to put up with it, just like the rest. Keep my mouth shut and do the work.

In the winter the women would go out in the fields and take cuttings and make piles and then bring them into the shed. We would go out to the fields around eight in the morning, and we'd have a fifteen minute break partway through the morning, and then we'd work in the fields until lunchtime. Sometimes one of the girls would say to our boss, "We're too cold, Sally, too cold. Let us in the pickup for a little while." She would be watching us in the pickup.

Sometimes she'd say, "OK, just for a little while." So we'd go in there and just all get close together and it was awful.

After a while she'd say, "OK. I can't let you sit here too long." So we'd go back again and really hurry up working so our bodies would not get so cold. It was stoop labor, too. It was cold, very cold.

Once when we were out going around the farms in the winter, our van broke down and no one would give us help, even though we begged them for it and promised to pay them. Finally, we had to walk a long ways in the snow, and I started crying and wouldn't go on, and Pablo forced me to keep moving so I wouldn't freeze. I tell you, I do not like this weather for nothing, and all the people who come from the South dread it. The people that were born and raised in Mexico are so afraid of it.

There are always tensions for people to live with. The last raid we had from immigration was hard on everybody. All at once, one morning, a group of guys from immigration went out and rounded up a bunch of undocumented men. Pablo and I learned they were in town, and we went and found them on one of the streets, leading them into the van. I felt very, very desperate and was crying. So I said to the immigration men, "Why do you do this? Why don't you take another job? Quit this dirty job. These people, can't you tell how much they suffer. You know that."

Pablo and I are trying to do everything we can to make life

better for all these people, but it is hard. We are organizing as part of the United Farm Workers, but they don't have money to help us with. They've got too many people on strike to send us money. But they've given us their support and have tried to help teach us. So it's up to us, really, to make this thing go. It is a very big job.

We are trying to work in lots of different counties; we've been trying to circulate where the farm workers are. Sometimes we even go as far as Chicago to talk to people. I'm always talking about the problems of farm workers. I'm always talking about organizing. I'm always looking for people's reactions, any signs that will give me an indication they are interested. If I can see that, then I know that I've got something to work from. I know that if people believe in justice, I can start. What we have to do is get all the people organized. But I haven't lost faith in what we're doing. I've got lots of faith.

I try to help people in lots of little ways, and, for those who feel alone, I'll come in and say, "Hey, you're not alone." And then I say, "This is what's happened; this is what could be changed; and this is what we could do all together." Then it's up to everybody to make the changes together.

We're just beginning and we have the hope of getting a service center going. That's how Cesar Chavez started the organizing in California. They gave service to the people with all of their problems, so people knew they cared and then they started to work together to form a union.

If we get the service center, oh, I'm going to see that we get some education for the people. I don't think we need professionals to do it, just someone that is bilingual and willing to teach the people how to write and to spell a little bit, how to read a little bit, just to get by. Learning these things would certainly help a lot. The most basic needs need to be taught, like how to get groceries, going to the post office and buying envelopes, asking for gasoline for the car, knowing how much $9.95 or whatever in quarters or cents or dimes is. Also, going to the bank and saying at least, "I want to open a checking account," something like that. Things that they can learn to do for themselves. 'Cause I have seen that they have learned. When I see these very little things that are accomplished, to me they are very big things.

I come on pretty strong sometimes, especially with men. I know that I'm a woman and sometimes they look at me and they talk, and I hear rumors that they say that for a woman I come on very strong, very militant sometimes. There's a lot of guys where it sort of hurts their pride to see that a woman would be the one to tell them how we can change things, especially in our race. The man is the boss and there is the macho image.

But when I talk to them I say, "What have you got to lose by organizing? We have to sacrifice a little bit."

The men say back, "Well, my job."

"Your job! You're worried about losing your job? I'm worried about losing my life over this." Boy, that hits them pretty hard.

I say, "I don't want a revolution but we can change things together," and that shakes them up a little bit, and then they look at me as if I was a very macho woman too and they listen.

We still need more of our own people. There's still a lot of fear and doubts. I've got some other people who say, "We'll go with you from farm to farm, Maria Elena." We need each other and we need to work together, but our people don't have much time because they've got to work so hard to survive, so we need to be able to pay our people. We need one person for the office, to answer the phone and take care of paperwork. We need another person to provide social services, and we need two people to go out to the farms. Those are our needs; we don't have them but we are just beginning.

Living is sometimes hard for Pablo and me. Our time together's been good, but we have had a lot of trouble, financial problems. We've never been able to, how should I say it, to make any progress. Not that I want to have a lot of money. It's just that we've had financial problems since we got together.

We've had trouble with our house. We were living right next door in a little old house, but it was in worse shape than this house. Then we had to tear down that house, and a man was trying to get rid of this place because there was all single men here and the house was in very, very bad condition. So the man sold us this house on contract; that way he could make a little money. With that we got this place, at least. It's ours. Of course, we're paying for it.

Then Pablo had some bad troubles with income taxes. When he was working the fields, he would always take his tax papers back to Texas to this lady to fix them up, and after a while he kept sending them but the girl that was fixing them never did fix them anymore. After we got married I didn't know how he was doing his, and I told him, "I don't want to have any problems, so I'll just continue like I was."

But then we found out his taxes hadn't been paid, and we have to pay the Internal Revenue over $9,000 for back taxes and penalties. Most of it is interest. We've been up to the Internal Revenue so many times, and every time we have to go it's about

$30 just for gas. We went to see a lawyer but he didn't help us much, and we went from one person to another and asked them if they could waive our interest so that we would just have to pay what we owed. They said, "No, we can't do that, we're sorry."

Then we told them, "Well, we've got this house."

The woman said, "Well, sell it."

"We're trying but we can't."

"Well, we're not after blood, but sometime you'll have to pay us, and we can't waive the interest."

This is so bad, especially when you're so poor. It is something that we constantly worry about. Sometimes I tell Pablo, "I wish the government would just come and take everything over so I wouldn't have to worry so much." Before we found out about the taxes, we had donated a little plot of land we had to be used for a service center. I'm glad we had done it before we knew about the taxes; we've made so many promises to the people.

Pablo and I can get along real good, but now these problems have begun to hurt us. We love each other but this has made a very, very big difference in our lives. The financial situation has really changed our life a lot and what can I do? It's terrible. But I never was the type to go from one marriage to the other. When I started going with Pablo I didn't want to get married again. It was a coincidence that it happened like that. But I was still young and I guess things happen. And now that we've got all this pressure because of our condition, that's a constant worry. I feel so helpless that I can't do anything about it, and he feels so much tension and I can't help it. The house, the condition it's in, I don't have any hopes of getting any repairs. I don't even have hopes of getting the gas back on, even this winter.

Now Pablo's always tense and we used to get along better before we got in this really bad situation with the bills. We owe the van, this little house, and the Internal Revenue. And now that I'm doing this work, everything has doubled, my housework, the conditions, everything. I'm hardly at home. Most of the time I'm away, and when I get home then other people come, and so I have to help them out too. Sometimes we don't even get to eat till very, very late and Pablo's very picky about food. He wants beans and tortillas but I can't do everything. Either you're a housewife and a mother and a wife or you're out working. All I can do is try.

Last winter we went to Texas, but the winter before we went without gas for heat because of money and it was horrible. I cried and cried with the cold, and I really was very, very terribly sick. It seemed to me it was bronchitis. We kept coming from inside to the van and turning the motor and we'd go riding around. We'd go visiting but everybody's so crowded in the winter. One family had about twenty-nine people, all sleeping in the living room and everywhere. I went to my daughter Christy's house, and she had all her husband's family too and it was pretty bad.

I got a cough and I couldn't get rid of the cough, and my chest was like I was being choked. We used up all our blankets, and at that time Oscar would sleep with us when it was too cold, and we'd try to keep warm in bed together. We would sometimes bring some hot wood coals into the house and put them in the living room, but it would smoke and it burned the floor, and it's not good to bring burning wood inside the house.

I worry about fire and the wires in our house because it's so cold and not in good shape. I guess I try to keep all my papers handy here because then, in case of an emergency, I can run out with a box of vital papers. I think about fire a lot and I think about being asleep and being caught in a fire, but then I think about freezing. I say I'd rather burn than freeze, so I've got a choice in here. I don't know if I can stand the cold another winter. [Cries hard.]

There are little things that hurt too. We had a real beautiful old glass window in our door. Inside the glass it was carved and it was very lovely. But these people came to buy it and we said no. So one day we came back home and it was all broken, all smashed up, and I got so disgusted and felt so bad. So, our door is still without a window. We just have a towel hanging there now, and I guess we'll put up plastic in the winter.

We try to make people feel better about us. Only twice have I ever asked for food stamps, once with all my kids and then last year I had to ask for food stamps again. It's not because I'm proud or anything that I don't want to ask, it's just that we want to show the department and everybody else in the agencies that we can do it on our own, even though it's being very hard. We would like them to know that we're willing to sacrifice. We hear so many people saying, "Yah, they live on the food stamps. Yah, they're on welfare. Dumb people, lazy people." We don't want to be called that. People only take food stamps because they really, really need them, and undocumented workers don't qualify. The man that's down there in the office, oh, you should see him. He puts on such a terrible face. Like you'd think it was coming out of his pocket.

It just takes a lot to keep going. I think that my job has increased a whole lot. Now that we're trying to organize the farm workers we have to go out a lot more and talk to people and so it's more work. And what happens when I have a little break is I just sleep. I go to sleep real tired and when I wake up I'm tired too.

It's frustrating to never get everything done, like my housework. Sometimes I get depressed and I don't know what to do. The situation is pretty bad in here. We have lots of roaches and sometimes we don't even have the money to buy the poison. It was very bad when the roaches were crawling all over, and I'd have people coming here and I'd see the roaches go up and around their collar. I'd say, "Oh, my God, I feel terrible." But then we had some money to start spraying so we tried real hard. But I tell you, it's impossible to stop them. So, when we get a little money, we go buy some medicine and spray. And I've always got piles and piles of dirty clothes because I don't have time to do my washing.

I guess, in a way, having so little makes it easier for me to talk to people. I come and I say, "Well, we're in the same situation. Mine is not any better than yours. So we can understand." That way we can communicate. Most of the people agree that we need to change things. There's just little things that have got to be taken care of before this is realized.

All these people are my friends but I'll tell you what; there are a lot of things that I don't talk about to them about. They know my situation and how bad it is, but there's a lot of things that I don't ever say, not even to Mom, maybe just to God. I think some things you just don't ever talk about.

Most of my kids are doing OK. My oldest child, Eva, she's just like a lawyer. She's smart and very outspoken, and she's not afraid to talk to people or nothing. But Eva, she says, "I wouldn't do your work, Mother. Not if you're paying a high price for it." She thinks that it's costing me not in money but in worry.

But my daughter Gloria understands about my work because she was with me longer, and she got so involved with my work at one time that she knows exactly what it's about and she's seen the situation. So she understands.

Gloria meant so much in our dance troop. She was a great dancer and she twirled with fire. That was just an extra number we'd always save as a tribute to the United States, especially on the Fourth of July. I made her this little outfit with glittering red panties and white and blue glittery shirt outfits, and she would twirl and put on a dance that was all American. They would turn off the light and she would really put on a good show. She was so pretty and she did it so good, but she married when she was sixteen. It was so hard for me to have her leave so soon. She's got one baby girl and I told her, "That's our next twirler. Try to teach her."

I think sometimes, if Gloria could only go back to school, she would really do something, because she is very, very smart, and she likes the things I do too, and she was a great help too. Five of my kids are in Texas. I wish I was with them.

It's good to be near Christy and my grandkids, of course, and Oscar is still with me. I worried for my kids a lot. When I had my kids here I was always with them, because there was so much beating up around here. I still do the same with Oscar. And I tell Oscar, "Please, no matter who offers you any drugs, don't take it." He says he gets hassled and is called a sissy because he doesn't go along with the rest of the kids. They say, "Mama's boy," and things like that, but I pray to God that he stays away from trouble, 'cause it's so much available in here. And he is such a good kid.

I think about my mom a lot. She's still being a midwife now. She's about fifty-six and is a very, very strong woman and very kind. She helps a lot of poor women. She doesn't have any young children now, my youngest sister is fifteen years old, so no more babies.

Now my mother's been doing the midwifing for many years and she's got a certificate. She had to go to some kind of training so that she could get it. It wasn't against the law to be a midwife in my younger days, but nowadays they're very strict. My mom rents a little place, and she's got like a clinic, with beds and cooking facilities and everything else. So now when she delivers babies, she not only brings the babies, but for a whole week she takes care of the baby so the mother can really recuperate. She sleeps with the babies, and if she's got too many, she's got friends to take over. She really takes care of the ladies. She feeds them homemade soup and good food. But she is so busy that when I go to Texas, I really don't get to see her, not to talk. So, in that way, I miss her.

I know I've got a lot of friends that come and confide in me. They tell me just about everything, all their life and their problems, and I listen because whatever, even if a lot of people don't consider some things to be important, I can see they are. So, regardless of whatever it is, I listen.

I think I can help them, but lots of times they can't help me. So maybe God can help me. Pablo and I, we work good and we get along all right, but there are some things we don't agree on. Also, he's older and so sometimes we don't have the same ideas. But most of the time, I try to go along with his ideas and just altogether to make life easier. And I tell him over and over again, "You have to trust God and depend on God, Pablo. I'm sure all these problems are the way it's meant to be, so don't give up."

Because of all my mom's kids and seeing her being a midwife and all my kids and all of my work with so many ladies, I know of what these women need. I'm totally against abortion, but I'm all for hysterectomy and tubal ligation and birth control. Our religion tells us that we shouldn't use birth control, and most of the Spanish ladies, they know that, but over here they turn around and they still do it. I've known this for years. They do it because they need it.

We women have been doing it for ages, taking care of ourselves. We know we're to accept what's from God, but what can you do when you know that you're also going to have to bring and raise those children? I know it's a sin to take care of it, but those children need food.

My work is so important to me. When I was younger and when my children were able to walk at least some, I took them to church, but it was not until I went to the Baptist church and started helping with their work among my people that I really had that strong desire. I was like, for all that time, looking for something, trying to find something that I didn't even know what it was.

It is now, after all these years, that I can say, "It was just that God wanted me to do something, some important work." I guess I found the answer. It took a lot of suffering and a lot of heartbreak, but I know that this is what God wants me to do. All of it, the dance group, the music, the organizing, I think it's part of it too.

I've asked God to give me the power to be able to do something about the suffering of all these people. I ask for God to please give me the energy and the knowledge and the strength to do something about things like this. When you live with these people, you work with them and you see them suffer, how can you not feel?

It's bad. I've seen so many of these people, hundreds of these people, and the more I go out, the more I meet people, the more people come to my house, the more I realize how much they're hurting.

I have this strong feeling inside me that God intended my life to be this way and that there is something special that God wants me for, maybe that's why I'm uneducated and I lack a lot of things. I tell Pablo, "Hey, listen, Pablo. Maybe what God wants us to be is very simple, to be a symbol to the people that we're suffering but can endure. Maybe that's why we don't have a very nice place with all the commodities. Maybe if we didn't have a thing to worry about, we wouldn't have this feeling, this kind of belief that's so powerful that we want to make social change and fight for justice for the rest. Maybe that will keep us going."

Epilogue

Later that fall I traveled to be with Maria Elena again during a time of great excitement. The Migrant Ministry had donated a trailer home to be put on the land previously owned by Maria Elena and Pablo and to serve as a United Farm Workers Service Center, the first such in the Midwest. The UFW president, Cesar Chavez, was traveling from California and was going to formally dedicate the Center in a celebratory mass to be held the following day. Hundreds of visitors were expected, especially migrant workers from throughout the region.

Maria Elena, Pablo, AFL-CIO union organizers, and others stayed up almost all of the night before, decorating the hall with UFW union colors of red and black, making banners with such slogans as "Viva Cesar Chavez, Campesinos de Rochell, Boycott Purina Pet Foods," and alternating as guards for the hall when the preparations had been completed. A group of women also cooked through most of the night and prepared hundreds of tamales. I went to speak with them, and the red chilies boiling away on the stove were so strong that my voice choked in my throat.

The next day a private ribbon-cutting ceremony was held with Cesar Chavez, Olgha Sandman, Maria Elena, and Pablo, and then a standing-room-only mass and rally took place in front of hundreds of people. Chavez and others spoke in Spanish and English, and Pablo and Maria Elena also told of their hopes for the center, with Maria Elena saying, finally, "Better to die on your feet that to live on your knees the rest of your life."

The ceremony was followed by music, dancing, and eating. Then Cesar Chavez had to leave, gradually the crowd thinned out, and those of us who were left began to clean up. Except for the ceremony itself, the same group of women who had cooked the night before, stayed in the steaming kitchen preparing food all day. After the others had left, they simply shifted to washing dishes and cleaning. Finally, only these women and their children remained and, at last, everyone was done.

I went with Maria Elena to one of the women's homes, where Maria Elena and her friends laughed and talked about the day. Finally, she and I went out for coffee before I began my trip back to Wisconsin. This was, she said, the biggest moment of her life. We talked of her exhaustion and her hopes for the future and just sat together, considering the day. It was dark and very cold when I dropped her off at her home, and as I pulled out of town, I thought about her hopes and dreams, her nonstop work, and the reality that she still had no heat in her home with which to face the approaching winter.

Selected Bibliography

Allen, Paula Gunn. *The Blind Lion*. Berkeley: Thorp Springs Press, 1974. Allen is a Native American poet.

———. *Star Child*. Marvin, S. Dak.: Blue Cloud Quarterly, 1981.

Allen, Walter R. "Family Roles, Occupational Statuses, and Achievement Orientations among Black Women in the United States." *Signs: Journal of Women in Culture and Society* 4, no. 4 (Summer 1979): 670–86.

Berch, Bettina. *The Endless Day: The Political Economy of Women and Work*. New York: Harcourt Brace Jovanovich, 1982.

Berk, S. F., ed. *Women and Household Labor*. Beverly Hills, Calif.: Sage Publications, 1980.

Blauner, Robert. *Racial Oppression in America*. New York: Harper and Row, 1972.

Blaxall, Martha, and Reagan, Barbara. *Women and the Workplace: The Implications of Occupational Segregation*. Chicago: University of Chicago Press, 1976.

Blicksilver, Edith. *The Ethnic American Woman: Problems, Protest, Lifestyle*. Dubuque: Kendall/Hunt, 1979.

Bowles, Gloria, and Klein, Renate Duelli, eds. *Theories of Women's Studies*. London and Boston: Melbourne and Henley, Routledge and Kegan Paul, 1983. Contains many excellent articles on feminist methodology in the social sciences.

Breines, Wini, and Gordon, Linda. "The New Scholarship on Family Violence." *Signs: Journal of Women in Culture and Society* 8, no. 3 (Spring 1983): 490–531. A comprehensive and up-to-date review of the literature on child abuse, wife beating, and incest.

Buss, Fran Leeper. *La Partera: Story of a Midwife*. Ann Arbor: University of Michigan Press, 1980.

Cabello-Argandona, Roberto. *The Chicana: A Comprehensive Bibliographic Study*. Los Angeles: University of California, Los Angeles, Chicano Studies Center, 1976.

Cherlin, Andrew J. *Marriage, Divorce, Remarriage*. Cambridge, Mass.: Harvard University Press, 1981. Cherlin examines trends in the statistical patterns of the last thirty-five years and presents them in this readable book.

Chodorow, Nancy. *The Reproduction of Mothering: Psychoanalysis and the Sociology of Gender*. Berkeley: University of California Press, 1978. An interpretation of women's psychological development that explains the flowering of relational skills created by mother-daughter psychological connections.

Chodorow, Nancy, and Contratto, Susan. "The Fantasy of the Perfect Mother." In *Rethinking the Family: Some Feminist Questions*, ed. Barrie Thorne, with Marilyn Yalom. New York: Longman, 1982.

Coles, Robert, and Coles, Jane Hallowell. *Women of Crisis: Lives of Struggle and Hope*. New York: Delacorte Press, 1978. The Coles present the life stories of five poor women interspersed with their own commentary and analysis.

Contratto, Susan. "Mother: Social Sculptor and Trustee of the Faith." In *In the Shadow of the Past: Psychology Portrays the Sexes*, ed. Miriam Lewin. New York: Columbia University Press, 1984.

Davis, Angela. *Women, Race and Class*. New York: Random House, 1981.

Davis, Lenwood G. *The Black Woman in American Society: A Selected Annotated Bibliography*. Boston: G. K. Hall, 1975.

Degler, Carl N. *At Odds: Women and the Family in America from the Revolution to the Present*. New York and Oxford: Oxford University Press, 1980. In this excellent history, Degler, a Stanford historian, develops the thesis that woman's struggle for autonomy requires that she place herself in contradistinction to the family.

Delaney, Janice; Lupton, Mary Jane; and Toth, Emily. *The Curse: A Cultural History of Menstruation*. New York: Mentor, New American Library, 1977. Illustrates the cultural shaping of this biological event with cross-cultural data as well as data from Western industrialized societies.

Dill, Bonnie Thornton. "The Dialectics of Black Womanhood." *Signs: Journal of Women in Culture and Society* 4, no. 4

(Spring 1979): 543–55. This essay presents a research model that illuminates black women's courageous responses to powerlessness.

Dinnerstein, Dorothy. *The Mermaid and the Minotaur: Sexual Arrangements and Human Malaise.* New York: Harper and Row, 1976. Dinnerstein looks at the psychological and social consequences of mothers being an infant's primary caretaker.

DuBois, W. E. B. *The Souls of Black Folk.* Greenwich, Conn.: Fawcett, 1961.

Dye, Nancy Schrom. "History of Childbirth in America." *Signs: Journal of Women in Culture and Society* 6, no. 1 (Autumn 1980): 97–108. A review essay of history of childbirth ranging from early to contemporary America.

Ehrenreich, Barbara, and English, Deirdre. *For Her Own Good.* Garden City, N.Y.: Anchor Press, Doubleday, 1978. The authors have written a history that analyzes over 100 years of "expert" health and social advice to women.

Ferber, Marianne E. "Women and Work: Issues of the 1980s." *Signs: Journal of Women in Culture and Society* 8, no. 2 (Winter 1982): 273–95. This review essay deals with works published since 1976 that treat the contemporary United States. The author focuses on women's nonmarket work, labor market earnings, and the earning gap between men and women.

Fisher, Dexter, ed. *The Third Woman: Minority Women Writers of the United States.* Boston: Houghton Mifflin Co., 1979.

Friedman, Richard C.; Hurt, Stephen W.; Aronoff, Michael S.; and Clarkin, John. "Behavior and the Menstrual Cycle." *Signs: Journal of Women in Culture and Society* 5, no. 4 (Summer 1980): 719–38.

Frieze, Irene Hanson. "Investigating the Causes and Consequences of Marital Rape." *Signs: Journal of Women in Culture and Society* 8, no. 3 (Spring 1983): 532–53. Report of findings from interview data gathered from almost 300 women. Focuses on definition of marital rape, consequences of forced sexual relations for the marriage and finally, the types of marriages in which forced sex occurs.

Fujimoto, Isao, et al., comps. *Asians in America: A Selected Annotated Bibliography.* Davis, Calif.: University of California, Davis Asian American Research Project, Department of Applied Behavior Science, 1970. The emphasis of this work is on Chinese, Japanese, and Filipinos.

Gilligan, Carol. *In a Different Voice: Psychological Theory and Women's Development.* Cambridge, Mass.: Harvard University

Press, 1982. A well-written book that presents data seriously questioning the relevance of the dominant theories of psychological development for women.

Goodman, Madeleine. "Toward a Biology of Menopause." *Signs: Journal of Women in Culture and Society* 5, no. 4 (Summer 1980): 739–53.

Gordon, Linda. *Woman's Body, Woman's Right: A Social History of Birth Control in America*. New York: Penguin Books, 1977.

Gordon, M., ed. *The American Family in Social-Historical Perspective*. New York: St. Martin's Press, 1978.

Gould, Meredith. "The New Sociology." *Signs: Journal of Women in Culture and Society* 5, no. 3 (Spring 1980): 459–67. A review article that looks at work since 1979, concentrating on emerging theoretical and methodological issues.

Green, Rayna. "Native American Women." *Signs: Journal of Women in Culture and Society* 6, no. 2 (Winter 1980): 248–67. An excellent and comprehensive review essay. To quote the author: "Since, for most readers, the literature prior to the sixties is not known, I have framed the review of current work in the context of work done since the seventeenth century in the United States and Canada which encompasses popular and scholarly production and spans several academic and professional fields—anthropology, history, psychology, literature, medicine, law, and journalism."

Gutman, Herbert G. *The Black Family in Slavery and Freedom, 1750–1925*. New York: Pantheon Books, 1976.

Gwaltney, John Langston. *Drylongso: A Self-Portrait of Black America*. New York: Vintage Books, 1981.

Hacker, Andrew, ed. *U/S: A Statistical Portrait of the American People*. New York: Viking Press, 1983. An excellent, readable summary of statistical information from the 1980 census. Particularly useful in that it gives breakdowns using race and sex as well as other relevant categories.

Hartmann, Heidi I. "The Family as the Locus of Gender, Class, and Political Struggle: The Example of Housework." *Signs: Journal of Women in Culture and Society* 6, no. 3 (Spring 1981): 366–94. Hartmann argues that the working lives of individual family members have an impact on the relationships that shape family life.

Hirsch, Marianne. "Mothers and Daughters." *Signs: Journal of Women in Culture and Society* 7, no. 1 (Autumn 1981): 200–222. Presents an overview of feminist work on mothers and daughters and argues their on-going relationship to the theories of male intellectuals.

Hooks, Bell. *Ain't I a Woman*. Boston: South End Press, 1981. A book about black women.

Houston, Jeanne Wakatsuki, and Houston, James. *Farewell to Manzanar*. San Francisco: San Francisco Books, 1973. A memoir of World War II internment camps for Japanese Americans.

Howe, Louise Kapp. *Pink Collar Workers: Inside the World of Women's Work*. New York: Avon Books, 1977. The experiences of women who are working for pay.

Hull, Gloria T.; Scott, Patricia Bell; and Smith, Barbara; eds. *But Some of Us Are Brave: Black Women's Studies*. Old Westbury, N.Y.: Feminist Press, 1982. A collection that deals with the relationship between black women and feminism.

Johnson, Allan Griswold. "On the Prevalence of Rape in the United States." *Signs: Journal of Women in Culture and Society* 6, no. 1 (Autumn 1980): 136–47.

Jordan, June. *Things That I Do in the Dark: Selected Poems*. New York: Random House, 1977. A collection of poems by an important black woman poet.

Joseph, Gloria I., and Lewis, Jill. *Common Differences: Conflicts in Black and White Feminist Perspectives*. Garden City, N.Y.: Anchor Press, Doubleday, 1981.

Joyce, Lynda. *Annotated Bibliography of Women in Rural America with a Review of the Literature about Women in Rural America, Bibliography of Women in Rural Areas Worldwide, and Resource Material*. University Park, Pa.: Agricultural Experiment Station, Pennsylvania State University, 1976.

Kahn-Hut, Rachel; Daniels, Arlene Kaplan; and Colvard, Richard; eds. *Women and Work: Problems and Perspectives*. New York: Oxford University Press, 1982.

Kelley, Jane Holden. *Yagui Women: Contemporary Life Histories*. Lincoln: University of Nebraska Press, 1977.

Kessler-Harris, Alice. *Out to Work: A History of Wage-Earning Women in the United States*. New York: Oxford University Press, 1982. An excellent history of women who work for pay.

Kingston, Maxine Hong. *The Woman Warrior: Memoirs of a Girlhood Among Ghosts*. New York: Knopf, 1976.

Ladner, Joyce. *Tomorrow's Tomorrow*. Garden City, N.Y.: Doubleday, 1971. A collection of pieces about black women.

Lawson, Ronald, and Barton, Stephen E. "Sex Roles in Social

Movements: A Case Study of the Tenant Movement in New York City." *Signs: Journal of Women in Culture and Society* 6, no. 2 (Winter 1980): 230–47. A study of the tenant union movement that seeks to explain why women have until recently been the organizers and followers in this movement and men the leaders.

Leavitt, Judith Walzer. "Birthing and Anesthesia: The Debate over Twilight Sleep." *Signs: Journal of Women in Culture and Society* 6, no. 1 (Autumn 1980): 147–64. An interesting account of the women who led the twilight sleep movement and their attempts to gain control of the birthing process through, paradoxically, falling asleep, and the medical profession's response to the movement.

Leifer, Myra. "Pregnancy." *Signs: Journal of Women in Culture and Society* 5, no. 4 (Summer 1980): 754–65.

Lerner, Gerda. *Black Women in White America: A Documentary History*. New York: Random House, Pantheon Books, 1972.

_____. *The Female Experience: An American Documentary.* Indianapolis: Bobbs-Merrill Co., 1977. A collection of women's writing from the colonial period to the present.

_____. *The Majority Finds Its Past: Placing Women in History.* New York: Oxford University Press, 1979.

Lorde, Audre. *The Black Unicorn*. New York: Norton, 1978. Lorde is a black woman poet.

Lurie, Nancy. *Mountain Wolf Woman, Sister of Crashing Thunder, a Winnebago Indian*. Ann Arbor: University of Michigan Press, 1961. An autobiography narrated to Nancy Lurie.

McCrindle, Jean, and Rowbotham, Sheila, eds. *Dutiful Daughters: Women Talk about Their Lives*. Austin: University of Texas Press, 1977. A book of fourteen "oral testimonies" of mostly lower- and middle-class British and Scottish women talking about their individual lives.

Malos, Ellen, ed. *The Politics of Housework*. London: Allison and Busby, 1980.

Miller, Jean Baker. *Toward a New Psychology of Women*. Boston: Beacon Press, 1976. Miller focuses on the deleterious effects of living in a male dominated society on women's psychological development.

Miller, Patricia Y., and Fowlkes, Martha R. "Social and Behavioral Constructions of Female Sexuality." *Signs: Journal of Women in Culture and Society* 5, no. 4 (Summer 1980): 783–800.

Moraga, Cherrie, and Anzaldua, Gloria, eds. *This Bridge Called*

My Back: Writings by Radical Women of Color. Watertown,
Mass.: Persephone Press, 1981.

Niethammer, Carolyn. *Daughters of the Earth: The Lives and
Legends of Native American Women*. New York: Macmillan
Co., 1977.

Oakley, Ann. *Sex, Gender and Society*. New York: Harper
Colophon Books, 1972.

———. "A Case of Maternity: Paradigms of Women as Maternity
Cases." *Signs: Journal of Women in Culture and Society* 4, no.
4 (Summer 1979): 607–31. Oakley describes "the ways in
which science, whether medical or social, has approached,
described, and defined the task of women as childbearers."

Parlee, Mary Brown. "Psychology and Women." *Signs: Journal of
Women in Culture and Society* 5, no. 1 (Autumn 1979): 121–
33. An excellent review article. Brown highlights the particular
problem of feminist psychologists and their relationship to a
parent discipline that has a commitment to the experimental
method.

Rowbotham, Sheila. *Hidden From History: Rediscovering Women in
History from the 17th Century to the Present*. New York:
Vintage Books, 1976.

Rubin, Lilliam Breslow. *Worlds of Pain: Life in the Working-Class
Family*. New York: Basic Books, 1976. An interview study with
considerable analysis of the family lives of fifty white working-
class families.

Ruddick, Sara. "Maternal Thinking." In *Rethinking the Family:
Some Feminist Questions*, ed. Barrie Thorne, with Marilyn
Yalom. New York: Longman, 1982.

Schecter, Susan. *Women and Male Violence: The Visions and
Struggles of the Battered Women's Movement*. Boston: South
End Press, 1982. A valuable overview of the early history and
current problems of the battered women's movement.

Seifer, Nancy. *Nobody Speaks for Me! Self-Portraits of American
Working Class Women*. New York: Simon and Schuster, 1976.
Ten interviews with working-class women with little
commentary.

Signs: Journal of Women in Culture and Society 8, no. 3 (Spring
1983). This is a special issue on women and violence.

Signs: Journal of Women in Culture and Society Supp. 5, no. 3
(Spring 1980), *Women and the American City*. This is a special
issue of the journal that ranges from articles on "Women and
Urban Policy," "The Health Careers of Urban Women: A

Study in East Harlem," and "City Lights: Immigrant Women and the Rise of the Movies," to research reports on rape prevention, child care, and networking.

Silko, Leslie Marmon. *Ceremony*. New York: Signet, 1978. Silko is a Native American fiction writer.

———. *Storyteller*. New York: Seaver Books, 1981.

Smedley, Agnes. *Daughter of Earth*. Old Westbury, N.Y.: Feminist Press, 1976. This is a novel about white, poor, working-class women that was originally published in 1929.

Sokoloff, Natalie J. *Between Money and Love: The Dialectics of Women's Home and Market Work*. New York: Praeger Publishers, 1980. Sokoloff effectively reviews the work of other social scientists who have studied this problem from different theoretical perspectives. In addition, she brings a Marxist-Feminist analysis to issues of women's workplace participation.

Soltow, Martha Jane, and Wery, Mary K. *American Women and the Labor Movement, 1825–1974: An Annotated Bibliography*. Metuchen, N.J.: Scarecrow Press, 1976.

Sone, Monica. *Nisei Daughter*. Boston: Little Brown, 1953. An autobiographical novel about this Japanese American woman's experience in World War II.

Stack, Carol. *All Our Kin*. New York: Harper and Row, 1974. Stack, an anthropologist, presents a study of black family life and the extensive support networks that develop.

Tong, Te-Kong, comp. *The Third Americans: A Select Bibliography on Asians in America with Annotations*. Oak Park, Ill.: CHCUS, 1980.

Trambley, Estela Portillo. *Rain of Scorpions*. Berkeley: Tonatiuh International, 1975. Short stories by a Chicana woman.

Walker, Alice. *The Color Purple*. New York: Harcourt Brace Jovanovich, 1982.

Wertheimer, Barbara M., and Nelson, Ann H. *Trade Union Women: A Study of Their Participation in New York City Locals*. New York: Praeger Publishers, 1975. An important case study of the barriers to women's participation in union leadership.

Zinn, Maxine Baca. "Mexican-American Women in the Social Sciences." *Signs: Journal of Women in Culture and Society* 8, no. 2 (Winter 1982): 259–72. A review essay by a sociologist who focuses on recent work about Mexican-American women in order "to narrow the gap between social science works on Chicanas and feminist social science."